Selling the Amish

Young Center Books in Anabaptist & Pietist Studies

Donald B. Kraybill, *Series Editor*

Selling the Amish

The Tourism of Nostalgia

Susan L. Trollinger

THE JOHNS HOPKINS UNIVERSITY PRESS
Baltimore

2 4 6 8 9 7 5 3 1

Library of Congress Cataloging-in-Publication Data

Trollinger, Susan L., 1964–
Selling the Amish : the tourism of nostalgia / Susan L. Trollinger.
p.   cm. — (Young Center books in Anabaptist and Pietist studies)
Includes bibliographical references (p.) and index.
ISBN-13: 978-1-4214-0419-6 (hardcover : alk. paper)
ISBN-10: 1-4214-0419-2 (hardcover : alk. paper)
1. Heritage tourism—Ohio—Amish Country. 2. Amish—Ohio—Amish Country—
Public opinion. 3. Mennonite architecture—Ohio—Amish Country. 4. Amish Country
(Ohio)—Description and travel. 5. Public opinion—Ohio—Amish Country. I. Title.
G156.5.H47T76 2012
338.4'791771—dc23   2011021670

A catalog record for this book is available from the British Library.

The maps, on pages 44, 46, 82, and 116, were created for this book by
Grounded Design Studio. Photographs are by the author.

*Special discounts are available for bulk purchases of this book. For more information,
please contact Special Sales at 410-516-6936 or specialsales@press.jhu.edu.*

The Johns Hopkins University Press uses environmentally friendly
book materials, including recycled text paper that is composed of at least
30 percent post-consumer waste, whenever possible.

To Bill

For his love and faith

Contents

Acknowledgments

During the more than fifteen years that I have been researching and writing this book, I have accumulated many debts of gratitude for the assistance given to me. Among the helpful persons in the Holmes County settlement in Ohio, I want especially to thank Elsie Sommers (co-owner with her husband, Junior Sommers, of Sommers General Store), who graciously talked with me at length about tourism in Berlin. Leslie Keser and Patricia Keser were crucial for helping me to understand the history of Sugarcreek as a tourist destination. Others, such as Ruth Schlabach, Rebecca Miller, Gloria Yoder, and Steve Mullet, generously shared information from their experience in business and with tourists and helped to nuance my readings of Amish Country tourism. I also wish to recognize the crucial assistance of Mike Huber, at the Elkhart County Travel and Visitors Bureau, and Shasta Mast, at the Holmes County Chamber of Commerce and Visitors Bureau, for sharing statistical data with me and answering my many questions concerning that data. Also, I remember Raymond Stutzman, now deceased, who introduced me to his friends in the Swartzentruber Amish community, who, trusting him, allowed me to photograph and study their plain style of living. I owe the greatest debt to Joan and Jake Mast. Welcoming me warmly and thoroughly into their lives, they shared with me a great deal of wisdom about Amish life and Amish Country tourism. And they tirelessly and always lovingly embraced the opportunity to spend time with my children, their grandchildren, as I spent countless hours exploring Ohio Amish Country tourism in their hometown and elsewhere.

To the communities of academics to which I have had the great privilege of being connected, I owe many debts of gratitude. As I formulated, wrote, and revised my arguments, many scholars helped me to sharpen my focus as well as my prose. I thank scholars within the field of speech communication, like Gregory Spicer and G. Thomas Goodnight, who read one or more of my chapters or listened to my conference presentations, encouraged me to continue the project, and offered specific ideas for improvement. I thank scholars within the field of Amish and Anabaptist studies, such as John Roth, Steve Nolt, Tom Meyers, David Weaver-Zercher, and Diane Zimmerman Umble, who took my work seriously, engaged it in their own scholarship, and/or gave me good reason to reconsider one or another claim. Perry Bush provided ongoing inspiration to me to complete the book, not only through his explicit words of encouragement but also in his wonderfully visible passion for his own work, which reminded me of my enthusiasm for mine. And I owe a special debt of gratitude to John Kampen, who served as proof that it is possible to serve one's institution and one's students while maintaining an active research program, and who, when I really needed it, challenged me to devote time to my research.

Faculty and staff at the University of Dayton have also provided me with crucial assistance and support. Ria Kapluck, an IT support specialist, helped me to get all of my photographs well cropped and in the proper format. Heidi Gauder, coordinator of instruction at the Roesch Library, gave me essential help in locating current studies and statistics as well as regular encouragement. Sheryl Brittig, a librarian with expertise in art and architecture, assisted me in identifying a work of art important in one of the chapters. Una Cadegan's clear and elegant prose inspired me to keep revising mine, and her enthusiasm for celebrating every step toward completion brought countless moments of joy to the project. By her relentless efforts, as dear friend and wonderful department chair, Sheila Hassell Hughes minimized administrative demands on my time so that I could complete revisions. I want especially to thank Anthony Smith, scholar of religion and popular culture, who not only read each chapter carefully but also talked through each one with me at length. His insights were brilliant and his enthusiasm for the project was infectious, so that I always left those conversations with renewed energy. In addition to these individuals, I express my deep gratitude to Dean Paul Benson, Associate Dean Don

Pair, and all of the members of the English Department at the University of Dayton for their warm welcome of me to this grace-filled community.

At a conference long ago when I presented one of my first papers on this topic, Donald Kraybill took an interest in my project. His affirmation gave me confidence to move forward with the project. Years later, as the project started to take shape, he gave me crucial advice for developing the manuscript. Most important, when a dramatic turn in my life gave me doubts about finishing the project, his unwavering support helped me to know that I should persevere. And, finally, his guidance, as well as the essential assistance of Cynthia Nolt, helped me find my way to the finish line.

During the final stages of preparing the manuscript, several individuals offered invaluable assistance. David McConnell shared wisdom from his experience publishing his book on the Amish and put me in touch with Doyle Yoder, who took wonderful photographs for the front and back covers of the book. Vicki VanNatta, longtime employee of Der Dutchman, provided important details about the restaurant when I could not make the trip to Walnut Creek. Becky Hornyak created a wonderfully clear, organized, and useful index. To Anne Whitmore, senior manuscript editor at the Johns Hopkins University Press, I owe an immeasurable debt for her painstaking work to ensure that my prose was clear, the headings were appropriate, and the citations accurate. And to Greg Nicholl, my editor at the JHU Press, I am deeply grateful, for his belief in the project and for his expertise in shepherding it through to publication.

I could not have completed this project without my close friends and family. My daughter, Anna Biesecker-Mast, and my son, Jacob Biesecker-Mast, gave me the immeasurable gift of joy throughout the project, reminding me that it is good to write and it is essential to play. Abigail and Dan Trollinger Hatch, Rebekah Trollinger, and Ahmed Khanani lovingly inquired about the progress of the project, expressed such wonderfully genuine interest in the project, and joyfully celebrated accomplishments along the way. I thank Dan, in particular, and his colleagues at Grounded Design for the artfully designed maps of Amish Country included in this book. Paul and Cindy Trollinger happily spent long evenings in conversation about the project, asking questions that challenged me to think more deeply about my answers. I am grateful to Gerald Mast, who introduced me to the world of the Amish and Amish Country tourism, for the generosity with which he shared his knowledge as an Anabaptist and rhetorical scholar. His willingness to read every draft I put in front of him and to answer every question I asked him were great gifts. I thank Brad and Jeanne Kallenberg, Ed Wingham, Rod and Johnelle Kennedy, Marc and Sue Sawyer, Tim and Luann Meador, and Andy Black, who sustained me week after week as I sought the energy and vision to keep moving forward. To my sister, Barbara Biesecker, I am thankful not only for her wisdom in pointing me in the direction of the literature on visual rhetoric and for her own brilliant theoretical insights central to the arguments of this book but also for her abiding love and care for me as a scholar and a sister.

Finally, I thank William Vance Trollinger, Jr., who, in addition to spending countless hours working through arguments and revisions with me under trying conditions, listened hard to me and read my prose so carefully (again and again) as to hear in it my voice, my heart-felt argument. With generosity and love beyond measure he then helped me to write in that voice much more clearly. It is to him that this book is dedicated.

Introduction

A Snapshot of Amish Country Tourism

On a hot summer afternoon some years ago, I witnessed a bewildering event. I was sitting on a bench outside a snack shop on Main Street in Intercourse, Pennsylvania, with friends. We were taking a break from browsing the shops of this charming tourist town in Pennsylvania's Amish Country.[1] As we sipped our freshly squeezed lemonade, a minivan pulled into one of the parking spaces in front of us. Two middle-aged white couples climbed out of the van. They were talking amongst themselves in a jovial way and seemed to be, like us, tourists.

As the group moved toward the shops to our right, one of the women spotted an Amish buggy heading in our direction at a brisk pace. Very excited, the woman thrust her hand into her purse, dug around a bit, and pulled out a camera. She then took off running toward the street. By the time she reached the street, the buggy had passed her. Not deterred, the woman ran down the street after the buggy. About a half-block down the road she stopped and, with her feet planted in the middle of the road, took a picture of the back end of that buggy. Thrilled, she ran back to her group and announced that she got the shot.

Amish Wisdom on Tourism

In late August 2004, I, along with a few friends, attended a New Order Amish worship service in Holmes County, Ohio.[2] Held in an outbuilding across the lane from the home of the Amish family who were hosting church that Sunday, the worship service lasted for a little over two hours. About a hundred people attended. For the duration of the service, we sat on backless benches, with the women on one side of the room, the men on the other, and the ministers in the middle. In the course of the worship service, one minister gave the main sermon, another minister followed with a shorter one, the congregation sang several hymns in the characteristically slow style of the Amish, and the congregation prayed together, each of us kneeling with head bowed over the bench on which we had been sitting. Shortly after the service, we shared a meal consisting of sliced cold meat and cheese, homemade bread, peanut butter spread (a mixture of peanut butter and marshmallow creme), pickles, and water. A dessert of cookies and coffee followed. While eating, as during worship, women and men sat separately.

After the meal, the Amish men escorted us visitors to a shaded area, where we sat on the grass and talked for an hour or so. The Amish women sat in another group about ten yards from us. The men talked to us about New Order Amish life. We learned, for instance, that the New Order Amish are deeply committed to Sunday school. For them, Sunday school is essential for explaining the biblical bases of their beliefs and practices. Rather than expect Amish youth to follow the rules because that is tradition, they argued, it is far better to explain the rationale behind the rules and expectations of Amish life. This is the better way, they said, even though doing so invites questions and, thus, increases the chances that some of their youth might arrive at different answers and even leave the New Order. These Amish men conceded the point that the Old Order Amish, who do not hold Sunday school or encourage such questioning, retain their youth at significantly higher rates than the New Order do.

As our conversation came to a close, I asked these Amish men what they thought about the tourists who come by the millions every year to Amish Country. Expecting them to express frustration with their overwhelming numbers, ubiquitous cameras, and ignorant questions, I was surprised to hear these Amish men talk about the important opportunity tourism provides for sharing their Christian witness through their visibly different common life and daily practices. They also spoke gratefully of the privilege they have to live a peaceful life, and they expressed compassion for tourists who, struggling with the rush and pressures of modern life, appear fascinated by the simplicity and slower pace of Amish life.

Questions and Inquiries

These two experiences of mine, each surprising in its own way, raise interesting questions about Amish Country tourism. Why would a middle-aged woman run down Main Street to capture a picture of the back end of a buggy? While the level of this woman's enthusiasm is unusual, her fascination is typical of the desire many visitors have to encounter the Amish and to capture their unusual lifestyle in photographs. Indeed, her eagerness invites questions about Amish Country tourists in general. What is it about the Amish that inspires millions of Americans to visit and revisit Amish Country each year? What is it that they want to see, capture, and experience? Even more important, what do tourists actually get when they visit Amish Country? Judging from the number of tourists carrying shopping bags out of gift shops, heritage centers, and bulk food stores, one thing they are certainly getting is a lot of merchandise. But is Amish Country tourism only a matter of consumption? Is it just about eating, browsing, and buying all things more or less connected to the Amish? Or is something beyond consumption going on here?

The second experience also raises questions. How do tourists see the Amish? Are they historical relics? A peculiar people frozen in time? Members of a bizarre religious sect? Do they merely offer a charming peek into an idealized version of premodern life? Or do they inspire important questions in tourists? Are the New Order Amish men right? Do the Amish witness to another, more peaceful, and perhaps even more humane way of life that visitors, weary from the hectic pace of modern life, find appealing? Or do the Amish function as little more than props for a tourism that promises visitors a trip down memory lane?

In this book, I address these and related questions. Although I talk about the Amish, my primary goal is not to describe them. Many others have offered excellent accounts of the Amish, and references to their books and articles can be found in this book's bibliography. Instead, my purpose is to understand Amish Country tourism and, specifically, how it attracts and sustains the interest of millions of visitors each year. The purveyors of Amish Country tourism use a variety of strategies to draw tourists in and give them pleasure during their stay, and I explore those techniques. I focus especially on the role the Amish play, wittingly or unwittingly, in providing visitors with satisfying experiences.

Because I am interested in the significance of the Amish in Amish Country tourism, I describe how the image of the Amish is constructed by the stories that are told and the experiences that are created for the enjoyment of tourists. However, because the Amish cannot be reduced to what tourism techniques make of them, I am also interested in how the Amish challenge the images of them that tourism constructs.

Shaping the Lives of Tourists and Amish

It is easy to imagine that nothing important happens when tourists visit Amish Country. For anyone who has toured such areas or who has watched visitors move through them, it is tempting to conclude that whatever tourists get in Amish Country, it is certainly not authentic encounters with Amish people. After all, visitors to Amish-settled areas do not spend their time getting to know the Amish, who (for good reason) do not necessarily want to get to know the tourists. Instead of encountering the Amish, tourists experience tourist attractions. Some tourist attractions provide helpful information about the Amish, such as where they came from, how they live in community, what their commitments are, and so forth. However, most do not. Most say little if anything about the Amish but instead focus on selling the tourist a souvenir, an amusement park ride, or a home décor item. Even if tourists meet an Amish person in the role of a tour guide, buggy-ride driver, or clerk at a produce stand, they do not in the course of such brief interactions come to know the Amish.

A visit to an Amish tourist area does not afford visitors an authentic encounter with the Amish. As I argue in chapter 2, it cannot. This is because all tourism is a form of mediation. Like a photograph, a television set, or a newspaper, tourism presents an image of something, not the thing itself. In doing so, it tells tourists how to see what is in front of them and guides them in making meaning of it. When visitors tour a Civil War battlefield, for instance, they do not experience the Civil War. Instead, they look at a field, listen to a guide tell them a story, or remember some account of a battle they saw on the History Channel. What they see, hear, read, and remember helps them conjure up an idea of what the Civil War was like. In the same way, Amish Country tourism consists of a collection of attractions, images, and stories that tells visitors what to notice about the Amish, how to interpret what they see, how to think about themselves in relationship to what they see—in short, how they should understand the Amish. Visitors would be mistaken to assume that everything the tourism industry tells them about the Amish is true. Indeed, the Amish are always more complicated and more interesting than any representation tourism offers of them.

However, to say that tourism cannot provide visitors with an authentic experience of the Amish is not to say that nothing meaningful happens when a tourist spends time in Amish Country. On the contrary, I argue that what transpires among tourists and the Amish is important. This is because Amish Country tourism consists of a system of representation that shapes the way Americans think about a significant and growing religious minority in this country and Americans' relationship to that minority. In addition, it influences how tourists see themselves, as well as their past, present, and future.

A system of representation consists of various signs. Each sign connects a signifier (such as a word, an object, a sound, a taste) to a signified (the meaning associated with each signifier). Within any system of representation, meanings are associated in fairly reliable ways. This system makes it possible for human beings to make sense of their world relatively easily. For instance, in the system of representation that governs ground transportation in the United States, the color red (a signifier) is often associated with danger, alarm, and urgency. This being so, whenever one sees, say, red flashing lights, one knows that danger lies ahead and that one should be alert.

Of course, not all signs are so easily read. Take the new car market, for example. As a system of representation, the new car market consists of many signs—each new car being one. Each sign within the system is designed to mean something that at least some prospective buyers are supposed to find appealing. With the creation of more and more niche markets, the meaning of the Scion versus the Nissan versus the Ford has become increasingly complex. Human beings are good at making sense of even such complex systems of representation. Thus, anyone who pays even a little attention to this system of representation knows that, whereas "Escalade" means big, powerful, luxurious, and gas guzzling, "Prius" means small, high-tech, socially progressive, and "green."

Human beings not only understand complex systems of representation, they are also heavily influenced by them. Thus, which cluster of meanings they find most appealing—that associated with the Escalade, the Prius, or some other vehicle—will have a great deal of impact on which car they buy.[3] In ways such as these, systems of representation shape not only the meanings that human beings make of their world but also the commitments they develop, the values they embody, and the decisions they make.

Like the new automobile market, Amish Country tourism is a system of representation; it associates the Amish with some meanings and disassociates them from others. Within Amish Country tourism, for instance, the Amish are connected with terms such as "simple," "peaceful," and "hardworking" but not "sophisticated," "violent," or "lazy." In this way, tourism tells visitors who the Amish are. By associating these words with the Amish, the tourism industry encourages visitors to evaluate the Amish in more or less positive ways. For instance, brochures often praise the Amish for these attributes. Thus, tourists come to know the Amish as not only simple, peaceful, and hardworking but also as good.[4]

Likewise, Amish Country tourism also offers images of tourists. It tells tourists who they are and suggests how they might evaluate and even alter their manner of living. Indeed, those same Amish Country brochures often talk about the speed of American life and how it causes visitors to experience excessive stress. Further, by contrasting the positive attributes of Amish life to the negative terms they associate with modern life, these brochures often make the suggestion that taking a certain course of action (such as spending more time around the Amish in Amish Country) is likely to make visitors happier. Amish Country tourism constructs these meanings about the Amish and tourists not only through the words and images of brochures, advertisements, and the like, but also by the environments that consist of buildings, interior décor, merchandise, and so forth. These tourism environments, within which tourists spend a day, a weekend, or longer, construct these meanings in various and powerful ways.

One of the most powerful tools for creating these meanings is story. Each of the tourist towns featured in this book retells one or more stories. The architecture, interior décor, merchandise, and other elements come together to invite the visitor to imagine that they are part of these narratives. The stories retold in a town, such as those about gender or the nation or the frontier, are popular myths that have long shaped American identity.[5] As tourists move through the spaces of the town, those myths are called to mind. The Amish, who have traditionally not been included in those myths because they were understood to stand outside mainstream American culture, are repeatedly woven into these myths as if they too were part of them. As a result, they seem to take on qualities of the characters in those myths.

The central argument of this book, then, is that Amish Country tourism creates a lot of meaning and that the meaning it generates matters to visitors. As millions of tourists move through the inns, shops, restaurants, and gardens of Amish Country every year, they are invited to imagine themselves as figures in the myths these environments tell. Insofar as these narratives give visitors compelling ways of understanding the Amish and their world, they also have the potential to shape the identity of the tourists, their view of the world, and their decisions. Since the millions of tourists who visit Amish Country each year appear to enjoy their experiences there, it is important to understand the myths they are taking up, how those myths produce pleasure for them, and how the myths might influence the visitors' self-understandings and aspirations for the future.

Amish Country tourism should be taken seriously. Although it is tempting to infer that Amish Country tourism is culturally unimportant because it does not involve an authentic encounter between tourists and Amish, it would be a mistake to do so. Amish Country tourism is not meaningless entertainment, just a distraction from everyday life. It impacts the lives of millions of tourists each year and influences the lives of hundreds of thousands of Amish.

Although Amish Country tourism is powerful in its constructions of meaning about the Amish and tourists, it is important to remember that no system of representation can completely or forever fix the meanings that it makes. Things are always too complex and changing for that. Thus, it is wise to take seriously what those New Order Amish men told me that Sunday afternoon. They said that tourism affords them an opportunity to witness to the millions of visitors who cross their paths each year. Put in the terms I am using here, the Amish are themselves a system of representation and, as such, are saying something to tourists. If those New Order Amish men are right, then the meaning that the Amish create by their witness might differ significantly from or even contest what Amish Country tourism would have visitors see and believe about them.

Scope and Method

Amish Country tourism happens in many places throughout the United States, but it occurs on an especially large scale in the three largest Amish settlements in the world, which are located in Pennsylvania, Indiana, and Ohio. Across these three settlements, what Amish Country tourism offers is quite similar. As I discuss in chapter 2, in all three locations, tourists encounter such attractions as huge Amish-style restaurants accompanied by bakeries and food shops, as well as amusement parks or water parks, furniture stores, and comfortable inns. Given the similarities among these three tourism areas, I have chosen to focus on Amish Country tourism in Ohio.

Ohio Amish Country tourism offers good study material for two reasons. First, although Ohio is home to the largest Amish settlement in the world, comparatively little scholarly research has been done on the Ohio Amish.[6] By contrast, much scholarly attention has been given to the Pennsylvania Amish and quite a few articles and books have been published on the Indiana Amish. Second, Amish Country tourism in Ohio grew rapidly during the fifteen years (1995–2010) that I conducted my research. Many inns, restaurants, and shops were built or expanded during that time. The Amish settlement in Ohio experienced huge economic growth during that time, largely because of tourism.[7] These developments warrant scholarly attention.

This book focuses on one of the Ohio Amish settlements, in order to do a close reading of the complex representations that make up Amish Country tourism. To understand how some signs are related to other signs and how they thereby tell stories and make meaning, it is necessary to look at them closely. Focusing on Amish Country tourism in one settlement enables such a close reading.

The particular kind of close reading offered in this book pays attention to what in the field of rhetorical studies is called "visual rhetoric."[8] Rhetoric is about how systems of representation persuade human beings (more or less successfully) to understand themselves, others, and their world in particular ways; to value people, ideas, events, places, and so forth in certain ways; to take or not to take one or another form of action; or to identify or dis-identify themselves with a person, a community, a nation, or an identity.[9] Traditionally, the field of rhetorical studies has focused on spoken and written texts. However, in the last decade or so, many rhetorical scholars have turned their attention to other kinds of visual texts, understood in a broad sense, in recognition of the fact that a great deal of persuasion makes use of communicative modes beyond speech and writing, such as objects and spaces. Visual rhetoric, then, is about how these other modes of communication shape the way human beings think, value, act, and identify.

Because the tourism industry uses signs in the forms of images, buildings, interior décor, and merchandise, it is right to take a visual rhetorical approach to understanding Amish Country tourism. By taking this approach I am able to attend closely to the three-dimensional and multisensory spaces that address tourists in complex, meaningful, and sometimes surprising ways. My readings are based in ethnographic research that was conducted over the course of fifteen years and included (among other research strategies) personal observations, extensive field notes, hundreds of photographs, and several interviews.

Overview and Organization

As a case study, I consider three of the most heavily trafficked tourist towns in Ohio's Amish Country. Noting that each of these towns features a distinct theme, I look at how these themes are constructed in the architecture and in the interior décor of those buildings. I consider how those themes are further developed in the merchandise that is sold within the buildings. I also attend to how tourists move in these spaces and engage the objects found within them.

Along the way, I talk about the tourists. As it happens, they are a relatively homogeneous group. Of course, there are differences among them. On the whole, however, they are white middle-class Americans who come from areas within a day's drive of an Amish settlement. Given the location of the three largest settlements, that means that they tend to come from the Midwest and the Northeast. They share anxieties typical of their demographic in this time and culture. Recognizing this, I argue that the pleasure that comes from Amish Country tourism has a lot to do with the fact that it offers symbolic resolutions to those anxieties.[10] By retelling myths that appear to provide solutions to their concerns, Amish Country tourism reassures visitors that the future looks bright; it thereby brings them pleasure.[11] I explain how the Amish fit into these narratives and how they are made to legitimate these myths and authenticate the solutions offered by them.

In the first chapter, I introduce the Amish by describing their origins, theological and biblical beliefs, and distinctive practices, as well as some recent changes that have significantly affected their common life. In chapter 2, I provide an overview of Amish tourism in the three largest settlements of Amish in the world, describe the average tourist to Amish Country, and summarize the current wisdom on Amish Country tourism. In chapters 3, 4, and 5, I focus on three themed tourist towns in Ohio. The first is Walnut Creek, a town that only twenty years ago could boast of little more in the way of tourist attractions than one Amish-style restaurant. Today, with its Victorian theme made visible in its shops, inns, and restaurants, Walnut Creek encourages millions of visitors each year to experience time, gender, and nation in what is portrayed as soothing and reassuring ways. In chapter 4, I turn to Berlin, with its American frontier theme, and consider how the story of the American frontier told there helps ease American anxieties about the relationship between technology and human agency. Chapter 5 is about Sugarcreek, the town with the longest history of tourism in Ohio's Amish Country. I consider how this town, known to tourists as "The Little Switzerland of Ohio," addresses tourists' concerns about race and ethnicity in a multicultural age. In the final chapter, I take a look at a distinctive tension in all Amish Country tourism between one strong desire that tourists have and the Amish resistance to it. I close with an exploration of the possible consequences that tourists' frustration may have for their future transformation.

Selling the Amish

An Amish couple driving their open carriage into the center of Berlin, Ohio

CHAPTER 1

Who Are the Amish?

The hurrier I go, the behinder I get.
—Amish folk wisdom, printed on a coffee mug

B y now, most Americans know something about the Amish. They know that the Amish are a distinctive religious sect whose members wear plain clothes, drive horse-drawn buggies, and have peculiar views about violence and forgiveness. Americans are familiar with these aspects of Amish life largely because of media coverage of the West Nickel Mines shooting in 2006, the UPN reality show *Amish in the City* (2004), and the Cinemax documentary *Devil's Playground* (2003), as well as fictional accounts of Amish life in films like *Amish Grace* (2010), *For Richer or Poorer* (1997), and *Witness* (1985). Of course, the degree of accuracy in these media representations of the Amish varies widely. A clearer picture of Amish origins, history, and contemporary life, based in the scholarship of Amish studies, will make it easier to see how Amish Country tourism draws upon Amish culture in its appeals to tourists.

Amish Origins

The Amish locate their origins in Europe during the first quarter of the sixteenth century. At that time, the Middle Ages were drawing to a close and the Enlightenment was just about to dawn. It was the time of the Protestant Reformation, during which people of intense religious conviction, like Martin Luther and Ulrich Zwingli, posed historic challenges to the theology, unity, and authority of the Catholic Church. One of the most important challenges that the Protestant Reformers made to the Catholic

Church involved the assertion that religious authority rests in Scripture alone. Working from this idea of "sola scriptura," Luther argued that the Bible should be translated from Latin into the vernacular, so that anyone could read it. Now his argument seems both obvious and harmless, but in his time Luther's argument constituted a major blow to the structure, practices, and authority of the church.[1]

For centuries, lay people had been unable to read the Bible because it was written in a language they did not know. As a result, they were obliged to take their understanding of it from clerics, who had been trained by the church to interpret the Bible in certain ways. When Luther argued that the Bible should be made accessible to any literate person, and when he later translated it himself into German, things began to change. By enabling lay people to read and, therefore, make their own meaning of the Bible, Luther and other Reformers created the possibility for multiple interpretations of God's word. But the Reformers did not just make the Bible more accessible. They also urged all Christians to become full participants in the project of figuring out what God was saying and what God's word meant for Christians. Embracing this call, many earnest Christians developed new interpretations of Scripture and became committed to them. Not surprisingly, their interpretations varied not only from those of the Catholic Church but also from one another. Thus, new versions of Christianity began to emerge, and Protestantism, in all its fascinating and bewildering diversity, was born.[2]

The Reformation transformed the landscape of Christian faith and practice dramatically. Still, some Christians thought that the Reformation had not gone far enough. They came to be known as the Radical Reformers. According to them, the early church was the true church of Jesus Christ because it fearlessly proclaimed the Gospel and was persecuted for doing so. In contrast to the early church, they argued, the sixteenth-century church (in both its Catholic and Reformed varieties) was not persecuted and remained closely tied to the state.[3] According to the Radical Reformers, no church could truly follow Jesus Christ if it was in any way structurally connected to the state. They therefore called for separating church and state.

By the time of the Reformation, the church had been officially connected to the state for well over eleven centuries. Indeed, it was in 380 CE that Theodosius made Christianity the official religion of the Roman

Empire. When Theodosius brought the church under the protection of the state, the Radicals argued, the church ceased to be the true church of Jesus Christ. This was so, they reasoned, because once the church became dependent on the state for its protection, it also came under the control of the state, thus forfeiting its power to tell the truth to and about the state

Worse yet, the Radical Reformers continued, within a relatively short period of time the church became the primary means for legitimating the actions and policies of the state, especially in the case of war. Already, in 312 CE, the Roman emperor Constantine had argued that his armies had been victorious on the battlefield because God had favored them. In particular, he claimed, God had given them the victory because all of them were wearing a Christian symbol during the battle. For the Radical Reformers, it was wrong for the Christian church to be used to legitimate or justify violence. According to their interpretation of the New Testament, Jesus taught that Christians should never take up the sword.[4] Instead, they argued, Jesus called on his followers to be peacemakers. In support of this interpretation, they pointed to the Sermon on the Mount, wherein Jesus said that Christians should not defend themselves even when attacked but should turn the other cheek. The church of Jesus Christ, the Radical Reformers argued, should never cooperate with the state's efforts to wage war and should, instead, embrace nonviolence and teach peace.[5]

After over twelve hundred years of church-sanctioned war, the Radical Reformers asserted, it was time for the church to separate itself from the state. One of the ways in which the Radical Reformers sought to do this was by rejecting the practice of infant baptism. According to them, infant baptism was one of the primary means by which the church and the state were connected. Legally, through the sacrament of baptism a child became both a Christian and a citizen of the state. By fusing state citizenship with church membership, the Radical Reformers argued, infant baptism brought every Christian under the protection and the power of the state. One implication of this situation was that the state could oblige Christians to act contrary to the teachings of Jesus by forcing them to kill other human beings in war. Given that one's allegiance to God must always supersede any other allegiances, and given that a Christian should always follow the teachings of Jesus before the commands of any monarch or general, only if the church were separate from the state could a Christian really live as a Christian.

The Radical Reformers also opposed infant baptism because they believed that baptism required making a lifelong commitment to following God in all things. Because babies were incapable of making any decisions, never mind one of such eternal significance, baptism should be a choice made by adults who understood the gravity of their decision and the challenge of remaining faithful to it.

On January 21, 1525, a small group of Radical Reformers gathered in Zurich and performed their first adult baptisms. Because of this practice, they came to be known as Anabaptists. This was a term of derision coined by their critics and meaning "re-baptizers." It was intended to chide the Radical Reformers for performing what Catholics and non–Radical Reformers considered a second, and thus unnecessary, baptism. Of course, the Radical Reformers did not see their adult baptisms as repetitions, since according to their theology their infant baptisms were not true baptisms.

Since it was through infant baptism that the state claimed all Christians as its subjects and the church counted all citizens as Christians, both the state and the church opposed adult baptisms. Indeed, adult baptism posed such a fundamental threat to the longstanding connection between church and civic authority that both entities endeavored to eliminate Anabaptists and, thereby, their dangerous ideas. For nearly a century after that first adult baptism, both the church (in its Catholic and Protestant forms) and civic authorities tracked, arrested, tried, tortured, and executed thousands of Anabaptists.[6]

Church and civil authorities had some difficulty eliminating Anabaptism because it turned out to be more popular than expected. Over time, Anabaptists also became more capable of avoiding detection and capture. In order to reduce Anabaptists' ability to attract more converts, the authorities focused on eliminating Anabaptist leaders. Many were captured, tortured, and executed.

One Anabaptist leader who managed to escape persecution was Menno Simons. While serving as a Catholic priest, Simons became convinced by Anabaptist readings of the Bible. He left the Catholic Church in 1536, became a leader among Anabaptists, and spent the rest of his life on the run. Amazingly, Simons managed to produce extensive Anabaptist writings even as he fled one town and then another. Books, tracts, and essays written by Simons were published and disseminated. They encouraged many others to adopt his view of Christian faith, community, and disciple-ship. Such converts came to be known as Mennists or Mennonites.[7]

To escape ongoing persecution, many Anabaptists fled their homelands in Switzerland (where most of the persecution occurred) for the Nether-lands, the Rhine region of Germany and France (particularly the Palati-nate and the Alsace), and Moravia. Persecution continued throughout the seventeenth century in Switzerland and in some of those areas to which Anabaptists had fled. Consequently, another wave of immigration oc-curred, this time to Russia and North America. Throughout their history, Anabaptists have continued to experience periods of persecution owing to the clash between their beliefs and those of their host cultures, although clearly, the persecution in the sixteenth and seventeenth centuries was the most severe and widespread.

In certain times and places, Anabaptists have enjoyed periods of toler-ance in which they have thrived, especially economically. When that hap-pened, typically one or more among them would become concerned that, as a people, they were becoming assimilated to the values and practices of their host culture and, thus, were no longer serving their prophetic role as faithful witnesses to the Gospel of Jesus Christ. This was the concern that inspired Thieleman van Braght to assemble the stories of Anabaptist mar-tyrs in 1660. Addressing Dutch Anabaptists who were living comfortably amidst peace and prosperity, van Braght exhorted his readers in the first pages of his eleven-hundred-page account of the Anabaptist martyrs to read these stories as reminders that to be a Christian is to be one who, like Jesus, should always be prepared to sacrifice life for faith.[8]

In the 1690s, Jacob Amman made a similar critique of the Swiss Ana-baptists, whom he lived among in the Alsace region. According to Am-man, these Anabaptists had assimilated to Alsatian culture and, as a re-sult, were lax in their response to brothers and sisters in the church who strayed from proper Anabaptist convictions and practices. For Amman, the church was always threatened by the potential for believers to drift from central Christian teachings. In order for the church to remain the church, he argued, it was necessary to impose excommunication and "the ban," or shunning, whenever a believer acted counter to core beliefs and refused to repent for having done so.[9]

Amman's aim was to reform the Anabaptist church by returning it to its core beliefs and practices as articulated more than a century earlier. Many

Anabaptist ministers agreed with him. Many others did not. To the surprise of some church members, Amman excommunicated the ministers who disagreed with him. In 1693, his followers created a new Anabaptist sect, which came to be known as the Amish.[10]

Within a few decades or so of their birth, the Amish were again fleeing persecution. In the 1700s, many crossed the Atlantic and settled in eastern Pennsylvania. By the 1800s, some were on the move again, this time not because they were being persecuted but because the Lancaster settlement was becoming more populated and they wanted additional productive farmland. They found rich soil in eastern Ohio, and soon other Amish followed them to the area that became Holmes, Wayne, and Tuscarawas counties, now known as Ohio's Amish Country. Similarly, in the 1840s Amish from Ohio and Pennsylvania traveled to Indiana and established what is now the Elkhart-LaGrange settlement.[11]

Amish Beliefs Today

The same beliefs that formed the Amish originally continue to shape them today. The Amish are strongly influenced by the biblical and theological convictions inherited from their Anabaptist forebears. One such conviction is that one's faith in God can never be reduced to a private or internal matter. For the Amish, as for the sixteenth-century Anabaptists, one's faith in God must be made manifest through one's obedience to the teachings of Jesus. Since they believe Jesus' teachings to be God's clearest revelation to humans, they must follow his teachings if they wish to be faithful to God. Because of this belief, the Amish take seriously the way they practice everyday life. That includes how they dress, how they make a living, how they worship, the languages they speak, and their means of transportation. All of these practices are matters of faith for the Amish.[12] To understand the ways of the Amish that many tourists find fascinating, it is therefore crucial to understand the faith commitments that drive them.

In addition to traditional Anabaptist commitments—adult baptism, separation from the state, and nonviolence—the Amish also hold to separation from the world, communalism, and "yieldedness." Like their sixteenth-century forebears, the Amish believe that in order to be the church of Jesus Christ, they must separate themselves from the state. At the heart of that commitment is their belief that Christians are called by Jesus to love everyone, including the enemy and, thus, to do no harm to anyone. Since states usually use force or the threat of force to enforce their policies, no Christian should serve the state. On this conviction, the Amish separate themselves from the state as much as they can by, for instance, refusing to serve in the military, not putting themselves forward for political office, and never taking a job as a police officer. Of course, the Amish have other reasons for separating themselves from the state. By rejecting certain forms of assistance from the state, like public assistance payments, for example, the Amish are obliged to rely on one another, thus strengthening the ties of their community.

The Amish also seek separation from the world. They understand the world to be driven by violence, competition, individualism, and scarcity. By contrast, they see the Kingdom of God as a place of peace, grace, community, and bounty. Some Christians believe that their task is to bring the Kingdom of God into the world right now, and so they, for example, lobby politicians to pass laws that they think are aligned with the Kingdom. For the Amish, this is a mistake. The call of the Christian, they believe, is not to make the world into the Kingdom of God. Instead, it is to watch for all the ways in which the Kingdom of God is already present in the here-and-now. According to the Amish, Christians should focus on witnessing to God's presence and truth whenever and however they can. When they help a stranger or extend grace to an offender or lend a hand to someone in need or put away their anger, they believe they are making God's already-present Kingdom visible to the world.

According to the Amish, the world continues its violent, competitive, individualistic, and materialistic ways. It does so, they believe, because it has not seen or refuses to acknowledge what Jesus did on the cross. For the Amish, Jesus' death and resurrection are God's clearest revelation that by God's grace all humanity is reconciled to God and one another.[13] This being so, the Amish reason, it makes no sense that anyone should be angry, hateful, judgmental, competitive, or violent. Because the world does not recognize the truth and presence of the Kingdom of God, it goes on thinking that reality demands that human beings be competitive, judgmental, and violent. Confused about what is really real, the world continues to reproduce its false reality through its laws, contests, business schemes, shopping centers, security systems, armies, and the like. Unfortunately, say the Amish, that false reality is as dehumanizing as it seems compelling.

For the Amish, it is imperative for Christians to recognize that the Kingdom of God is true whereas the so-called reality of the world is false. Moreover, they believe that Christians are called to live in accordance with the nonviolent, graceful, and forgiving character of the Kingdom of God even as they live in the world. The Amish know that it is difficult to live in the world and yet resist its tempting ways. Thus, they try to live apart from the world and, thereby, be as free as possible from its influences. By staying separated from the world, they believe, they have the best chance of living according to the truth, values, and practices that constitute the Kingdom of God.

In addition to separation from the state and the world, the Amish also believe strongly in communalism. Like their commitments to adult baptism, nonviolence, and separation, this tenet also dates back to the early Anabaptists. As indicated by the name of their first confession of faith, the Schleitheim Brotherly Union, the Amish live their religious commitments in community, or what they call the brotherhood.[14] They do so believing that the Christian is called to live in a manner contrary to the ways of the world. Living in reconciliation with all other human beings in a world of hate, violence, and war requires a lot of help; it cannot be done in isolation. For the Amish, to truly be a disciple of Jesus in the world requires living in community with others who also follow Jesus.

To be more specific on this point, the Amish believe that a true Christian must practice nonviolence. To do that in a world convinced that in the end violence solves problems and resolves injustices requires immersion in a community that thinks and acts otherwise. Within such community, an individual who believes he or she has been slighted and wants to lash out can get counsel and support for acting instead with grace and forgiveness. Even more important, an individual who has been steeped in the attitudes and practices of a nonviolent community is not likely to think that a violent response is good or even makes sense. Without training in the mindset and ways of violence, such a person is highly unlikely even to be able to raise a hand against another. Of course, the Amish know that the community provides no guarantee that every member will be able to practice nonviolence. Still, they are convinced that a Christian community separated from the world provides the best chance to follow Jesus' commands.

The Amish recognize that the world has a great deal to offer that looks, feels, and sounds both good and true. If Christians are going to resist its offerings in all its many, tempting, and changing forms, they are going to need their brothers' and sisters' help. When Christians do begin to succumb to temptation, as they surely will now and again, they will need their community of faith to get them back on the right path. Or, if they are struck by misfortune—their house burns down or a husband becomes ill or a crop yield is bad—they will need the community of faith to get them through materially and spiritually. In all these ways, community is central to Amish faith.

A final crucial commitment for the Amish is to *Gelassenheit*, a German word that means "yieldedness." Although the term is rarely used by the Amish, it captures the idea that living nonviolently means more than never willfully harming another person, even an enemy. It also means that they should not try to make history come out right. They believe that it is not their job to make sure that the good guys win or that justice is done but that the work of justice is God's. Moreover, they believe that God already made everything fundamentally right when Jesus died on the cross for everyone and then was raised three days later. For the Amish, Christians can do no better and no more than Christ did on the cross.[15] Furthermore, since God continues to work in the world through the Holy Spirit, the Amish believe that Christians should leave it to God to work things out in God's own way and time.

Thus, instead of taking matters into their own hands, the Amish believe they should yield. Rather than fight, sue, or prosecute when threatened or harmed by another, the Amish accept that a Christian should turn the other cheek as well as forgive and forget. Rather than join a protest or run for office when it appears that the civic order is becoming a mess, the Amish are convinced that their focus should be on living the Christian life within their own community. Yielding in ways such as these is Gelassenheit, and it is the Amish mode of being in the world. Gelassenheit allows them to love their enemy and, they believe, is the mode of being in the world that most closely resembles Christ on the cross.[16]

Amish Practices Today

The Amish are a complex people. Even to speak of *the* Amish is problematic. There are many different kinds, or affiliations, of Amish, ranging from the very change-resistant Swartzentruber Amish, who are not allowed to have gravel on their dirt driveways or windshields on their buggies, to the very change-minded Beachy Amish, who drive automobiles. Even within a particular affiliation, such as the Old Order Amish, there is significant variation depending upon which settlement they live in and the approach to change that their local Amish bishop takes.[17] Additionally, no matter how hard the Amish work to maintain their traditional way of life, they are nevertheless influenced over time by changes in the world. When, for instance, a new technology becomes available, some Old Order Amish may begin to use it. If the use of that new technology does not seem to threaten the character of Old Order Amish life, it may become accepted for use more broadly.[18]

The settlements in which the Amish live may consist of only a dozen families or contain tens of thousands of Amish people. A settlement consists of one or more districts. A district is a single congregation typically consisting of twenty-five to thirty-five families who live in a relatively small geographical area.[19] Since Amish worship services are held in homes rather than in church buildings, districts are limited to the number of families that the homes can accommodate.[20]

The Family

Within the district, Amish life is organized according to family units. Amish families tend to be large, typically consisting of two parents, six or more children, and one pair of grandparents. Families usually live in one or more houses on a farm.[21] Farming has always been the preferred occupation among Amish, both because they are very good at it and because they believe that living by the land enables a Christian to be close to God. The husband is the head of the household, and the wife is expected to defer to his authority. For those families that farm, the husband is primarily responsible for working the fields and caring for livestock, but all members of the family work the farm together. The wife's duties center on the house and include the laundry, cleaning, sewing, and cooking. In addition, she typically tends to a large vegetable garden and preserves most of its produce for use throughout the winter months. She is also primarily responsible for child care. From an early age, children assist their parents by working alongside them in the house, barn, fields, and garden. Children tend to be given chores that are gender specific. Girls work in the house and garden with their mothers while boys work in the barn and fields with their fathers. However, during the seasons of planting and harvesting, everyone works in the fields.

Education

For the Amish, the family is the primary location for raising and educating children. By working with their parents all day, Amish children learn not only the skills but also the attitudes and values required for Amish life. Thus, while acquiring the ability to bake bread, drive a team of horses, or plant crops, they are also taught that they must bend their will to the wisdom of the sect and that idleness is a gateway to sin. Within the family, the children also learn about their Amish heritage and faith. The Bible is read and discussed in daily devotions; stories of Anabaptist martyrs are handed down from one generation to the next. Beyond the family, Amish children are educated in reading, writing, and arithmetic. They attend one-room schools close to their homes and are usually taught by young Amish women who, like all Amish, receive no formal education beyond the eighth grade.

The Amish are strongly committed to limiting their children's schooling. They had few problems when the norm for all rural American children was a one-room schoolhouse and few children were educated beyond the eighth grade. But beginning in the 1920s, when some state governments tried to force Amish children to attend consolidated elementary schools or to stay in school until they were sixteen years old, some Amish resisted by refusing to send their children to school. For their defiance of state law, well over a hundred Pennsylvania Amish were imprisoned. The issue was largely resolved in 1972 when the US Supreme Court ruled that allowing the Amish to educate their children in a manner consistent with their religious beliefs was in keeping with the Constitution.[22]

The Amish go to such lengths to control their children's schooling because they are convinced that their children need an education designed to prepare them for Amish life, not for mainstream American life. If Amish children were to attend mainstream schools, they would study subjects regarded as unnecessary for Amish life. More importantly, they would learn values and ideas contrary to those of the communal life of the Amish. For instance, in mainstream American education, children learn to compete with one another, to articulate distinct positions, to think critically, and to value the individual. These ideas and values are not compatible with

Amish life, which requires individuals who readily yield to tradition and the common will of the community.[23]

From the time Amish children finish school at about fourteen years of age until they reach sixteen, they work all day at home with their parents. Throughout the day, they work, learn, and play under the watchful care of their Amish family. When they reach the age of sixteen, however, they are granted freedom both to spend more time with their Amish friends and to experience aspects of the outside world that have so far been forbidden. The Amish call this period in the life of Amish youth (from sixteen to about twenty-two) *Rumspringa*, which translates as "running around" time.

Rumspringa is for spiritual exploration as well as learning about the world. During this period, Amish youth consider both how best to live a Christian life, if they choose to do so, and whether or not to live in the world according to Amish ways or to take up the ways of the "English," as the Amish call the non-Amish. For the Amish, candidates for baptism and membership in the Amish church must think carefully about whether they are ready to commit their life to faithful discipleship. They must also have the opportunity to experience the world that they will be obliged to reject if they join the Amish church. For this reason, the Amish give their youth (and especially young Amish men) freedom during Rumspringa to wear the clothes of the world, to own and drive a car, to have their own cell phones, and even to attend wild parties.[24] It is also during this time that Amish youth typically choose their life partner from among their Amish friends. Marriage typically follows closely upon baptism.[25]

Worship and Ordnung

The church and, in particular, the worship service is at the center of Amish life. Typically, the Amish gather for worship every other Sunday. Their worship services last about three hours and consist of two sermons, the distinctively slow singing of sixteenth-century hymns, and prayer. Worship services are held in homes on a rotating schedule, and each Amish family hosts church about once a year. On Sundays when they do not gather for worship, they typically visit Amish family and friends in other districts and often attend church with them.

Amish do not sit as families in church. Instead, they sit as brothers and sisters in Christ, with the men on one side of the room facing the women, who sit on the other side of the room. While one minister stands to preach the others sit in the center of the congregation. After church, the whole congregation (numbering, on average, 130 people in the Holmes-Wayne settlement and 165 in the Lancaster settlement) shares in a light meal prepared by the hosting family.[26] During the meal, as in church, they divide themselves by gender; the men eat together and the women eat together. After the meal, fellowship continues with further conversation, often still in gender-specific groups.

Each church district has a bishop, ministers, and a deacon. Only men may serve in these leadership positions, and all men who join the church promise to serve as unpaid ministers if th,ey are called upon to do so. When there is a vacancy in such a position, all church members are invited to nominate candidates. When nominations are complete, the new leader is chosen by lot: The bishop places a slip of paper in one hymnal. Then a set of hymnals equaling the number of candidates and including the one with the slip of paper is put before the candidates. Each candidate then selects a hymnal. The candidate who selects the hymnal with the slip of paper is considered the one "chosen by lot."

In addition to providing opportunities to worship God, the church serves the crucial function of establishing and protecting the rules of community life known as the *Ordnung*. The Ordnung (or order) consists of a collection of unwritten rules that govern their communal life. These rules establish how they should dress, what technology they may and may not use, what kind of behavior is prohibited, and so forth. When an Amish youth joins the church, he or she makes a commitment to follow the Ordnung for the rest of his or her life, thereby helping to preserve and protect the traditions of Amish life. Further, they agree to yield to the wisdom and discipline of the group. If the church finds a member to be in violation of the Ordnung, the offender is expected to confess his or her transgression. For infractions considered minor, the confession may be made to a church leader in private. If the infraction is considered major, the offender may have to confess it publicly to the church. Depending on the nature of the infraction, the offender may also be denied communion and/or shunned for a period of time. A member who is unwilling to be disciplined in this way risks being permanently excommunicated and shunned by the church district. Excommunication and shunning are a most fearful prospect for all

Amish, since they mean that one is put out of the only community one has ever known and a community upon which one's entire life style depends. However, any member who has been disciplined in this way may return to full membership in the church following a proper confession.[27]

Visible Signs in Amish Life

The Amish believe that if one truly believes in the saving grace of Jesus Christ, that belief will become manifest in just about everything one does. Further, because following Jesus means living according to the Kingdom of God rather than according to the world, a true Christian cannot help but look and act differently from the ways of the world.

Over the centuries, the Amish have carefully discerned within the context of community which daily practices they think best reflect the Kingdom of God and which run counter to it. The former they have adopted and the latter they have rejected. In the course of this process, they became a people visibly distinctive from the world in a variety of ways. They embrace this visible difference as part of their Christian witness to the truth that the Kingdom of God is not some idealized place located in the hereafter but, instead, is visible in the present.

Dress

One of the most visible marks of Amish discipleship is Amish dress.[28] Perhaps the most notable characteristic of Amish attire is its apparent uniformity. Seen from the perspective of an outsider, all Amish women seem to dress one way and all Amish men dress one way.[29] Adult Amish women wear solid color dresses typically of blue, green, gray, or wine that fall below the knee or lower, depending on the age of the woman. Adult women also usually wear a white apron over the dress. In some settlements, such as the one in Lancaster, Pennsylvania, the dress is accented with a small triangular shaped cape made of the same fabric as the dress. For the most part, Amish women's dresses are fastened with straight pins or snaps rather than buttons or zippers. Amish women also wear black stockings and black shoes and a white head covering (called a prayer covering), a cap that conceals most of their hair and ears. Adult Amish women are required to wear their prayer coverings in all public settings and to cover their heads in some fashion during all waking hours.[30] Women do not cut their hair; they pin it up under their covering. When they go outside, especially in the colder months, Amish women wear a black bonnet over their prayer covering.

Amish men are expected to wear long-sleeve dress shirts in solid colors such as green, blue, wine, or purple. They tuck their shirts into black or dark blue pants that have a wide flap, or broadfall, in the front that is secured with buttons. Suspenders hold up their loosely fitting pants. No belts are allowed. Amish men wear solid color vests over their shirts. Like Amish women they must cover their heads in public, so they wear a broad-rimmed hat made of straw in spring and summer and one of black wool in fall and winter. All adult Amish men who are either married or are single and over the age of forty must wear a beard, which they are expected not to trim (though some do to keep it neat), but must not wear a mustache. They wear their hair in a distinctive bowl cut.

The dress for Amish children is a variation of the dress for their adult counterparts. Like their mothers, Amish girls wear solid color dresses. However, they may or may not wear the head covering or apron, depending on their age and what they happen to be doing. Similarly, like their fathers, boys wear broadfall pants, dress shirts, suspenders, and hats.

For the Amish, their distinctive manner of dress is important for marking their separation from the world. It also communicates significant features of their Christian community and faith. The general uniformity of Amish dress, for instance, shows that they are a people who conform to communal norms, and their style of dress indicates that the norms by which they live are unlike those of the world. Whereas mainstream American fashion focuses on turning heads with the newest trend, Amish dress renders everyone's appearance the same (at least to outsiders). Moreover, the details of its style change very slowly. Also, unlike worldly styles, Amish clothing conveys a strong desire for modesty and humility.[31] Finally, whereas mainstream fashion emphasizes costliness and self-expression, Amish attire is often sewn at home with inexpensive fabrics, signaling frugality and economic equality.

Technology

The Amish are also visibly different from the world in the way that they live with technology. Although they do not see technology as evil, they are keenly aware that any technological device can alter daily life.

For the Amish, humane living is anchored in and focused upon family and community life, so any technological device that inhibits that communal life is suspect. The Amish put a premium on spending time together and actively engaging one another. Not only do they prefer to spend the day working as a family and/or with other members of their community, they also want to spend their evenings gathered together in the living room talking, reading, sewing, and so forth. Televisions, computers, iPods, and the like are not welcome in Amish homes, because such devices tend to separate individuals from one another. The Amish do not want to spend their evenings with one child engrossed in a video game and another listening to music through a set of headphones while dad watches a game on TV and mom checks her email. So important is social interaction for the Amish that they devote a considerable amount of time and energy to discerning which technological devices they will allow in their communities and how they will use them. They are always asking themselves what impact a particular technology will have on family and community life. If they find that a certain device pushes the members of their community apart from one another, they are likely to reject it.[32]

It is well known that the Amish largely reject the combustion engine in favor of the horse.[33] Rather than drive cars, the Amish use horse-drawn carriages, commonly called buggies, to take them where they need to go. Likewise, instead of tilling their fields with diesel-powered plows, the Amish pull their plows with teams of mules or horses. The Amish eschew automobiles because they are determined to protect a mode of living that maximizes time and interaction within the family and community, and the Amish maintain that cars take people away from one another. Given the significant amount of effort required to hitch a horse to a buggy and the slow pace of buggy travel, people are much more likely to stay home or, if they do go somewhere, not to go far, than if their transportation is automotive. In addition, by restricting farming technologies to those dependent on the horse, the Amish increase their dependence on one another. Harvesting without a combine means calling on extended family and friends.[34]

Beyond encouraging dependence on one another and a slow pace of life, the horse also serves as an unmistakable sign of Amish separation from the world. In a culture with interstate highways, drive-up windows, and long commutes, it is very difficult not to notice a people who travel in buggies and live at the pace of a horse. Indeed, the horse and buggy is probably the most distinctive sign of the otherness of Amish life.[35]

Language

A third major distinctive feature of the Amish is their mother tongue. Most Amish speak a dialect called Pennsylvania Dutch, also known as Pennsylvania German.[36] From infancy until they begin school, Amish children speak only this dialect. Once in school, they begin to learn English. Even after learning to speak and write English, the Amish child will depend upon Pennsylvania Dutch, since it is the language of the Amish home and community. English is the language of commerce, especially commerce with the world outside the Amish community. However, the Amish often mix their mother tongue with English, as is common in many immigrant communities.

The fact that all Amish speak Pennsylvania Dutch first and continue to speak it throughout their lives also separates them from the rest of the world. This is so, most obviously, because it gives them a way of communicating among themselves that excludes outsiders; the dialect clearly marks who is in and who is out. Moreover, the dialect connects them to their religious heritage. It is particularly significant that the Amish read two central texts of their faith in German: the Bible and the *Ausbund*. The latter (first published in 1564) contains hymns written by sixteenth-century Anabaptists who were imprisoned and awaiting their executions; the Amish sing from it at every worship service.[37]

Economic Changes and New Developments

Three aspects of the traditional, agrarian form of Amish life bear special mention. First, it was this form that dominated Amish culture throughout most of the twentieth century. Second, it is this form that Amish Country tourism uses to attract and sustain the interest of visitors. Third, traditional Amish agrarian life was and is more complicated than it appears to outsiders, than it is represented in Amish Country tourism, and than I am able to convey in this brief account of it.

Amish life is always changing as contingencies arise and the Amish respond to them in distinctive ways. Sometimes the Amish adopt the changes that they encounter in the outside culture. Such was the case when the Amish began using polyester as a primary clothing fabric. They welcomed polyester because it makes laundry easier and in no way compromises family or community life. Other times, they adopt a new device but control its use in some way. This was the tack they took with the tractor, which they brought onto their farms but refused to drive through their fields. While they will use the tractor engine to drive, say, a conveyor belt carrying hay to the loft of the barn, they will not hook it up to a plow in order to prepare their fields for planting.[38] Still other times they reject a technology because they find it to be too threatening to the values of their communal life. This has been their response to the electrical grid. Anticipating that easy access to electricity would make for longer work days throughout the year, which would, among other things, reduce time spent relaxing in the evening with family, the Amish rejected its convenience and, to this day, remain unplugged.

While the Amish have adapted their traditional agrarian life to new circumstances throughout their history, in the last twenty years or so they have felt obliged to make especially significant changes. This is so because the change that they have been adapting to is so fundamental to their common life—the economics of farming. For over four centuries, the Amish have built their common life on the farm. As a people, they have been rooted in the soil, dependent upon the seasons, and living closely with animals. Their days have been structured by sunrise and sunset, the constant need to manage manure, and all the many tasks associated with farming. This mode of life has nourished the Amish in their faith as they cared for God's creation, strengthened family life as worked together, and reinforced the practices and values of their communal life as they gathered in large groups every harvest season.

However, in the last twenty years or so, the presumption that Amish life is centered on the farm has begun to weaken as farmland has become so expensive as to be out of the reach of most Amish families. This change was due to several factors. The demand for land among the Amish increased as the Amish became more numerous. The expansion of cities, suburbs, and exurbs has encroached on Amish settlements. And, as Amish Country tourism became an increasingly popular form of entertainment, more hotels, restaurants, shopping centers, and other attractions were built in Amish-settled areas. With all of these market pressures on land, prices soared, leaving young Amish farmers unable to purchase or make a living off the land in their communities.[39]

As the economics of Amish farming became less viable, Amish families had to find alternative ways of making a living. Of course, there have always been Amish who made their living off the farm, for instance, by providing special products and services such as blacksmithing, leatherworking, and buggy repair. However, the number of Amish employed in such occupations was always low compared to those who farmed. As the price of land escaped the reach of most Amish, some opted to migrate to other agricultural areas, usually farther west, but many more stayed in their home settlements and sought other employment.[40] Without high school diplomas (never mind college educations), many Old Order Amish men who wanted to raise their families in their home settlements looked to jobs in manufacturing.

A leading scholar of Amish culture, Donald Kraybill, identifies four concerns that Amish leaders had about this shift from the farm to the factory. First, they worried about how family life would change when the father was removed from the home for full-time work elsewhere. What impact would his absence have on children who would not have the chance to work side by side with their father throughout the week? What would it mean for husbands and wives if they could no longer work together throughout the day? Second, they feared that Amish men might take on the values of the factory and the non-Amish men with whom they worked day after day. Would Amish men, like their non-Amish coworkers, eventually become focused on the clock? Would their attitudes toward work change such that they would think of it only as something they do while the clock is punched? How would a weekly paycheck change the way they think about and use money? Third, Amish leaders were concerned about how factory work would impede Amish men's commitment to communal life. Would they be able to participate fully in Amish life by attending weddings, funerals, and barn raisings given the demands of a factory work schedule? Finally, the leaders were uneasy about the fringe benefits that accompanied factory employment. Would the availability of health insurance diminish Amish dependence on mutual aid, their longstanding practice of turning to one another in times of need? Would Amish families move toward independence from the Amish community?[41] If they did, what would come of Amish life?

The Old Order Amish have taken these concerns and questions seriously. Over the last couple of decades, they have developed strategies for embracing non-farming employment. These strategies so far seem to be making it possible for them to make a good living off the farm yet retain the character of traditional Amish life.[42]

One approach that they have taken is to avoid employment in large factories owned by people outside their communities. By restricting manufacturing work to jobs in relatively small factories, typically owned by Amish or Mennonites, they do not have to worry about an overwhelming worldly influence on their men. Indeed, in many instances, Amish men find themselves working along side one another.

Examples of this approach are numerous. Keim Lumber in Charm, Ohio, is an extensive lumberyard, manufacturing facility, and retail store owned by a Mennonite family and located in a predominantly Amish area. The vast majority of its employees are Old Order Amish men. They do all kinds of work, from hand hewing wooden beams to operating computerized routers to engaging in telephone sales. Keim Lumber accommodates them in many ways, including giving them days off for weddings, funerals, and Amish holidays. The company even provides transportation for their Amish employees who live too far from the facility to make horse-and-buggy transportation feasible.[43]

Another strategy has been to develop cottage industries that can either support a family or subsidize a small farm. These small businesses create a wide variety of merchandise. Men make outdoor furniture, sheds, backyard play equipment, and much more. Producing these items is often made much easier and more profitable by the use of power tools. In an effort to encourage the success of these new cottage industries without dramatically changing Amish life, the Old Order Amish now allow power tools; but because they continue to prohibit access to the electrical grid, they use diesel engines and air compressors to power them.

Women's work has also changed with the move off the farm. Although the vast majority of Amish women (especially married Amish women) see homemaking as their primary focus, increasing numbers of them also work in these cottage industries. Sometimes they keep the books. Other times they make and/or sell their own goods, including quilts, baked items, and dried flowers. Single Amish women increasingly work outside the home in small factories applying finish to furniture, managing inventory records in lumber yards, or waiting on tables in Amish-style restaurants.[44]

These moves away from farming and toward manufacturing and small business are having a significant impact on Amish life. To be sure, there is much to commend in how the Amish have adapted new modes of making a living to longstanding values of Amish life. The Amish are thriving. The scarcity of farmland has not translated into Amish impoverishment. On the contrary, the Amish have done well financially throughout this transition. They have also done a good job of staying relatively close to home and available for important family and community events. Indeed, in many ways, contemporary Amish life looks much as it has done for a century, with its emphasis on close-knit community, traditional gender roles, and large families.

Still, important changes are emerging in Amish life. Some Amish women are running their own businesses. Some Amish families live in ranch-style homes in town and thus do not own a horse for either farm work or transportation. Some Amish have become multimillionaires by making the most of the Amish Country tourist's desire for Amish-made furniture or gazebos or cabinets. As Kraybill observes, what all this will mean for the Amish in the years ahead is impossible to know.

> The occupational bargain the Amish struck in the 1980s when they left their plows for cottage industries has served them well for a generation. It kept their work within their control and allowed it to flourish in the context of family and community. However, it remains uncertain whether this was a good compromise or a worm that will eat their soul from within over time. Will the transformation of work undermine community stability and erode Amish identity?[45]

It might seem reasonable to expect that some day soon the Amish will disappear altogether. It is not impossible that in a few years or so the Old Order Amish will be driving cars, hanging flat-screen TVs on their walls, and Tweeting. Similar predictions have been made before. Yet, two decades or so into this process, they still light their gas lamps every evening, put on their plain clothes every morning, and welcome one another into their homes for church. Despite important changes to the very structure of Amish life, this people remains peculiar—and the object of fascination for American tourists.

Ohio Amish Country tourists resting on one of the many shop porches in Berlin

CHAPTER 2

Tourism in Amish Country

Just eating my way through Amish Country.
Goin' buggy in Amish Country.
—Confessions of Amish Country T-shirts

The Amish remain a peculiar people. Most of them live in the heart-land of the United States, yet in many ways they defy the very character of American culture. They resist much of its wisdom, challenge some of its most sacred values, and reject many of its practices. Still, they flourish. They are growing in number as they find new ways to prosper even while they reject the speed, competitiveness, individualism, and much of the advanced technology of American culture. Even as the Amish contest the ways and beliefs of US culture, Americans are attracted to them. It is not too much to say that many Americans are captivated by the Amish.[1] Many non-Amish Americans seem to like being around the Amish, watching them and partaking of their culture. A trip to Amish Country is the primary means by which the non-Amish encounter these peculiar people.

Locations and Numbers

There are three major Amish Country tourism areas in the world, and all of them are in the United States.[2] They are: Lancaster County in Pennsylvania, Holmes and Wayne counties in Ohio, and Elkhart and LaGrange counties in Indiana. These three areas correspond to the three largest Amish settlements in the world: the Holmes-Wayne settlement has 227 church districts, Lancaster County (which is the oldest settlement) has 179 districts, and the Elkhart-LaGrange settlement has 137 districts.[3]

Lancaster County attracts the greatest number of tourists, for reasons of location and history. Just 65 miles west of Philadelphia, 135 miles north of Washington, DC, and 165 miles south of New York City, Lancaster County is a convenient destination for tens of millions of potential visitors seeking to escape city life and suburban sprawl.[4] Lancaster County is also the longest-standing destination for Amish Country tourism in North America; its first explicit efforts to attract tourists date back to the mid-1940s. Finally, the Lancaster County terrain is beautiful, with rolling hills and lush farmlands. Given these factors, it is not surprising that as many as 11 million tourists visit Lancaster County each year. With these impressive numbers, Amish Country tourists bring a lot of resources to Lancaster County, including $818 million in direct economic impact.[5]

While the numbers for Amish Country tourism in Ohio and Indiana are not as high, they are still impressive. Approximately 4 million tourists visit Holmes County each year, accounting for $154 million of direct economic impact annually.[6] The volume of tourists is about the same in the Elkhart area, with more than 4.2 million tourists visiting each year, resulting in $243.9 million in direct economic impact to the county.[7] While both the Holmes-Wayne settlement and the Elkhart-LaGrange settlement are, like Lancaster, located in fertile, rolling farmland, neither is near such large population centers as is the Lancaster County settlement. Moreover, efforts to promote the Amish in the Holmes-Wayne and Elkhart-LaGrange areas did not start until the late 1950s and 1960s, respectively, fifteen to twenty-five years after similar efforts in Lancaster.

A Brief History of Amish Country Tourism

In the early decades of the twentieth century, the Amish received little attention from outsiders. What notice they did get, whether on postcards or in travel magazine articles, portrayed them as a backward religious sect that did not fit within the progressive landscape of US culture.[8] All that changed in the late 1930s when national news outlets got wind of a group of Amish in Lancaster County who were resisting the state's effort to eliminate their one-room schoolhouses in the process of consolidating school districts. As the Amish appeared frequently in the pages of the *New York Times* and other national publications during the years of the dispute (1937–1938) and were characterized as defenders of the one-room

school and the old-fashioned American virtues for which it stood, outsiders became increasingly interested in learning more about the Amish.
That growing interest received a hearty response in what one scholar has
called a "surge of Amish-related literature" that "helped pave the way for
a full-blown tourist industry."[9] Novels, children's books, feature articles,
and the like appeared that further encouraged not only public interest in
learning more about the Amish but in visiting their home in Lancaster
County as well.[10] By the mid-1940s, tourism had developed into a well-
recognized phenomenon in Lancaster County. Guides led visitors on bus
tours through the rolling hills and pastoral valleys that would come to
be known as Amish Country.[11] Then, in 1955, *Plain and Fancy*, a musical
about a New York couple who travel to Lancaster County to sell a piece of
land and while there become involved in a romantic drama involving an
Amish family, opened on Broadway. With a successful run of over a year
and additional runs in other major metropolitan areas, this largely sympa-
thetic treatment of the Amish further encouraged potential tourists.[12]

Traveling to Lancaster County was made much easier in the 1940s with
the opening of the Pennsylvania Turnpike and with growing post–World
War II prosperity. With money in their pockets, many Americans took to
the new highway for weekends and holidays among the "Pennsylvania
Dutch." By 1963, 1.5 million tourists were visiting Lancaster County annually. By the mid-1990s, that number had more than doubled, to 3.5
million.[13]

An important inspiration for tourists in the latter half of that period
was yet another positive portrayal of the Amish, this time in the form of a
blockbuster film. Set on a farm in Lancaster County, Peter Weir's *Witness*
(1985) told the story of Philadelphia police detective John Book (Har-
rison Ford) and Amish widow Rachel Lapp (Kelly McGillis) who fall in
love in the course of their extraordinary efforts to protect Lapp's son, who
witnessed a murder. The sharp contrast between Book's violent world and
the deadly betrayals he encounters there, on the one hand, and the nonviolent Amish with whom he rediscovers life-giving work, friendship, and
love, on the other, inspired millions of Americans to spend a few days in
Amish Country in hopes of experiencing something of what the fictional
character John Book had come to know.[14]

The positive portrayals of the Amish that brought tourists from the
eastern United States to Lancaster County also encouraged tourists from

the Midwest to visit the major Amish settlements in Ohio and Indiana. In Ohio, Amish Country tourism began in the late 1950s; in Indiana it started about a decade later. In Ohio it first took the form of organized tours that included a noon meal, typically prepared by an Amish woman with the help of her family. Brochures about "Amishland" followed. In 1976 the Amish Farm, an early tourist attraction, began offering tours of what was once an Amish homestead located on the premises. By 1989, 1 million tourists a year were visiting what had come to be known as Ohio's Amish Country and were spending $45 million annually.[15]

The first known brochure featuring the Amish in Indiana appeared in 1966. Just four years later, Das Dutchman Essenhaus, an Amish-style restaurant, was erected in Elkhart County near Middlebury. It opened on January 1, 1971. By 1985, the owners had completed three additions to the facility to accommodate the increasing flow of tourists. That same year, they began construction of a thirty-two-unit inn on the premises. In nearby Shipshewana, now a popular destination for Amish County tourists, tourism started at the Shipshewana Auction and Flea Market. The auction had opened in 1922 as a market for Amish farmers. By 1986 its flea market boasted 1,050 booths with as many as thirty thousand shoppers per day.[16]

The Tourists

The more than 19 million tourists who annually visit the Lancaster, Holmes-Wayne, and Elkhart-LaGrange settlements are a fairly homogeneous group. Although some Asian-American, African-American, and Latino tourists make the trip to Amish Country, these groups constitute only a small fraction of the visitors to these areas.[17] Without question, the vast majority of visitors to Amish Country are white.[18] There is some variation in age and grouping, but the most common tourist is a middle-aged to retirement-age man or woman accompanied by his or her spouse and another married couple.[19]

These visitors appear to belong to, or at least to identify with, what goes by the name "the middle class" in America. They drive late-model cars, usually American-made, and often minivans or SUVs. That is to say, it is rare to see a tourist arrive in Amish Country in a car that is more than ten years old and uncommon to see them pull into the parking lot of an Amish-style restaurant in a luxury sedan.[20] They dress modestly and casually: both men and women typically wear shorts and a T-shirt in the summer and jeans and a sweatshirt in cooler weather. Often their T-shirts and sweatshirts show their enthusiasm for sports teams, the American flag, or Harley Davidson motorcycles.

The vast majority of tourists to each of the three settlements appear to come from nearby counties and states. A 1998 traffic study conducted in Ohio, for instance, showed that 88 percent of the vehicles that came into Holmes County from outside it were from other Ohio counties. Further, those cars that were not from Ohio tended to be from nearby states, such as Pennsylvania, Michigan, West Virginia, and Indiana.[21] My observations in the Lancaster and Elkhart-LaGrange settlements suggest that tourists to those areas also tend to come from nearby states and counties.[22]

In general, Amish Country tourists are working-class or middle-class people of moderate income, average education, and moderately conservative views. They are found throughout the United States but are more prevalent in the Midwest and are often associated with the "American Heartland." In discussing this group, I will refer to them as middle Americans.[23] To be sure, tourists who visit Amish Country come with a range of desires, interests, and curiosities. Recognizing some diversity among them, I nevertheless focus on the characteristics that they share and that are addressed by Amish Country tourism purveyors. Further, I consider not only who the tourist is upon arrival to Amish Country but also how they may be shaped by Amish Country tourism.

Tourist Attractions in Amish Country

Amish Country tourism offers a variety of attractions to visitors. Particularly popular is Amish food. In all three settlements, the Amish-style restaurant attracts tourists with a menu that typically features fried chicken, real mashed potatoes, and various freshly baked pies.[24] Other food attractions include bakeries, bulk food stores, farmers' markets, roadside stands, and food concessions at auctions and flea markets. At any of these places, tourists can typically find loaves of whole wheat or white bread, a variety of pies and cookies, and fresh fruits and vegetables when they are in season. For the tourist who wants to talk with an Amish person, settings like these offer ample opportunities for doing so, since at these sites Amish themselves typically sell their goods directly to customers.[25]

In addition to providing plenty of Amish-made or Amish-style food to eat or take home, Amish Country tourism offers information about Amish life and organized ways to observe Amish culture. The earliest form of this cultural observation was the bus tour. By 1946, the Hotel Brunswick of Lancaster City was running bus tours through the Lancaster settlement that featured a guide who spoke at length about Amish life through a microphone at the front of the bus. The tour typically ended with a meal in an Amish home.[26]

Another way to provide information is access to an Amish farm that has been opened to the public. Often, these farms were previously owned by an Amish family and then purchased by non-Amish entrepreneurs. They offer tourists an opportunity to see and experience the interior of an Amish house and barn. Typically, guides lead visitors on tours of the premises and talk at length about daily life on an Amish farm. The guides also often relay something about how Amish beliefs and practices originated in the theological and biblical debates of the European Reformation. At the end of the tour, and usually for an additional fee, tourists are invited to take a ride in a buggy driven by an Amish man, affording them another opportunity to talk directly with an Amish person.[27]

Amish Country tourism also offers "heritage" or "information" centers that aim to provide accurate information about Amish life, history, and culture to tourists, who often harbor misconceptions about the Amish.[28] Mennonites concerned about the plethora of misinformation given to tourists about their religious cousins often own or run these centers.[29]

Each of the three largest settlements is home to such an information center. Menno-Hof, the heritage center in the Elkhart-LaGrange settlement, features a guided tour of a barnlike structure in which tourists learn about the sixteenth-century European origins of the Amish and Mennonites, their immigration to North America in the eighteenth and nineteenth centuries, and some of their more notable efforts at relief work throughout the twentieth century. The Lancaster Mennonite Historical Society and the Mennonite Information Center share a building just off US Route 30 in Lancaster County. Together, they offer a bookstore filled with titles on Amish and Mennonite topics, museum displays of Amish and Mennonite art and culture, a Ten Thousand Villages shop that sells fair-trade goods made by third-world artisans, and a reconstruction of Moses' tabernacle. In Berlin, Ohio, the Amish and Mennonite Heritage Center features a 265-foot-long, 10-foot high cyclorama depicting the origins and history of Amish and related groups.[30] Visitors may take a tour of the cyclorama with a local Mennonite, Beachy Amish,[31] New Order, or Old Order Amish guide and visit the bookstore, which is well stocked with books about Amish, Mennonite, and other plain groups. The center also offers a free, twenty-minute video that introduces the history and life of the Amish and Mennonites in the area.

Amish Country tourism also offers shopping opportunities and recreational activities. Although many of these attractions make reference to the Amish, often in oblique ways, their purpose is not primarily to convey information about the Amish. Indeed, if they make reference to the Amish, they typically do so as if "Amish" were a brand like "Levi" or "Nike" or "Apple." As a brand, "Amish" suggests the high quality associated with Amish craftsmanship (especially related to furniture and food) and/or certain aspects of Amish life, like its slower pace or its commitment to family, church, and community.[32] Even many of the tourist attractions mentioned above, like Amish farms or Amish-style restaurants, include gift shops that sell a variety of merchandise.

The merchandise in some of these gift shops and stores makes reference to the Amish: cookbooks for Amish-style food, Amish-style dolls dressed in plain clothes and typically lacking facial features, or books about the Amish. However, most of the items sold in these shops have no direct connection to the Amish, and Amish Country tourism offers many shopping opportunities that have no apparent relationship to Amish life. For example, Lancaster has both a host of small, independent shops that appear in "villages" (e.g., Kitchen Kettle Village in Intercourse) and along roads in tourist towns, as well as two major outlet malls that feature discounted brand-name merchandise from such brands as Gap, Kenneth Cole, Carter's, Pottery Barn, Nautica, Under Armor, and Coach. Not surprisingly, these stores make no explicit connection between these brand names and the Amish who refuse to wear or use their goods. The silhouette of an Amish buggy does appear on one outlet mall sign, high above the parking lot; perhaps this symbol is meant to connect bargain prices with Amish thrift.

In Shipshewana, Indiana, the tourist is presented with three major shopping options. The first is a group of shops that includes a gift shop, bakery, and furniture store, which are connected to the Blue Gate, an Amish-style restaurant complex housed in rambling, white, vinyl-sided buildings that loosely refer to the architecture of an Amish home.[33] The second option consists of small, independently owned shops located in what were once single-family homes along two streets behind the Blue Gate. These shops offer tourists a wide variety of merchandise—picture puzzles featuring Native American art, handmade doll clothes, various interior décor items. The third option is a newly constructed shopping mall built largely by local Amish construction workers and designed to echo the structure of a barn, with exposed solid wood beams and hardwood floors.[34] This multistory structure houses many independent shops that, like the small stores lining the streets, sell a wide variety of merchandise. One can buy stringed instruments (guitars, violins, dulcimers), quilt fabrics and ready-made quilts, men's and women's active wear, lots of interior décor items, and gourmet kitchen utensils.

Shopping in the Holmes-Wayne settlement resembles that of Lancaster and Elkhart-LaGrange settlements. There are many large stores. Typically, they are located near Amish-style restaurants. They tend to feature interior décor items but also sell merchandise like scented hand creams, gourmet coffee, inspirational books, and greeting cards. In addition there are smaller shops lining the main and side streets of each town in the settlement. In these shops tourists are offered a wide variety of merchandise, from gourmet kitchen utensils and appliances to Amish Country sweatshirts, from real antiques to John Deere tractor party lights. Furniture stores are common here as well. They typically sell high-quality solid-wood furniture for every room in the house made by local Amish craftsmen. Some furniture stores in the area also sell national brands of furniture from North Carolina and elsewhere. Antique malls are popular in the Holmes-Wayne settlement. Often located in huge barnlike structures, these antique malls provide space for many vendors to sell old books, dishes, furniture, toys, and the like.

Although eating in Amish-style restaurants, shopping in gift shops, and visiting Amish heritage information centers are perhaps the most common tourist activities in all three settlements, plenty of other attractions are available as well. In the Ohio and Pennsylvania settlements, tourists can take balloon rides. In Lancaster County, visitors can enjoy a day at an amusement park, taking carnival rides and playing games of chance. In Shipshewana, tourists may book a room in a hotel that features an indoor, Amish-themed water park consisting of water slides and pools amidst fake

Amish barn façades decorated with hex signs; a fiberglass horse head appears to be sticking out of a window in one barn wall. All three areas present festivals of many sorts, especially in the peak tourism months of summer and fall. Festivals celebrating animal-powered farming, Swiss cheese, 1950s classic cars, arts and crafts, the fall harvest, or gospel music, just to name a few, are typically hosted by a collection of area businesses whose aim is to promote a town, a tourist attraction, and/or a particular product to visitors.[35]

Although there are differences in tourism among the three major Amish settlements in the number of years each area has promoted tourism and the volume of visitors who pass through each area annually, there are many more similarities. All three emphasize the Amish as their draw and include attractions that make explicit claims to providing authentic connections to the Amish. Some do it by telling a story of the Amish experience. Others do it by giving tours through an Amish house or barn. Still others do it by selling food either prepared by Amish cooks or inspired by the traditions of Amish cooking. And some do it by selling Amish-made crafts such as furniture, quilts, or trinkets.

Given the volume of visitors that Amish tourism attracts, it is not surprising that all three of these areas have seen the development of other tourist attractions that make (at best) oblique connections to the Amish: the Amish-themed water park with its fake barn façades and fiberglass horse head, a gift shop that sells quilts manufactured in China, the silhouette of a horse-drawn buggy on the sign in the parking lot of the outlet mall. Indeed, each of these Amish-settled areas is now home to many restaurants, shops, festivals, and assorted paraphernalia that, despite use of the word "Amish," share little but proximity with Amish life and culture.

Authenticity and Amish Country Tourism

Since the mid-1940s increasing numbers of Americans have made the trip to Amish Country. On the face of it, their purpose has been to satisfy their curiosity about this peculiar people by experiencing them and/or their culture in some way. The ever-expanding variety of attractions in Amish Country raises the question as to the "Amishness" of what tourists experience. Do visitors encounter Amish people or culture? Are they able to experience Amish life in a meaningful way in the course of their visit? Or do all the distractions of the tourism industry render impossible anything like an authentic encounter with Amish life?

According to Thomas J. Meyers, a sociologist who has written on Amish Country tourism, not only are many visits to Amish Country absent anything like a meaningful encounter with the Amish, but most Amish Country tourists do not want one. In his essay on Amish Country tourism in Shipshewana, Indiana, Meyers argues, on the basis of more than seven hundred interviews with tourists, that the vast majority of them are not interested in an authentic encounter with the Amish. They do not want to talk to the Amish. They have no desire to get to know Amish people. They are not even especially interested in learning about the Amish. Instead, they just want to shop.[36]

The only sense in which the Amish are at all significant for the majority of Amish Country tourists, Meyers argues, is that these visitors want to shop in an area where the Amish are. They want to be in the vicinity of the Amish as they purchase merchandise, some of which is associated with the Amish. According to Meyers, visitors believe that when they buy merchandise that is connected with the Amish, whether by proximity (in Amish Country) or origin (Amish made) or merely association ("Amishness" is somehow linked with the item), they experience the goodness of Amish life. This experience is the pleasure of Amish Country tourism. As Meyers puts it, these tourists' "primary goal . . . is not to get an insider's view so much as it is to purchase a bit of the host culture and take it home with them."[37]

Meyers's survey research draws attention to the obvious point that visitors to Amish Country do consume a lot while there, whether by eating or shopping or receiving services. To understand Amish Country tourism, then, it is necessary to attend to the varieties of consumption that take place within it. Consumption is important, not only because it represents 70 percent of the gross domestic product,[38] but because it serves as one of the primary ways that Americans express their identities. Also, consumption and all of the advertising and marketing that support it play a major role in shaping those identities. Consumption is not just shopping, often viewed simplistically and disdainfully as a feminine activity that amounts to little more than a self-indulgent waste of time and money. Rather, it is a complex network of social practices that shapes American culture, communities, and identities.[39]

If Amish Country tourism is largely about shopping, what merchandise is being offered to tourists and what does it mean to them? If these tourists say that they do not care to know the Amish or learn about them but "just" want to shop, why is it that they take particular pleasure in consuming in Amish Country? Meyers reports that visitors to Amish Country feel that making purchases there puts them in touch with the goodness of Amish life. What is that goodness that visitors apparently enjoy consuming? Is there any sense in which that Amish characteristic of being "good" might challenge the values of the consumer culture?

Survey research is limited in that it can only report what tourists think they are doing or, even more narrowly, what they want the researcher to know. It cannot explain what actually happens when tourists plan a trip to Amish Country or all of what they experience when they are there. Human desires, motives, and experiences are more complex than any individual is likely to realize or be able to articulate. Can any consumer truly describe all of the desires, expectations, and effects involved in purchasing something, or why he or she is purchasing an iPhone versus a Blackberry or a Treo? Might purchases be driven by desires of which individuals not aware but which are nevertheless compelling?

While I accept Meyers's finding that tourists want to shop, in particular in Amish Country, I do not infer from the tourists' self-reports of not being curious about the Amish that therefore the Amish have little to do with why tourists are so attracted to Amish Country. A significant body of research argues that the Amish are crucial to the success of Amish Country tourism. This body of research is based not only in what tourists say to researchers but also in scholars' observations and interpretations of tourist behavior in Amish Country.

Based on research of a wide variety of tourist venues, Dean MacCannell, in his seminal book *The Tourist: A New Theory of the Leisure Class*, argues that the allure of any tourist site is that it promises authenticity. By authenticity, MacCannell means a genuine encounter with a mode of being in the world that is, unlike modern life, unmediated, unselfconscious, transparent.[40] This mode of being has no pretense. It hides nothing. It simply is what it seems, unlike modern life. Tourism promises authenticity in a variety of ways. It might take the form of a history museum filled with dioramas of a preindustrial culture or a heritage center that displays the artifacts of an extinct religious sect. It might be a luau showcasing ancient stories told in dance by an "exotic" people. Whatever the particular form, tourism promises meaningful access to a people and a way of life that are fundamentally different from modern life.

This is what tourism promises, MacCannell argues, but it is not what tourism delivers. Indeed, it is beyond what tourism can deliver. Tourism is, by its nature, a form of mediation. Tourism is the heritage center that interprets, the tour guide who describes a people in a certain way, or the restaurant that offers a certain "unusual" style of food. It is never *actually* that other mode of being in the world. It is, at best, a representation of it. Moreover, tourism is a particular kind of representation, one that aims to please tourists. In this sense, it is not some random depiction of another way of life; it is always an interested portrayal designed to intrigue, inform, and/or entertain the tourist, usually for a profit.[41]

When MacCannell's theory of tourism is applied to Amish Country, some interesting insights emerge. First, it becomes apparent that the allure of Amish Country *is* the Amish. Understood as a premodern and, thus, exotic other, the Amish are fascinating because they seem to live an authentic life. To moderns, they appear to have no pretense. They seem to hide nothing. They look as though they exist simply and unselfconsciously in the world. Theirs is an uncomplicated life, so it seems. Because life in contemporary America seems only to become more complex and stressful with time, moderns long for a simpler and more authentic life. Amish Country tourism promises meaningful access to these people who seem to have held on to something moderns have lost. That is its draw.

Although Amish Country tourism promises tourists a glimpse into that other, premodern life, it in fact does not provide it. Instead, as MacCannell's theory also suggests, it offers only a mediated experience of it, yet a mediated experience that tourists apparently find to be quite pleasurable. Roy C. Buck's sociological research confirms and extends these inferences. Based on his extensive participant observation of Amish Country tourism, Buck concludes that it does not give visitors real access to Amish life. Instead, it leads visitors away from the Amish by convincing them that "they are 'strangers in a strange land' and therefore in need of abundant assistance."[42] Once tourists are convinced by Amish Country tourism that they cannot understand the peculiar ways and beliefs of the Amish on their own, says Buck, they come to depend on tourism's tours, guides, brochures, and the like to instruct them. As a result of this persuasion, visitors stop trying to encounter the Amish directly by talking with them or even by venturing down country roads on their own. Instead, they enter what Buck calls "the tourist subculture" and accept the pamphlet, the tour, or the meal that tourism offers. For the most part, Buck argues, tourists appear satisfied with this mediated experience.[43]

In short, Buck confirms MacCannell's claim that as a form of mediation, Amish Country tourism cannot provide the tourist with an authentic experience of Amish life. However, Buck makes a second argument that, while not central to the concerns of this book, is nevertheless interesting. He was the first to argue that, although Amish tourism only further distances tourists from what they seek, it also helps to preserve Amish culture. In this way, the inauthentic character of Amish Country tourism may be a good thing, at least for the Amish.

In his seminal book, *Amish Society*, John A. Hostetler, who during his lifetime was recognized as the principal authority on the Amish, agrees with Buck that far from bringing the tourist and the Amish together, Amish Country tourism sets them apart. Like Buck, Hostetler appreciates the benefit that this separation brings the Amish. He, too, sees that one of the functions of Amish Country tourism is to protect the Amish from tourists who might otherwise overwhelm their simple life. That benefit notwithstanding, Hostetler takes a dark view of Amish Country tourism. Contrasting the perspective of any Amish person when touring the outside world to the experience of the visitor to Amish Country, Hostetler argues that, whereas the Amish person finds the outside world to be "a moment of illusion . . . a reality without community and therefore without spirit," the tourist to Amish Country is likely to think that he or she is encountering something that "may approximate a religious experience."[44] For Hostetler, Amish Country tourism provides only an illusion of authenticity, and the fact that the tourist nonetheless enjoys it only speaks to the rather low character of the tourist.

Given Hostetler's scholarly reputation, it is significant that he confirms MacCannell's and Buck's point that Amish Country tourism does not afford the visitor anything like an authentic encounter with the Amish. However, his negative evaluation of Amish Country tourism and, especially, of the tourist seems unhelpful. First, his conclusions are quick and dismissive, lacking curiosity about why millions of Americans make the trip to Amish Country each year. Second, he summarily disposes of the tourist as a category of people altogether different from himself and anyone else who aspires to a worthy form of life. Oddly, he mobilizes the Amish, a people deeply committed to humility, as his companions in the ranks of the morally superior.[45]

Unlike Hostetler, I explore the dynamics of tourism as a tourist myself. Because I too am a tourist—that is, an outsider who is drawn to the Amish and their communal life—I do not assume superiority, moral or otherwise, over other tourists. Indeed, whenever I speak of tourists in this book, I include myself in the category.

Rather than making evaluative judgments about tourists, sociologist Donald B. Kraybill offers a clear-eyed view of how Amish Country tourism functions. His focus is on the Amish and the ways in which Amish Country tourism affects their community life and culture. Building explicitly on MacCannell's theory, Kraybill argues that rather than offer visitors an authentic encounter with Amish life, Amish Country tourism functions like a stage upon which a social drama is performed. On the "front stage" tourists enjoy performances of Amish life in the form of tours, guides, heritage centers, and so forth. These front stage performances typically offer idealized versions of Amish life that are most often performed by non-Amish people serving as guides, wait staff, retail shop clerks, and the like. Sometimes the Amish are players in the front stage performance, for instance, when Amish men give buggy rides or Amish women sell their pies at a farmers' market. These front stage performances serve as a buffer zone that protects the "back stage," or reality, of Amish life.[46]

For Kraybill, recognizing that Amish Country tourism provides a buffer zone for the Amish is crucial to understanding how Amish Country tourism works and what its effects are. He argues that as a front stage performance Amish Country tourism provides tourists with a safe and predictable experience of Amish life. This produces pleasure for tourists who do not have to worry that they are going to be shocked or overly disturbed by this "exotic other" or that they are intruding on Amish life. As a front stage performance, Amish Country tourism is also crucial for the Amish because, again, it protects their life and culture from being overtaken by tourism. Additionally, by highlighting the admiration visitors have of Amish life, tourism helps the Amish remember that theirs is a good life.[47]

Kraybill's description and theorization of Amish Country tourism is helpful for a number of reasons. First, it avoids claims that there is nothing of value in this commerce between Amish and tourist. Second, it engages in a genuine inquiry about the function, dynamics, and effects of Amish Country tourism. And the results of that inquiry are valuable. It reveals much about how the specific dynamics of Amish Country tourism actually serve to strengthen Amish culture. More than this, Kraybill underscores the point that Amish Country tourism cannot be reduced to the question of authenticity; the fact that Amish Country tourism does not provide visitors with authentic encounters with the Amish does not mean that nothing meaningful happens there. This is a fundamental insight.

While Kraybill focuses on the function and effects of tourism on the Amish, David Weaver-Zercher and David Walbert put their emphasis on the tourist. Their purpose is not to figure out what Amish Country tourism does for or to the Amish. Instead, they want to know how the Amish have been represented to tourists. Looking at a wide variety of popular representations of the Amish in Hollywood films, novels, brochures, lectures, and so forth, they decipher what the Amish have been made to mean to Americans in a range of contexts that includes Amish Country tourism.

It is noteworthy that both Weaver-Zercher in his book *The Amish in the American Imagination* and Walbert in his book *Garden Spot* part company with scholars like Meyers and Hostetler who say that tourists are not curious about the Amish. In fact, their histories of how the Amish have been represented over time reveal how various constructions of the Amish have inspired intense curiosity among Americans. More specifically, both argue that in the nineteenth century, the Amish were mostly ignored or, if noticed, construed as exotic. Both claim that positive media attention paid to the Amish during their dispute with the state of Pennsylvania over schooling in 1937–1938 was responsible for constructing the Amish as a virtuous people dedicated to a strong work ethic and other American values, such as thrift, honesty, and self-reliance. Due to the cultural popularization of this portrayal, especially in Broadway plays and Hollywood films, Weaver-Zercher and Walbert argue, visitors have been inspired to travel to Amish Country in order to encounter these unusual people who have managed to preserve their rural way of life even as the family farm has largely disappeared from the American landscape.[48]

With these histories as their backdrop, Weaver-Zercher and Walbert present their analyses of Amish Country tourism. Both recognize that

Amish Country tourism does not give visitors an authentic encounter with the simple life they apparently seek. Instead, they argue, it constructs the Amish in ways that provide tourists with nostalgic experiences of the past in American culture.[49]

Although the approaches taken, histories recounted, and arguments made by these two scholars have much in common, Walbert puts forward a more negative view of Amish Country tourism than does Weaver-Zercher. This is so because Walbert has a political agenda, made explicit in the conclusion of his book, for saving rural America. His plan involves preserving agricultural land, encouraging contact between residents of the city and those of the country through local farm markets, supporting the development of farms of various sizes growing a greater variety of crops, and so forth.[50] Given his agenda, it is not surprising that Walbert is frustrated by the fact that Amish Country tourism discourages visitors who are curious about rural life from considering how to nurture that kind of life in a culture apparently determined to turn every cornfield into a residential development. Instead of fostering appreciation of the value of rural activities to current society, Walbert argues, Amish Country tourism constructs the Amish as relics from the past who, as such, are entirely irrelevant to the present. The Amish are made to appear to belong to a time long gone when America was largely rural, most families farmed, and people understood their dependence upon the land. Depicted as relics, they can serve no purpose beyond stimulating nostalgia for a bygone era.[51]

Weaver-Zercher focuses on providing close readings of the texts (whether musicals, films, novels, tourist attractions, etc.) that have shaped Americans' view of and relationship to the Amish In the process he articulates crucial insights, which appear in many ways in Walbert's book, for understanding the dynamics of Amish Country tourism. The first insight is that the Amish are constructed to inspire feelings of nostalgia for a more simple, peaceful, and virtuous America. The second is that this construction of the Amish is so popular that it has proved highly profitable for film director, novelist, and tourism entrepreneur alike. The third is that Americans enjoy that nostalgia because, while they are engaged with it, it relieves anxieties of modern life concerning work, family, and community.[52]

These insights inform the present volume. Although I offer an alternative understanding of the kind of nostalgia at work in Amish Country tourism than either Weaver-Zercher or Walbert does, the idea that Amish Country tourism plays on imaginative "memories" of better days in the United States is essential, as is the recognition that these strategies are successful. I look at how these representations of the Amish address present-day concerns and how Amish Country tourism seems to resolve real anxieties that modern Americans experience.

As Weaver-Zercher and Walbert assert, the ways Americans understand the Amish come from outsiders, not the Amish. The Amish do not market themselves, Weaver-Zercher argues. They do not put themselves forward as paragons of virtue or as ideal Americans or anything else. Noting this, outsiders have been quite happy to step into the gap and offer those representations of them, often doing this to great financial profit.[53]

Neither Weaver-Zercher nor Walbert explicitly makes the point (though both probably assume it) that those who take on this role have tremendous advantages over the Amish for disseminating their representations. Newspaper, magazine, and book publishers not to mention Hollywood producers have the means to make their constructions of the Amish attractive, readily available, and, therefore, dominant.[54] As a result, their representations of the Amish are much more likely to capture Americans' collective imagination than anything the Amish might say or do. Of course, the fact that the Amish avoid much communication technology only makes outsiders' advantage even greater.

Appreciating this fact, Weaver-Zercher and Walbert studied how the Amish have been constructed by outsiders, not how they have represented themselves.[55] I follow their lead by focusing on how Amish Country tourism uses or "domesticates the Amish," to borrow Weaver-Zercher's phrase, in order to give pleasure to the tourist. I also show how Amish Country tourism addresses the tourist in meaningful ways even as it does not, and cannot, deliver on its promise of authenticity. I closely read the visual rhetoric (architecture, interior décor, food, merchandise) of three important tourist towns to learn how these visual features of Amish Country tourism not only produce meaning but also provide pleasure for visitors.

Systems of representation typically construct meaning in reliable ways that make deciphering signs easy. These systems regularly associate one sign, like the word "woman," with a cluster of meanings, such as emotional, nurturing, communicative, and dependent, while commonly linking "man" with a different set of meanings, such as rational, providing,

quiet, and independent. These clusters of contrasting meanings bring order by giving relatively clear ways to understand complex ideas. In the
same way, Amish Country tourism (alongside other systems of representation like movies and novels) associates the Amish with a cluster of meanings. As Weaver-Zercher and Walbert argue convincingly, over time the
Amish have been constructed by these systems as a rural or simple people
who are plain, hardworking, honest, peaceful, thrifty, and so forth. They
have been represented as different from urban or modern people, whose
labor is seen as no longer productive and who rush around in a desperate
effort to achieve the highly materialistic life that is the measure of success.
By linking the Amish to one set of meanings and "the rest of us" to a contrasting set of meanings, Amish Country tourism gives tourists relatively
clear ways to understand this peculiar people as well as themselves. In
constructing the Amish as relics of the past, Amish tourism lets visitors
know that they need not be unsettled by the differences between themselves and the Amish since, after all, the Amish really belong to a bygone
era.

However effective systems of representation are at making meaning of
the world, no such system can completely or permanently fix the meaning
of any sign. This is because reality is always more complicated than language or visual image can capture. There is always some kind of remainder,
some sort of meaning or aspect of the sign that the system cannot quite take
into account. Thus, no system of representation is ever able to convey the
reality that seems to be expressed in the signs "woman" and "man." Another reason that systems of representation can never fix the meaning of
any sign forever is that over time everything changes. What "woman" and
"man" meant a half-century ago is quite different from what they mean
today; characteristics that once "signified as" masculine (such as unemo-
tional) or feminine (such as weak) may not do so now.[56]

Throughout this book, I attend to the ways in which the Amish exceed,
transgress, or elude the meanings Amish Country tourism makes of them
and the ways that Amish life does not always fit neatly within the cluster
of meanings assigned to it. When I come upon such a misfit, I explore how
it may unsettle the ways that Amish Country tourism instructs tourists
to see the Amish and themselves. I note ways that the Amish challenge
the meanings constructed by Amish Country tourism, for tourism cannot completely and permanently control the idea of what it means to be

"Amish." Although the Amish avoid the media as much as they can and by no means market themselves to outsiders, they are a conspicuously visible people. While they rarely address the world through words, they speak often through their appearance and practices. Thus, they too have a visual rhetoric by which they construct themselves as other than the world. By their dress, modes of transportation, selective use of technology, and so forth they communicate clearly that they are different, perhaps even strange.

In examining the visual rhetoric of the Amish, I ask what the Amish signify, how they disrupt the understanding that Amish Country tourism constructs of them, and how they act on their commitment to being a witnessing people. The Amish do not proselytize or preach about their way of life. They do not argue that their way of being in the world is superior to the way others live. This is because they do not think it is appropriate for a people who follow Jesus to insist. Instead, they witness by trying to live in a way that is true to the nature of the Kingdom of God and that, thereby, may help others see that the Kingdom is real and present in the here and now. One of my goals in this book is to see their witness.

An Overview of Ohio's Amish Country

Ohio's Amish Country stretches roughly from US Route 30 on its northern edge to Interstate 77 on its eastern side to the southern border of Holmes County on the south and to State Route 83 on the west. While tourism occurs at many locations within these borders, tourist attractions are concentrated along the main east-west artery through Holmes and Tuscarawas counties, State Route 39 (see map on page 44).

Tourist destinations come in a variety of types, from small roadside vegetable stands to furniture stores along county roads to flea markets just off SR 39. In addition to individual tourist spots, there are entire towns that have cultivated tourism. Some of them are small, like Charm, which is south of SR 39, and Mount Hope, which lies to the north of it. Such towns have a few attractions, usually an Amish-style restaurant, flea market, and/or furniture store. Often, in towns like these, visitors are directed to businesses that were not originally aimed at tourists, such as Mount Hope's livestock auction and Charm's extensive lumberyard (Keim Lumber).[57]

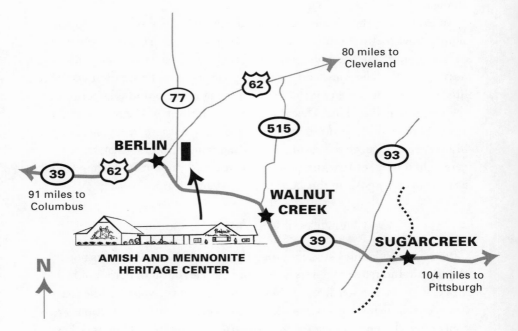

80 miles to
Cleveland

62

77

515

93

BERLIN

39 62

91 miles to
Columbus

WALNUT
CREEK

39

SUGARCREEK

104 miles to
Pittsburgh

AMISH AND MENNONITE
HERITAGE CENTER

N

The heart of Ohio Amish Country

Other towns are larger and have been heavily developed as tourist destinations, particularly Berlin to the west, Walnut Creek in the middle, and Sugarcreek to the east. Larger towns are home to multiple Amish-style restaurants, inns, gift shops, and other tourist attractions. This book focuses on these latter three towns for two simple reasons. First, they provide three examples of purposeful and complex efforts to attract and sustain the interest of tourists. Thus, these towns provide opportunities for studying the visual rhetoric of inns, gift shops, and Amish-style restaurants simultaneously. Second, because of their extensive development and their location, these towns have historically drawn the most tourist traffic in the Ohio Amish Country.

WALNUT CREEK

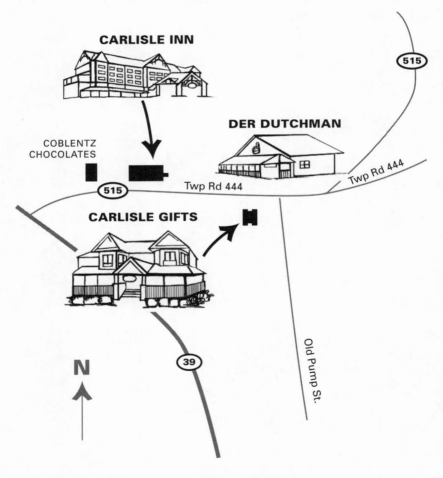

CARLISLE INN

DER DUTCHMAN

COBLENTZ
CHOCOLATES

515

Twp Rd 444

Twp Rd 444

CARLISLE GIFTS

515

N

39

Old Pump St.

Tourist sites in Walnut Creek, Ohio

CHAPTER 3

Time and Gender in Walnut Creek

A trip to the past makes an excellent present [and future]
—Magazine advertisement for Lehman's Hardware

In 1970 the first Amish-style restaurant to open its doors in what would become Ohio's Amish Country was Der Dutchman.[1] For more than two decades, Der Dutchman drew a modest number of guests to its seventy-five-seat dining room. All that changed in the early 1990s. Its seating capacity was increased nearly tenfold by various expansions and renovations. Also in the early 1990s, the Dutch Corporation (which then owned Der Dutchman) built Carlisle Gifts, a three-story gift shop, and Carlisle Inn, a fifty-two-room hotel.[2]

Today, Der Dutchman serves approximately four thousand guests on a busy evening,[3] totaling nearly two million diners a year.[4] Carlisle Inn has capacity for 104 overnight guests.[5] From spring through early autumn (May through September), the inn is often fully booked. Reservations for October, when tourists come in their greatest numbers, in order to enjoy the autumn colors, must be made a full year in advance.

Clearly, Amish Country tourism is thriving in Walnut Creek and by studying it we can learn something about how Amish Country tourism engages the interest of visitors.

A Tour of Walnut Creek

Tourists typically come to Walnut Creek via State Route 39, since it is the main artery through Holmes County and since it runs just south of the center of town. As tourists approach the town, they come to a traffic light on SR 39 and turn north onto SR 515 (which becomes Carlisle Street, the main street in town).[6] Near the center of town they pass a small cemetery[7] on the left and then the Coblentz Chocolate Company, a gourmet chocolate factory and retail shop.[8] Beyond Coblentz they come upon a huge parking lot, where many of them park, so that they can spend their time in Walnut Creek on foot.

For those who do get out and walk, a sidewalk runs along Carlisle Street past Carlisle Inn, an impressive three-story structure. Once past the inn, they can choose to continue on the sidewalk to Der Dutchman Restaurant and Bakery, which sits just beyond another big parking lot. Or they can cross the street and head toward Carilisle Inn's buggy ride stop, where an Amish man sits under an umbrella in a folding chair, waiting for customers. If they take the latter route they will continue heading into the center of town, following a winding brick sidewalk through a flower garden and past a large gazebo. In just a few minutes, they will arrive arrive at P. Graham Dunn gallery, which sells laser-engraved wood products, such as plaques bearing well-known biblical passages or popular hymn verses.[9] Next door, they will find Carlisle Gifts, which specializes in interior décor items. Just beyond Carlisle Gifts and finishing out the block is the Walnut Creek Country Store, which sells a wide variety of souvenirs, including Amish Country T-shirts and mugs, Christmas ornaments, and other collectibles. Looking across Carlisle Street from this corner, they will see the famous Der Dutchman Restaurant, which sits opposite these shops and houses a bakery, several banquet rooms, and multiple dining rooms.

If they continue along Carlisle Street, they will pass a small bank and then come to Rebecca's Bistro, a gourmet coffeehouse and restaurant. Down a side street, they will see the public library, German Culture Museum, Inn at Walnut Creek, and the post office. Behind the post office and up a small hill sits Schlabach's dry goods store and Miller's Country Pride Foods, two establishments regularly frequented by local Amish.

As tourists make their way through town, they cannot help noticing that there is a great deal of consistency in the appearance of the buildings that line its streets. Many have beige vinyl siding accented by white trim. Almost all of them have large front porches featuring white balustrades. A few have wraparound porches. Turned balusters also appear on the many balconies on both the front and back façades of Carlisle Inn. Other building features include steeply pitched roofs, ornamented gables, walls set on unusual angles, large bay windows, and textured shingles.

The Victorian-themed wraparound porch with its extensive balustrades at Coblentz Chocolate Company

Puzzling Victorian Theme

These architectural and decorative elements echo, albeit in late twentieth-century fashion, an American Victorian style that was popular in the nineteenth century. In particular, Carlisle Gifts, Carlisle Inn, and Coblentz Chocolates all emphasize elements of the Queen Anne style, which was a dominant building style in the United States in the late 1880s and 1890s.[10] The American Victorian style on the exteriors of these buildings is continued inside these shops, restaurants, and inns, with their saturated colors, crown and dental moldings, faux copper ceilings, turned balusters on staircases, wicker furniture, floral patterns, and lace window treatments.

There is no question that Walnut Creek has a Victorian theme. Indeed, over the last twenty years or so, business leaders have transformed Walnut Creek into a twenty-first-century conception of an American Victorian town.[11] Judging from the impressive growth of tourism in Walnut Creek, visitors seem to like Victorian Walnut Creek.

The popularity of Walnut Creek's Victorian theme presents an interesting puzzle. Tourists come to Walnut Creek largely because it is in Amish Country, and Amishness is supposed to be about plainness and simplicity.

But Walnut Creek's theme is neither plain nor simple. Indeed, it presents a striking contrast to the plain style of Amish life.

This contrast is most stark when one compares it to Old Order Amish houses. These simple yet spacious two-story dwellings are designed to accommodate large families through long winters and hot summers. In Ohio, these houses tend to take one of two basic forms and to display few decorative features. Perhaps the most common form is the I-house. This two-story, side-gabled home is just one room deep, often symmetrical on all sides, with porches running the full width of the house along the front and the back.[12] A variation of this form has a porch along the front of the house and a wing extending out the back. A second common form is the one-and-a-half or two-story, front-gable house that may or may not have a wing. These houses have moderately pitched roofs and are usually clad with wood siding that is painted white.[13] Interiors of Old Order Amish houses are kept simple as well, with only the occasional throw rug, solid-color curtain, or a piece of upholstered furniture added for comfort.[14]

The interiors of Walnut Creek's shops and hotels display an even greater contrast with Amish houses. Unlike the Victorian shops, filled with lace table runners, porcelain figurines, and Thomas Kinkade prints, Amish homes contain almost nothing that is not functionally necessary. Walnut Creek's ornate interiors have been created by the skillful arrangement of lace tablecloths, Tiffany-style lamps, and silk flowers, while Amish interiors are characterized by lack of ornamentation.

Why do Amish Country tourists come in such impressive numbers to Walnut Creek when its theme appears completely at odds with the lifestyle of the Amish? Is it that visitors care little, if at all, about the Amish and just want to shop? Is there any way in which Walnut Creek's theme connects to the Amish? A rhetorical analysis of this puzzling environment sheds light on these and other questions regarding Walnut Creek's attraction for its middle American visitors.

The Visual Rhetoric of Tourism in Walnut Creek

Walnut Creek's Victorian theme has been thoughtfully developed and often beautifully executed, though it is far from seamless.[15] Cracks and gaps in the illusion that visitors are passing through a nineteenth-century Victorian town are common and visible. For instance, several of the buildings that house tourist enterprises are obviously constructed of cement block. Often the Victorian theme is limited to a building's storefront, and even then the exterior may display modern construction materials such as vinyl siding and asphalt shingles. The structures that carry the theme most prominently are disproportionately large compared to other buildings in the town. This is the case for Carlisle Gifts, Der Dutchman, and especially Carlisle Inn. Given their unusually large size for the town, it is difficult not to be aware that they were constructed or expanded for a twenty-first century tourist industry. Further, to accommodate the increasing numbers of cars, campers, and buses that come to Walnut Creek, additional parking lots have been built and existing parking lots have been expanded. Finally, to enable non-Amish and Amish alike to use their cell phones, a Verizon Wireless tower stands between the post office and Schlabach's store.

These obvious intrusions of twenty-first century life into Walnut Creek's Victorian theme indicate that no one is trying to create the illusion of a return (even if that were possible) to nineteenth-century, small-town life in America. Instead, this theme seems to be aimed at inspiring nostalgia, and with it pleasure, in the tourist.

Walnut Creek's Victorian theme draws upon the last two decades of the nineteenth century in the United States. The late nineteenth century in America was a time of profound change.[16] At that time, the American frontier was closing. Factory work was displacing agriculture as the primary mode of making a living. As rural Americans moved into cities for employment and massive numbers of immigrants arrived on US shores, the populations in cities, and especially their slums, grew rapidly. Those who remained on the farm experienced intense pressures from a market driven by the steam locomotive to produce more crops from larger farms through scientific methods and industrial farming machinery. The age of electricity was dawning, telephone lines were being strung, and the internal combustion engine was about to make its appearance in Henry Ford's cars.[17] Labor movements were pressing for better working conditions and relief from fifteen-hour workdays. Women's movements were struggling to transform women into full citizens by, among other things, winning the right to vote. In this post–Civil War era, the United States was beginning to emerge as an imperial power.[18] At the levels of economy, technology, politics, social relations, and global influence, the United States was passing through a time of tremendous transformation.

The architecture of Carlisle Gifts echoes the Queen Anne style of the late
nineteenth century

It is significant that twentieth- and twenty-first-century Americans
have been and are experiencing similarly radical transformations. These
changes have been widely documented and discussed. Briefly put, they
include the shift from an industrial manufacturing economy to an information and service economy, the infusion of digital technology into all
aspects of life, the emergence of identity politics, changes in the racial
makeup of the population, and the rise of the United States as the remaining global superpower.

Thus, Walnut Creek's theme refers to a historical moment similar to the
present in the sense that during both times Americans were experiencing
profound changes at the most basic levels of culture. This parallel is not
made explicit by any literature promoting Walnut Creek, but it may be
implied, for the shops, restaurants, and inns do feature technological devices from both before and after the industrial revolution. Carlisle Gifts
displays candles throughout the store as well as many versions of reproduction Tiffany-style electric lamps. It dedicates one sizeable section of
the store to the celebration of horses and another to the car and tractor. It
offers sundials for the garden and nineteenth-century-style reproduction
clocks for the mantel or table. Implicitly, then, the theme points to tech-

nological changes within late-nineteenth-century American life that may be seen as analogous to the present insofar as they effected fundamental transformations in daily life.

Although the Victorian theme dominates Walnut Creek's visual rhetoric, significant aspects of contemporary life appear juxtaposed to the theme. Obvious examples include the modern construction materials, large parking lots, and wireless communication towers mentioned above. In addition, tourist businesses throughout the town offer many modern conveniences and pleasures, such as in-room spas, king-size beds, and decaf mocha lattes. The juxtaposition of a late-nineteenth-century Victorian style with aspects of contemporary American life serves two complementary rhetorical functions. First, by incorporating key features of American life that emphasize consumer comfort, convenience, and pleasure, these juxtapositions alert tourists that they are invited into this nineteenth-century theme as twenty-first-century Americans. Second, juxtaposing features of two cultural moments that are similar in certain respects helps the tourist enter the theme. Seeing signs of the tensions between residual and emergent technologies from nineteenth-century life, for instance, enables the tourist to identify with the theme. These juxtapositions encourage tourists to feel comfortable connecting with the theme and, thus, enable them to enjoy the nostalgic experience to come. The nostalgic experience itself produces pleasure for the tourist in large measure because it promises resolutions of contemporary anxieties.

The Time Famine

Middle Americans are feeling increasingly pressed for time. While debate in both scholarly and popular venues is sure to continue about whether middle Americans are working more now than they did at mid-twentieth century, there seems to be general agreement that they *feel* like they are working more and relaxing less.[19] In their book, *Time for Life: The Surprising Ways Americans Use Their Time,* John P. Robinson and Geoffrey Godbey call this experience of increasing time pressure the time famine: "At present, American society is starving . . . for the ultimate scarcity of the postmodern world, time."[20] They argue that Americans try to solve the time famine through "time-deepening behaviors" designed to increase how much they do in any given amount of time. Such behaviors include trying to do a single activity faster, substituting one leisure activity for another that can be done more quickly, endeavoring to do more than one activity at a time, and/or scheduling leisure activities more tightly.[21] Thus, Americans try to be more productive both at work and at play by completing tasks more quickly. Ironically, because these strategies do not expand time but only increase the number of activities or tasks done in any given amount of time, they have the effect of intensifying the experience of time famine. By doing more in less time, time seems to move more quickly, thus giving the impression of less, not more, time.

Walnut Creek's execution of its Victorian theme creates an imaginary memory of a late-nineteenth-century America in which middle Americans experienced time differently than they do today. As tourists enter into the theme, they are invited to experience time as if there were plenty of it. In sharp contrast to the tourist's experience of time famine, Walnut Creek offers an experience of a time feast by the way it presents food, space, and merchandise.

Slow Food amidst the Time Famine

There are two kinds of food for sale in Walnut Creek. There is the food prepared for the tourist's consumption and there is the food imagined in the plethora of cookbooks available for purchase. The first kind of food provides the tourist with the experience of eating "slow food," food that takes time to prepare and has traditionally been eaten at the table with others.[22] The second type invites the tourist to experience nostalgia for a future in which she or he might prepare and enjoy such food.

The opposite of slow food, fast food, relies on industrialized methods of food production and preparation that often strip the ingredients of their nutritional value and flavor, which are frequently then replaced artificially. Fast food actually contributes to the problem of time famine, since it is another tactic for doing more in less time. By contrast, slow food is made by hand and, thus, takes more time to prepare. Moreover, slow food is intended to be eaten at some leisure around a table with family and friends. Insofar as slow food requires more time both to produce and to consume, it works against the time famine.[23]

In Walnut Creek, Der Dutchman is the major provider of food prepared for the tourists' consumption. It serves Amish-style food, which in

Ohio's Amish Country typically means: (1) that the tourist will be invited to choose between a family-style meal and ordering off the menu; (2) that certain items, like real mashed potatoes, are certain to appear on the menu; and (3) that the food is the kind that takes time to prepare.

Many tourists who come to Der Dutchman for lunch or dinner opt for the family-style meal. When they do, everyone at the table serves themselves out of common serving dishes, as if they were sitting around the kitchen or dining room table at home. If they choose a family-style meal, they can select from one to three different meats from among four options; they are served real mashed potatoes, creamed corn or green beans, dressing (stuffing), gravy, and loaves of bread; and at the end of the meal each may select a slice of fresh baked pie for dessert. At family-style meals, serving dishes will be refilled until all at the table have eaten their fill.

Diners who order off the menu may select from a larger variety of meats that usually includes pan fried chicken, broasted (deep fried) chicken, baked ham, roast beef, baked turkey, and smoked sausage. Chicken and beef gravy are available to accompany these selections. Side dishes include real mashed potatoes, chicken noodles (akin to chicken noodle soup with only a bit of broth), dressing (stuffing), and corn. An extensive salad bar is also available either as a side dish (one trip) or as a meal in itself (unlimited trips). The salad bar offers the typical complements to a green lettuce salad like cucumbers, carrots, onions, chopped egg, and cheese as well as various other salads, including peas and cheese salad, a sweet carrot salad, macaroni salad, a sweet Amish-style version of potato salad, and coleslaw. In addition there are yellow (mustard) pickled eggs and red (beet) pickled eggs. At the end of the salad bar the tourist will find fruit salad, gelatin salad, puddings, and apple butter. Dinner rolls or a small loaf of white or wheat bread comes with any entrée. Dinner may be concluded with date pudding, a sundae, or a serving from one of the twenty or so types of fruit, cream, and custard pies made daily in the bakery.

The food that covers the dinner table and fills the long salad bar at Der Dutchman is not the food typically found on the plates of Americans today. Unlike the prepared food so many Americans remove from their freezers and cupboards and warm up in their microwaves, most of the food at Der Dutchman is prepared from scratch in its kitchen. Potatoes arrive at the restaurant's kitchen whole and in their skins. There they are peeled then shredded (for the Amish-style potato salad) or mashed. And while a machine does the peeling, shredding, and mashing, "two Amish girls pick out the eyes by hand."[24] Likewise, the broasted chicken is rolled in breading and deep pressure fried on site just as the roast beef is baked for nine hours in Der Dutchman's kitchen after tomatoes and onions have been added to it. The red and yellow eggs served on the salad bar are even pickled on site. And, of course, the dough for all of the bread, rolls, pastries, and pies (along with the accompanying fillings) is made in the kitchen. Indeed, bakers arrive in the middle of the night to bake these items fresh daily. In sum, the food that Der Dutchman serves its guests is the kind of food that takes time (sometimes many hours) and skill to prepare. Moreover, its preparation involves techniques that are learned with practice over time. This is particularly true of the loaves of bread, dinner rolls, and cinnamon rolls that involve yeast and the myriad of pies that depend on a flaky crust that typically is not made well on the first try.

Especially when Der Dutchman's slow food is served family style, the diners are participating in the recreation of a cultural memory of family. Whether or not they have ever eaten a meal with their entire family before, dining at Der Dutchman provides them with the opportunity to perform that highly idealized and, for many, lost tradition. Sitting amidst family or friends and passing dishes filled with slow food, tourists can remember (even if they have only seen it on TV) the warmth and good feeling of sharing a common meal of home-cooked food that was prepared with time, care, and a lot of practice.

Although cooking Amish-style food requires knowledge and skill, it looks simple enough. This is not, after all, French cuisine. Soufflés and flans are not the typical fare in Amish Country. Amish-style food is approachable. It involves no risk taking in terms of etiquette or flavor. In addition, it looks like food that any decent cook could make—even the tourist.

The racks of cookbooks at Der Dutchman and many other restaurants and shops in Amish Country encourage this impression. The back cover of Der Dutchman's thirtieth anniversary edition cookbook states, "If you have ever experienced Der Dutchman's cooking you know [the employees] are discriminate cooks. Now—enjoy THEIR favorites in YOUR kitchen" (emphasis in original). Visitors who purchase such a cookbook buy the means to prepare an Amish-style meal at home. More than that, they embrace the promise of a future in which the preparation of such meals will create the experience of plentiful time among their family and friends.[25]

Leisurely Space amidst the Time Famine

In Walnut Creek, nostalgia for a life characterized by plentiful time is also created through the visitor's experience of space. Three key kinds of space in Walnut Creek encourage this experience: resting spaces, shopping spaces, and the overall layout of the town.

Interior resting spaces, such as those found inside Carlisle Inn, invite the tourist to enjoy leisure time in the low-tech style of another era. A parlor just off the lobby contains a gas fireplace; several groupings of easy chairs, couches, and floor lamps; and a baby grand piano. Guests are encouraged to imagine evenings filled with conversation, reading, and music. A sunroom on the second floor features casual groupings of wicker furniture that is outfitted with soft cushions. With games stacked on end tables, guests are encouraged to enjoy one another's company against the backdrop of a picturesque valley that is home to several Amish farms. Absent the ubiquitous flat screen TVs found in sports bars, doctor's offices, and living rooms with their never ending stream of images and voices demanding attention, these resting spaces invite the tourist to imagine an idealized past when friends and family talked and laughed with one another or just sat quietly with a book, some needlework, or a wooden toy. In this way, visitors are encouraged to long for a future when leisure means a relaxed time of reading, talking, and playing in the company of loved ones.

The exterior resting spaces are also important for creating a different experience of time. Nearly every building that houses a tourist business in Walnut Creek has a porch. Moreover, those that emphasize Walnut Creek's Victorian theme tend to have deep front porches that extend the width of the building and often wrap around the sides. In addition to making clear references to the Queen Anne style, these porches invite tourists to rest. Because of their depth and length, they (and upper-story balconies, too) have plenty of room for hickory rockers (an Amish-made rocking chair crafted of curved hickory branches and strips of oak), wood benches, or plastic chairs. Throughout the day and into the evening, tourists are regularly seen sitting on these balconies and porches talking with their companions, watching other tourists and the Amish go by, or napping. Used in these ways, the porches and balconies of Walnut Creek invoke nostalgia for a time when people had or might have plenty of time to rest.

Shopping spaces in Walnut Creek also promise a leisurely experience of time, and one that contrasts sharply with how American consumers encounter time in, say, big-box stores. The layout of a big-box store promises speed. Merchandise is organized in long, parallel aisles and clearly identified by large signs suspended over shelving packed with merchandise. Moreover, each big-box store of the same name is organized in similar, if not identical, fashion; the shopper of any Wal-Mart, Best Buy, or Lowe's can find what they are looking for quickly. Of course, shoppers in these huge stores do often linger and buy more than they intended, but because the arrangement of merchandise is predictable, shoppers feel that these stores have delivered on their promise of efficiency and speed.

The layout of shops in Walnut Creek is quite different from stores organized for efficiency. In Carlisle Gifts, for instance, merchandise is displayed in boutique-like areas located on three floors separated by two curved staircases. On the first floor, fragrant soaps and hand creams line the shelves of display cases in one corner, tea sets sit among lace tablecloths and runners in a room at the rear of the store, and Thomas Kinkade prints are hung with other inspirational wall hangings in a gallery. Tourists moving through Carlisle Gifts are encouraged to browse in a leisurely manner as they meander about the many "boutiques" within the store.

The arrangement of displays within these boutiques also invites the tourist to slow down. Items related to a certain theme, like the garden, for example, are grouped together. However, unlike merchandise in big-box stores that is stacked in neat rows on parallel shelves, the merchandise in Carlisle Gifts is arranged as units on various sorts of cabinet shelves, baker's racks, and table tops. In addition, pictures, mirrors, and other wall hangings fill the walls and hang from the ceilings. Merchandise is also nestled into clusters on the floor. With different items appearing in every direction as well as on every plane and level, the tourist is encouraged to slow down so as not to miss anything.

Even the layout of the town encourages the tourist to move at a slower pace. Rather than drive from one location to another, visitors are encouraged to park their cars and move about on foot. Walnut Creek's central business area takes up only about six square blocks, and sidewalks connect all of the shops, restaurants, and inns. As they wander in the town, visitors can imagine a mode of living in which they would not need their vans, cars, or SUVs to get from place to place in their lives.

As tourists spend time in the interior and exterior spaces of Walnut Creek, they are invited to experience time in a different manner than they are accustomed in current US culture. Typically, the spaces of contemporary American culture are constructed or appear to be constructed efficiently, so that Americans can do more in less time. By contrast, space in Walnut Creek strongly encourages visitors to slow down, as they sit, watch, talk, browse, play, meander, and nap.

Merchandise for the Home and the Time Famine

Although Walnut Creek shops offer a wide array of merchandise, from gourmet jellybeans to compact disc music compilations to shot glasses decorated with Amish figures, the emphasis is on Victorian reproduction or pseudo-Victorian home décor items. There are abundances of lace curtains, ornate picture frames, Tiffany-style lamps, Oriental rugs, porcelain figurines, silk flowers, and framed prints of floral still lifes. Many of these items are reproductions of late nineteenth-century designs. A block off the main street, a small antique mall sells genuine items from the nineteenth century.

Carlisle Street's Victorian reproductions are thoughtfully displayed according to conceptual themes and color schemes. As tourists move through these shops, they are invited to assemble similar kinds of displays in their own homes. By doing so, they may imagine, they will create spaces in which they, their families, and their friends will be inspired to slow down and relax just like those Victorians presumably used to do. Of course, creating such a space will take a lot of time and effort, not to mention money. Moreover, just like preparing slow food, creating a home décor anything like what is seen in these shops takes a lot of know-how and practice. Attempting one silk flower arrangement could consume the better part of an afternoon for a novice and probably would not result in something very aesthetically appealing. Nevertheless, the displays of home décor in Walnut Creek evoke a yearning for a life that would allow for time spent both creating and enjoying such a décor.

In addition to encouraging visitors to redecorate their homes in a style that invokes a relaxed experience of time, the merchandise also invites them to spend time preparing for and entertaining guests. For instance, throughout the 1990s and into the twenty-first century, Carlisle Gifts devoted a great deal of retail space to teatime.[26] An area with a large bay window and an adjacent alcove were full of porcelain teapots and tea-cups. They could be seen everywhere on large and small tables as well as on shelves. In addition, whole sets of china devoted to teatime were laid out on oval dining tables covered with lace tablecloths. These sets included dinner and salad plates, candlesticks, eggcups, honey pots, and tea bag rests. These elaborate displays conveyed a teatime that involved sandwiches and biscuits, lace and china, family and invited guests. From the perspective of time use, displays like these inspire the desire for a life in which one has the time in the late afternoon to bake biscuits, set a table, and entertain guests.

Amish Time

The visual rhetoric in Walnut Creek is about slowing life down to a re-laxed pace in which pies are baked, flowers are arranged, and friends lin-ger. Read this way, the ornate Victorian theme of Walnut Creek does make a connection with common representations and popular understandings of Amish life. Perhaps the best-known symbol of the Amish is the horse and buggy.[27] Indeed, the first indication tourists have that they have arrived in Ohio's Amish Country is the yellow road sign showing the silhouette of an Amish horse and buggy, warning drivers to watch for these slow-mov-ing vehicles. Whenever a tourist is obliged to slow down behind a buggy on a Holmes County highway, he or she immediately understands that Amish life is slow. Donald Kraybill puts the point this way: "Horses not only symbolize the slower pace of Amish society but also actually retard its speed. It takes longer to plow with horses, and driving time on the road increases fivefold."[28] As the archetypal sign of Amish life, the horse and buggy signifies a slow pace of life in which nothing is or can be rushed.[29]

Many Amish live in and around Walnut Creek, so it is common to see them driving their buggies through town. In addition, Carlisle Inn's buggy rides give tourists the experience of seeing the local scenery at the pace of Amish life. Walnut Creek's emphasis on relaxing the speed of tourists' fast-paced lives endorses the slow pace of Amish life. Indeed, each time a buggy passes by, it seems to be saying that, even in a culture struggling with time famine, it is possible to live as though time were plentiful. Thus, the Amish who pass through Walnut Creek are constructed by its theme as living proof that tourists, too, can enjoy an expansion of time.

But how are visitors supposed to achieve the slower pace of life that Walnut Creek promotes? Although the theme encourages the visitor to imagine a future in which time is expanded, by what means could the tourist retard the pace of her or his life? Arguably, the visual rhetoric of Walnut Creek compounds the problem of the time famine. If a tourist is inspired by the slow food of Der Dutchman and purchases a cookbook, or by the décor of Carlisle Gifts and buys a bunch of silk flowers in the hope of transforming the experience of time at home, unless that tourist reduces other demands on his or her time, he or she will likely experience only an intensification of the feeling of time famine. Put simply, she or he will have simply added another task to an already busy life. However, when one attends to the construction of gender and then nation in Walnut Creek's theme, it is possible to see the beginnings of a solution to this problem.

Gender

Gender is not what it used to be, or at least not how it is remembered. Once, it consisted of two categories that seemed clear and distinct. "Woman" referred to the nurturer who was devoted to homemaking and childrearing; "man" designated the breadwinner who labored to support his family. Now gender is complicated and confusing. There are at least three categories: woman, man, and transgendered. Even the categories of man and woman are blurred. "Woman" may refer to someone whose life is focused on work outside the home, and "man" may mean a person who stays at home to raise his children. At the root of these changes may be a fundamental transformation in the US economy that is causing employers to prefer candidates at all levels of employment who exhibit women's traditional strengths in communication, consensus building, and nurturance. Whatever the causes, a profound historical shift has transpired such that women now constitute the majority of the US workforce for the first time in history.[30] Given changes like these, it is not surprising that for most married couples with children under eighteen, "man" and "woman" both refer to someone who works outside the home.[31] The news and entertainment media seem to compound the confusion and add to middle Americans' anxiety about gender with a steady stream of news reports, commentaries, talk-show panels, sit-com plots, and Hollywood narratives that offer all manner of opinion, story, and advice. Women and men confront a dizzying variety of depictions of gender roles.

Given all the confusion about gender roles, it is not surprising that middle Americans are ambivalent about changes in gender relations and anxious about the impact of those changes on family life. According to one survey, 76 percent of US adults think that gender relations in families, the workplace, and society have changed "quite a lot" or "a great deal" in recent years. More than two-thirds (68%) are ambivalent about those changes, saying that they are both good and bad for the country. When asked about the impact of changes in gender relations in the family, 80 percent said that they make it harder for parents to raise children, and 71 percent said that they make it harder for marriages to succeed. However, when asked whether it would be better or worse for the country if women were to return to their traditional roles, as in the 1950s, only 38 percent said it would be better, while 34 percent said it would be worse, and 25 percent said it would make no difference.[32]

Despite this ambivalence among respondents in the survey, more than two-thirds (68%) said it would be better if women stayed home to focus on the house and children, although they recognized that mothers may have to work for financial reasons.[33] Finally, the survey indicated that both women and men struggle with their feelings about work and family. Among working parents, more than half of both females (53%) and males (54%) reported that they felt bad about leaving their children when they went to work, and a similar percentage (54% overall) said that they often experienced stress juggling commitments between work and family.

When this ambivalence about changes in gender roles and anxiety about the implications of those changes for the family is coupled with the growing sense of time famine, a more complex picture of middle-American life begins to emerge. According to this picture, middle Americans are unsure about who they are as men and women, anxious about how they are managing their responsibilities at work and at home, and nervous about what it all means for their children. Furthermore, as they try to negotiate these changes in the context of their anxieties, a process that is itself time consuming, they experience a more intense sense that they do not have enough time.

Gender and Victorian America

A central binary opposition that organized Western culture throughout modernity, especially during the Victorian period, was between the public and private spheres. The public sphere designated the cultural space within which all the business of commerce, politics, war, and formal education was to be conducted under the watchful eye of the public and in the bright light of reason. This was masculine space. By contrast the private sphere referred to the cultural space within which all the nurturing of infant, child, and husband was done under the care of wife and mother and in the warmth of her affection. This was feminine space. For over three centuries, understandings of gender and of space were organized on these premises to create a reliable social sphere. In that sphere, it was clear who men and women were, what their strengths were, and where they belonged.[34]

The women's movement challenged these stable understandings of gender through most of the nineteenth century. It did so by contesting the simple opposition between public and private as well as the relegation of women to the private sphere. Perhaps the most visible disruption made by that opposition occurred when women dressed in tight corsets, long dresses, and white lace marched in city streets and demanded the right to vote. In addition to these highly visible protests, much more subtle disruptions in the opposition of public and private also occurred. As Ann Satterthwaite argues, women's appearance in the mid-nineteenth century invention known as the department store prefigured their emancipation: "The early department stores served an important role in transforming the role of women—bolstering women's sense of independence and helping them enter the public sphere on their own."[35] Amidst an emerging consumer culture that was becoming increasingly visible in city centers, shopping became an opportunity for women to move about the public sphere freely and without a chaperone. In this way shopping spaces helped to unsettle and encourage the renegotiation of the once stable gender categories.[36]

Like those nineteenth-century department stores, shopping and other public spaces in Walnut Creek serve as places where the meaning of gender is being renegotiated. Although nineteenth-century department stores challenged women's confinement to the private sphere, shopping spaces in Walnut Creek seem intent on encouraging women's return to the home.

The Feminine Space of Carlisle Inn

Although Carlisle Inn is open to the public, it signifies a private space. This is partly because it is privately owned and because, like all hotels and places of overnight accommodation, visitors are obliged to pay a fee to gain full access to it. But, while good hotels strive to make guests comfortable, Carlisle Inn is especially private in the sense that its design and décor remind visitors of a late-nineteenth-century Victorian home.

Both the exterior and the interior of the inn display characteristic features of Queen Anne—style houses. Exterior features that obviously refer to Victorian architecture include a wraparound porch, bay windows, walls set on angles, and turned balusters. From the outside, the inn looks like a gigantic Queen Anne single-family house. The same is largely true for the interior. Just beyond the entranceway, for instance, there is a spectacular curved staircase open to the second floor. With its fireplace, couches and chairs, and a baby grand piano, the room just to the right of the lobby resembles a parlor in a Victorian home. Even the lobby seems "homey"; a complimentary snack of popcorn and cookies is almost always available for the taking. Guest rooms suggest the bedrooms of a house, as each is decorated differently and includes handcrafted furniture. Because the interior of the inn conveys a strong sense of private space, it also signifies as feminine space. It is the kind of space once clearly understood as the domain of woman.

The interior décor of the inn underscores the idea that this is feminine space. Throughout the inn appear floral patterns in upholstery, wallpaper, and carpets; lace patterns in valences, table runners, and doilies; curved lines along scalloped valence edges, couch backs, and staircase banisters; and saturated colors in carpets, upholstery, and floral arrangements. Lighting provided by table lamps, floor lamps, track lighting, and fireplaces is warm and soft. Artwork features floral still-life images. In short, the interior décor of the inn creates an intensely feminine look and feel to a building whose architectural features call to mind a private residence.

Although the interiors of Carlisle Inn signify as feminine spaces, they do not imply that the inn is designed exclusively for women. On the contrary, the message they convey is that, like a nineteenth-century Victorian home, this space is in the care of women—its interiors are decorated and maintained by women—but that work is done on behalf of all guests, be they women or men. Men are welcome in this space in the same way that a breadwinning man would have been received into a nineteenth-century Victorian home. Just as the private space of the home would have been viewed as a respite from the hubbub of the public sphere in the nineteenth century, so too is Carlisle Inn constructed as a refuge in a fast-paced culture. In this way, the visual rhetoric of Carlisle Inn encourages guests to long for a future when the home, understood as private space created and maintained by women, once again serves as a refuge from a relentlessly busy and stressful world.

Masculinity at Der Dutchman's

On the face of it, the visual rhetoric of Der Dutchman Restaurant and Bakery is quite different from that of Carlisle Inn. While the exterior of Der Dutchman does display Victorian features like a wrap-around porch, turned balusters, and multiple gables, its overall style is not as ornate as either Carlisle Inn or Carlisle Gifts. Similarly, its interiors are less feminine than Carlisle Inn, although "feminine touches" can be seen throughout, including valences with scalloped edges on the windows, brass chandeliers with curved lines and candlesticks, and framed Thomas Kinkade paintings depicting romantic scenes.

Beyond these "feminine touches," the rest of the interior has a more institutional and efficient look. The main dining room is a huge open space filled with approximately ninety dining tables flanked by metal chairs with upholstered seats and backs. The tables are organized into neat rows and covered with burgundy oilcloths. The ceiling throughout the main dining room is uniform in height at just over nine feet and is covered with rectangular, white ceiling tiles. In the much smaller front dining room there are fourteen solid-wood booths that seat up to four people and one large table that can seat thirteen people.[37] The two salad/breakfast bars are housed in two large, rectangular wooden cooling cases.

Of course, the point of going to Der Dutchman is to enjoy some Amish-style food, and Amish-style food is meat-and-potatoes food—simple, substantive, and hearty. In this simpler and more efficient environment, in which many Amish men eat every day, Der Dutchman food invites visitors to participate in a cultural memory of a time when American men insisted on meat and potatoes. This is the food of a man who works his body hard all day so that by dinner time he requires the kind of substantive replenishment that a meal like fried chicken, mashed potatoes and gravy, corn, bread with apple butter, and a piece of pie supplies. In fact, it is difficult to imagine food that contrasts more sharply than Der Dutchman's does with the calorie-counting, carb-counting, fat-gram-counting sort of food that greets many sedentary Americans after a day of sitting at computers.[38] In this sense, the food at Der Dutchman is as much about work as it is about leisure. Because it evokes a cultural memory of hearty food eaten after a hard day of physical labor, it encourages nostalgia for the kind of productive labor that brings sweat to the brow and makes one's muscles ache.

Although this space and the food served within it emphasize a cultural memory of masculinity that is traditional, woman also figures importantly here. The wait staff are all females, and as they move about the restaurant in their plain dresses and white aprons they are reminders that this sort of food has traditionally been prepared by women for their husbands and children. Although only one male works among the cooks behind the swinging doors of Der Dutchman's enormous kitchen, and although industrial-size mixers are regularly used back there, the visual rhetoric of the food is that the meals served here are like those that women all over the country used to prepare for their families on a daily basis.[39] As guests enjoy their Amish-style food, they are encouraged to long for both a masculinity that is synonymous with the kind of physical labor that inspires a hearty appetite, as well as the return of a femininity that responds to all that hard work and robust hunger with heaping bowls of mashed potatoes and piled-high platters of meat.

The Curves of Carlisle Gifts

The space within Walnut Creek shops takes the shape of curves, cubbies, and corners. In Carlisle Gifts, for instance, to move about the shop is to move along the lines of curls and curves. Visitors maneuver along irregular lines that wind around displays and into bay windows and back into corners. They spiral up and down the two curved staircases as they go from one floor to another. They are encouraged to proceed at an irregular pace moving here and lingering there. This is also a space characterized by multiple planes—ceilings are at various heights and with beams; display tables and cabinets may be short or tall; walls are covered with a wide variety of three-dimensional objects. The narrow gallery that runs the depth of the store on one side and the "lace room" located in the back of the first floor divide the store into smaller, intimate spaces. Even the central, open space of the store is broken up into smaller spaces by the many boutique-like areas created by the arrangement of displays and furniture.

In the context of Walnut Creek's Victorian theme, which reiterates traditional understandings of gender, this too is feminine space. This is not efficient, angular, or logical space. Rather, it reflects the curved lines and warm recesses of the female body that might encircle one and within which one might linger.

Similarly, lighting throughout the store is varied, generally warm, and often decorative. One large brass candlestick chandelier hangs from the second floor ceiling through a central opening over the first floor. Recessed incandescent lighting provides general soft light throughout the store, and track lighting focuses on specific areas and displays. In addition to a multitiered display of nineteenth-century reproduction lamps on the second floor, table lamps appear throughout the store casting warm pools of light on nearby surfaces. Lighting tucked under cabinet shelves or integrated into figurines and knick-knacks directs attention to objects of interest. Focused lighting invites the visitor to abandon efficiency and take the time to appreciate attention to subtle detail.

The inventory within Carlisle Gifts is dominated by items like lace doilies, silk flowers, crystal vases, scented lotions, and porcelain figurines that invite the tourist to imagine a lifestyle that includes time to relax, be creative, and enjoy beauty. Moreover, such merchandise is designed to inspire the shopper to consider how she could create a similar environment and, thus, a similar lifestyle at home. Obviously, both the merchandise and the vision encouraged by it are gendered; both presume a shopper whose preferences are traditionally feminine.[40]

Without a doubt, it is women, not men, who are meant to leave Amish Country with the intention of re-creating, as a refuge from the hurry and stress of middle American life, the kind of environment seen in Walnut

Feminine space in Carlisle Gifts

Creek. But neither the merchandise offered in Walnut Creek nor the projects the theme is designed to inspire are entirely about women. Although
women are targeted as the agents of change, their purpose clearly should
be to construct a space not principally for themselves but for their husbands, children, and guests. That the focus should be on others is made
obvious by the merchandise. Decorative items feature masculine themes
like hunting, polo, and old clocks; teatime is all about laying out an impressive spread for a guest; toys, wall hangings, and coverlets are clearly
designed for a child's room.[41] The point of all this merchandise is to inspire
in women a desire to embark upon a time-consuming effort to create a
space that enables others in her care to experience the extension of time in
private space.

While Walnut Creek's visual rhetoric inspires nostalgia for a life in
which time is plentiful, its vision for achieving such a life through slow
food and feminine spaces would only exacerbate the time famine. Cooking fried chicken takes considerable time, and assembling a beautiful room
takes much more. Walnut Creek's focus on women as the agents of this

new relationship to time seems to provide the answer. If women would return to their traditional role and domain, then everyone would experience not only plentiful time but an end to gender confusion.

Time, Gender, and the Amish

One feature of Amish life that no observer can miss is the differentiation in appearance between men and women. Tourists invariably see Amish men in broadfall pants, usually dark blue and solid in color, long-sleeved solid-color dress shirts, and, when outdoors, distinctive and uniform hats. If they are married, Amish men also wear a mustache-less beard. Amish women are always seen wearing dresses in solid colors, with dark hose and dark shoes, their uncut hair pinned up beneath their large white prayer coverings.

Beyond dress, the Amish are seen in daily labor that is strictly divided according to traditional gender roles. Visitors regularly witness Amish men plowing fields with a team of horses, driving a forklift at one of the many area lumberyards, or working on a construction crew. Similarly, Amish women are observed in their gardens tending to beautiful flowers and taking care of fruits and vegetables that they will later put up for the winter. They are also encountered waiting on tables at Der Dutchman and making pies in its bakery. Through a glass partition at Coblentz Chocolates, tourists watch them hand dip chocolates. Throughout Walnut Creek, visitors frequently see Amish men and women performing the kind of gender differentiation that the visual rhetoric of Walnut Creek prescribes. In these ways the Amish seem to prove that even in the twenty-first century, it is possible for men and women to have clarity about gender differences, to take up their traditional roles, and in so doing to enjoy a lifestyle that makes an experience of plentiful time possible.

Even as the Amish of Walnut Creek seem to confirm the idea that it is possible to achieve a slower pace of life by returning to traditional gender roles, they probably do not make a good case for its ease or viability in contemporary American culture. If such a return also means that the tourist has to trade in his car for a horse and buggy, for instance, then such a solution remains implausible. What if there were a way to slow down without giving up all the conveniences and comforts of contemporary life? Would this resolution to time famine and gender anxiety via a return to traditional gender roles be plausible? Such a way is offered, wittingly or unwittingly, in the national patriotism represented within Walnut Creek's Victorian theme.

The National Context

There is much evidence of American patriotism in Walnut Creek. In honor of Memorial Day and Independence Day, American flags are displayed on telephone poles all along Carlisle Street through the months of May and July. Stores regularly develop elaborate displays of merchandise around the theme of the stars and stripes. At Carlisle House, Thomas Kinkade's series of paintings of the flag, Statue of Liberty, White House, and so forth are showcased on a wall dedicated to patriotic themes. Elsewhere in the store, miniature replicas of the Jefferson Memorial, Lincoln Memorial, and White House are sold, as are statues of Thomas Jefferson and other Founding Fathers.

These visible expressions of patriotism may seem strange in a town that draws visitors because of its proximity to the Amish. After all, the Amish are well known as a people who refuse military conscription, are forbidden by their church to hold public office, and are discouraged from voting.[42] Indeed, whenever obedience to the state threatens to compromise their allegiance to God or the integrity of their communities, they resist it. Thus, in addition to refusing military duty, they have also resisted the consolidation of their one-room schools and participation in Social Security and Worker's Compensation. Less well-known of them is that the Amish will not recite the Pledge of Allegiance or fly a flag in or around their schools or homes.[43]

A simple explanation for the many patriotic displays in Walnut Creek is that, since the terrorist attacks on September 11, 2001, and the ensuing wars in Afghanistan and Iraq, American consumers have a heightened desire for patriotic merchandise. Seeking to capitalize on this desire, merchants in Walnut Creek have provided both displays and merchandise, even if doing so is incongruous with the ethos of the Amish. These displays convey powerful messages about the nation as both a political and an economic force in the world, but these messages have been conveyed during a time when middle Americans have often been uneasy about the United States' role in the world. While over the last couple of decades Americans have often expressed intense support for the nation, especially in the immediate aftermath of September 11, at other times they have been skeptical about US involvement elsewhere in the world (particularly when the wars in Iraq and Afghanistan have appeared to be failing). The persuasive messages put forth by patriotic displays in Walnut Creek offer reassurance to middle Americans of the basic goodness of the nation while at the same time suggesting solutions to the practical challenges concerning time and gender that the tourists face.

The Nation as Global Political Force

During his 2000 presidential campaign, George W. Bush advocated a foreign policy in which the US military would become involved in a foreign country only when specific US interests were at stake, success was a probable outcome, and an exit strategy was well developed. He argued that such an approach was the proper corrective to the Clinton administration's policy of nation building. A US foreign policy characterized by nation building, Bush argued, was in error because it often did not work, it put American troops at unwarranted risk, and it communicated an arrogant posture on the part of the US to the rest of the world. When Bush made these claims on the campaign trail, he spoke to an important concern among Americans in a post–Cold War era in which the US had emerged as the last remaining superpower.

In the wake of the terrorist attacks on September 11, 2001, the United States invaded Afghanistan and then, seventeen months later, Iraq. While the war in Afghanistan was largely understood as a defensive move against an attacker, Bush explained the war with Iraq as a "preemptive" strike against a nation that posed an imminent threat by way of its alleged possession of weapons of mass destruction. Initially, most Americans supported Bush and his new view of US military involvement on foreign soil, but five years into the war in Iraq, Bush set a record for presidential disapproval ratings at 69 percent.[44] Americans' disapproval of Bush's presidency evidently was connected to his handling of the war in Iraq.[45] By December 2006, 71 percent of Americans disapproved of Bush's handling of Iraq and 63 percent of Americans were pessimistic about the outcome of the war.[46] By March 2008, 60 percent of Americans said the war was a mistake.[47]

Since at least the 1990s, then, many Americans have been uneasy about the US role in the world. In the last several years, the protracted efforts around invading, occupying, and rebuilding both Iraq and Afghanistan have made many Americans wary once again of such foreign involvements. As Americans looked beyond US shores, they found much confirmation of their concern. According to the 2007 Pew Global Attitudes survey, the largest survey of global opinion ever taken, over the period from 2002 to 2007, the percentages of respondents "with favorable views of the United States" fell "from 60 percent to 30 percent in Germany, 61 percent to 29 percent in Indonesia and 30 percent to 9 percent in Turkey."[48]

For middle Americans who remain uneasy with America's role in the world and who visit Amish Country, Walnut Creek's visual rhetoric reassures. One clear message of Walnut Creek is the strong identification with the nation that emerged in response to September 11. For instance, the Thomas Kinkade gallery in Carlisle Gifts encourages reverence for the nation by showcasing prints like "The Light of Freedom." In that print the American flag is in the foreground and the Statue of Liberty and the New York City skyline, minus the Twin Towers, are in the background. The dramatic light of a setting sun breaks through the clouds to shine upon the flag as it flies in a strong breeze. Another print, "The Lights of Liberty," depicts the White House on a cold and snowy winter evening with the warm glow of its interior lights and the lights of a Christmas tree on the lawn. Through these and other Thomas Kinkade prints on display throughout Walnut Creek, tourists are invited to focus their emotions on the US as a powerful beacon for democracy in a world changed forever by September 11.

Other displays of merchandise around Walnut Creek strike a much less serious tone. Indeed, they are better characterized as festive displays of patriotic symbols. There are all manner of items bearing the image of the flag—stuffed snow men, pads of paper, ball point pens, candles, figurines, lighted balls, statues, tin buckets—or otherwise making reference to patriotic themes. These celebrative patriotic displays invite tourists to experience their identification with the nation as a happy feature of their lives rather than as an occasion for asking questions about the role of nation in the world.

This celebrative experience of the nation is enhanced by the fact that it is set in Walnut Creek's Victorian theme. The way the theme is presented does not remind visitors of the social antagonisms that erupted, sometimes violently, between labor and capital or women and the state during the Victorian period. Instead, the late nineteenth century is remembered here as a time when all was right in America, when work was meaningful, families were well ordered and leisure was plentiful. Set within that constructed memory, these patriotic displays invite the tourist to think of the nation's response to September 11 as evidence that the United States always stands as the warm, welcoming, and strong sign of freedom no matter the threat. Placed in the context of Walnut Creek's Victorian theme, then, these patriotic displays encourage visitors to imagine a future in which the present unease about the role of the United States would be remembered as just another moment when the nation's resolve to sustain its historic role in a hostile world was being tested. Or, as the Thomas Kinkade catalogue sold in Walnut Creek instructs us, "Now is the time when each of us must summon our courage and strength so that the 'Light of Freedom' will forever illuminate this glorious country."[49]

At first glance the patriotic displays in Walnut Creek seem at odds with the Amish who draw visitors to the area. With a closer look, however, it can be seen that this is not so. The presence of the Amish underscores the idea that the United States is a beacon of democracy that welcomes and protects all who seek freedom. The Amish are a religious people who resist the power of the state, yet they are also seen to be thriving in the very heart of America. As a people who depart visibly from the norms of American culture and who move about Walnut Creek contentedly, the Amish function as living proof that the United States protects freedom even when a particular expression of freedom runs counter to the interests of the state. The Amish, especially in the context of the tourism grown up around them, serve as visible evidence that the United States remains the benevolent protector of all religious freedom, financial prosperity, and personal happiness. In such a context, patriotism is presumed. The implied question to tourists visiting Walnut Creek is not about the rectitude of US involvement in wars and such around the globe but whether the tourists have sufficient resolve to sustain their support of the nation and adequate courage to express it.[50]

The Nation as Global Economic Force

Just as Americans have asked questions about the nation's relatively new political role as sole superpower, so too have they wondered about its position in the new global economy. In the last decade, the news media have devoted much time and many column inches to a set of issues that affect working conditions and wages in the United States. With that attention, a confusing picture has developed about what it means to live and work in the United States amidst a global economy. On the one hand, middle Americans are instructed that a global economy means more access to foreign markets for US goods. With greater access to new markets, so the logic goes, US companies will grow in size and profitability, which will increase jobs and wages.[51] On the other hand, middle Americans are alerted to the fact that a global economy also means that US companies are free to move their manufacturing interests to the southern hemisphere, where they can employ cheaper labor and avoid US taxes and costly federal regulations. Moreover, those businesses that remain in the US are forced to operate more efficiently in order to remain competitive in a global market. According to this logic, neither the number of US jobs nor the wages paid for them are likely to increase with economic globalization.[52] What will increase are the demands that workers be more productive.[53] Whether in the end the global economy will serve as the engine for prosperity or will cause protracted financial distress to middle Americans, there can be little doubt that the uncertainty of the US role in a global economy and its effects on middle Americans is palpable.[54]

Consuming the Good Life in Walnut Creek

Given that Amish Country tourism is consumer oriented and takes place in a consumer economy, it is not surprising that visitors are addressed as those who use and enjoy the products of other people's labor rather than as the laborers who make products and perform services for a wage. At this very basic level, then, Walnut Creek's visual rhetoric simply sidelines the whole issue of what the global economy will mean for US workers. This is another way in which Amish Country tourism provides visitors with an escape from the concerns that accompany life as a middle-American wage earner today.

The presentation of the Victorian theme in Walnut Creek is characterized by abundance and attention to detail for the pleasure of the visitor. The newly built and renovated buildings are spacious structures surrounded by thick lawns, full shrubs, and overflowing flower baskets. Their charming interior spaces include architectural details like curved staircases, faux copper ceilings, and crown molding and are decorated richly. Similarly, restaurants and shops convey a feeling of abundance. Portions are always generous at Der Dutchman, and the long salad/breakfast bars are always brimming with many fresh selections. Merchandise in the shops is plentiful and displayed densely, filling walls, cabinets, and tables.

But, whenever tourists turn over an item in one of the shops to see its price, they also typically see where the item was made and are thus repeatedly reminded of the larger economic structure that makes such an abundance of merchandise possible in the twenty-first century. A reproduction Oriental rug from Egypt, a teapot from England, lace from the USA, figurines from China, dinnerware from Thailand, scarves from Korea, and crystal from Poland indicate that living in the United States within the larger context of a global economy means enjoying the power to adorn one's life at affordable prices. In this way the tourist is encouraged to experience the global economy as a condition of the good life, which to the consumer presumably means a life of affordable luxury.

But when tourists turn over those items and see the name of a developing country, they may also be reminded of the cheap labor that makes so many items affordable. The tourist may experience some discomfort at the recognition that their good life depends upon the underpaid work of a stranger. Walnut Creek's visual rhetoric reassures on this point too, by its representation of the laboring Amish.

The Happy Amish Laborer

One of the largest (and clearly the most visible) segments of the tourism labor force in Walnut Creek is young Amish women. They make the chocolates at Coblentz Chocolates, cook and serve the food at Der Dutchman, and work behind the counter in the bakery. It is significant that these women are not only young but also typically single. They are usually living with their parents and working in these businesses until they marry and begin bearing children. They are paid a modest hourly wage, and they are dependable, honest, and hard workers.

When tourists look upon them, they cannot help but notice that they are Amish women, since they wear the plain dress and prayer coverings required by their church. Thus, they do not signify as individual working women but as Amish women who belong to a people that differs dramatically from mainstream culture. They represent a culture that harvests wheat with horse-drawn wagons and pitchforks and lights its kitchens with gas lamps. In these visible ways at least, theirs is a preindustrial culture. Yet, these young women work in a postindustrial economy where they may be seen as similar to other laborers around the world who produce goods for an economy quite different from their own. Like the Third World worker, an Amish woman baking pies at Der Dutchman signifies as the kind of cheap labor that produces most of the merchandise that the US consumer buys.

In recent years tourists have gained increased (albeit mediated) access to these laboring Amish women. As always, tourists may exchange words with an Amish woman serving them dinner, selling them a pie, or weighing their box of chocolates, but recently tourists have gained a new form of visual access in Coblentz Chocolates. With the renovation of the store in 2002, a chocolate factory was added to the store; so production of the chocolates, which used to occur elsewhere, now happens on site. During that renovation a clear glass partition was installed so that tourists could watch these Amish women work in the factory. Thus, tourists get a seemingly behind-the-scenes but very public look at Amish labor in Walnut Creek.[55] Presumably, the intent is to enable tourists to appreciate that the chocolates being sold are hand-dipped. However, along with that, they are also given a glimpse of these different people at work.

What visitors see as they look upon the chocolate factory, with its well-swept floors and gleaming stainless-steel pots, is a clean, hard-working, and happy laborer in her plain dress, white apron, and prayer covering. Clearly marked as an Amish woman, she appears to be doing exactly what she ought to do given the gender roles of her culture. She is not, after all, manufacturing cabinets (as are Amish men who may be watched in a nearby cabinet shop).[56] Instead, she is baking muffins, canning preserves, or dipping chocolates. This is the kind of work she will be expected to do in her own home once she is married and has children. To visitors, then, she appears to be laboring in ways that suit her position within her community's social order as an unmarried woman without children. Her work makes sense within the context of her life, and there is no reason to think she may be discontented.

Of course, visitors are likely to know that, as a humble people, the Amish do not pursue excessive wealth but, instead, prefer modest incomes in order remain plain, faithful, and humble. Knowing this, tourists readily conclude that the young Amish woman is not only a hard worker engaged in labor appropriate to her sex and her culture but also a happy worker who gladly receives a modest wage. To the extent, then, that she figures also as an analogy for the Third World worker, she reassures the tourist who wonders whether it is all right to consume so many goods made affordable by cheap labor. Looking through the glass partition at Coblentz Chocolates, the visitor is invited to conclude that there is nothing wrong with enjoying the fruits of such cheap labor.

From the perspective made possible by Walnut Creek's presentation of the Amish, the global economy enables relationships of production and consumption that are mutually beneficial for all. The worker gladly earns a modest wage for gender-appropriate labor in a clean working environment; the consumer enjoys high-quality yet inexpensive goods. In Ohio's Amish Country, this positive relationship between producer and consumer makes affordable, and is yet another encouragement for, an imagined future in which women fashion a lifestyle for their families that is characterized by plentiful time, beautiful surroundings, and social order.

Issues Resolved

Amish tourism is thriving in Walnut Creek. This is not because Walnut Creek offers tourists authentic encounters with the Amish. It does not. Instead, through its themed environment Walnut Creek constructs an experience for its visitors that they enjoy. The presentation of Walnut Creek's Victorian theme in its architecture, interior and exterior décor, food, and merchandise addresses important anxieties and concerns that tourists have. Taken together, all of these elements of Walnut Creek's theme reassure the tourist and encourage them to imagine a future in which time is plentiful, gender is clear, and nation is good. All this reassurance is made more pleasurable by Walnut Creek's construction of the Amish as proof that such a future is not some pie-in-the-sky dream but a real possibility.

In response to tourists' concerns about the political role of their nation in the world, Walnut Creek's visual rhetoric says that America has been and will remain a benevolent power that works on behalf of democracy around the globe. Further, it emboldens middle-American tourists to embrace that vision by instructing them that being patriotic is an act of courage that recognizes the United States' true essence as a nation. Regarding tourists' unease about the global economy and their place within it, Walnut Creek's visual rhetoric provides reassurance by demonstrating, through the merchandise sold there, that the global economy enables the good life in the United States. With its presentation of the Amish as contented laborers, it also shows that the global economy might be good for workers around the world, who gladly labor for their modest incomes. Thus, Walnut Creek encourages tourists to see themselves as benevolent consumers whose consumption is crucial for keeping the gears of the global economy well greased. Taking all this into account, it is not surprising that tourists find these resolutions to their anxieties pleasurable indeed.

In addition to offering resolutions to concerns about global politics and economy, Walnut Creek's environment also invites tourists to imagine alternative ways of being in the world, ways that address concerns about time famine and gender relations. The resolution for the time famine implied in the visual rhetoric of Walnut Creek is for women to return to their traditional role in the home and to transform the home into a space in which everyone within it experiences plentiful time. By planning and preparing slow food and by creating a feminine environment that invites others to lose track of time, women may, this visual rhetoric suggests, expand time. In addition, by reclaiming their traditional role, women may reassure all that it is still possible to experience clarity about gender roles.

But how are American women, the majority of whom work outside the home, going to find the time to create this experience? The visual rhetoric of Walnut Creek points, albeit implicitly, in the directions of two possibilities for resolving this problem. The first answer is that a global economy makes it possible for the US consumer to purchase high-quality goods at low prices, so middle Americans are able to enjoy the good life at less expense. Thus, while economic downturns may require significant belt-tightenings,[57] if the desire is strong enough, it may still be possible for the middle-American family to get along on one income or one primary income with augmentation from part-time work. The middle-American woman might be able to return home to pursue this imagined future.

The second answer this rhetoric offers is that it is good to hire the services of a domestic laborer to execute the plans of the middle-American woman. In this scenario, the middle-American woman would continue to work outside the home while at the same time overseeing the creation of a new lifestyle at home that is not characterized by microwave dinners and a disheveled interior. Such an arrangement need not necessarily be viewed as problematic if, as it is in Walnut Creek, one could hire a woman for such work who would welcome the income and see the work as appropriate for her.

Of course, the visual rhetoric of Walnut Creek does not explicitly advocate either of these solutions. Instead, it offers a beautiful environment in which visitors are encouraged in multiple ways to imagine a future characterized by plentiful time, ordered gender, and a benevolent nation. But Walnut Creek does suggest narratives by which visitors might achieve such a future.[58] Its Victorian theme and its representation of the Amish suggest that, with a little help from the global economy, and especially its cheap labor, this imagined future might be realized.

An Amish Style Critique

In the context of Walnut Creek's visual rhetoric, the Amish appear to be living proof that it is still possible to live at a leisurely pace, to have clarity about what it means to be a man or a woman, to feel patriotic about the role of the nation in the world, and to feel good about practices of consumption. The Amish appear to support this vision for a different future insofar as they are represented within Walnut Creek (and elsewhere) as a people that have maintained an apparently premodern way of life. With their gas lamps, horse-drawn buggies, and plain clothes, their life moves slowly and their social order is clear and secure. Thus, they seem to say to tourists that it may be so with them as well. If they will take home that cookbook, that tea pot, that hickory rocker, that inspirational wall hanging, then they might create that future by changing their style of life to one in which women serve tea and biscuits, men enjoy meat and potatoes, conversations linger on the front porch, and everyone assumes the fundamental goodness of the nation and the middle-American citizen-consumer.

But do the signs of the Amish—their plain dress, head coverings, beards, horses and buggies, bodies at work—really point toward this imagined future? Consider this: the visual rhetoric of Amish Country tourism in Walnut Creek presumes that lace and lotion, china and chocolates, rugs and rockers can change your life. Indeed, like much advertising, this rhetoric

An Amish woman and children arrive at the main intersection in Walnut Creek

is based on the premise that style is everything: how you signify visually constitutes you. As the Thomas Kinkade catalogue instructs: "Surround yourself with people and things that both define and reflect who you are."[59]

This central proposition of America's visual and consumer culture—that image is everything; that how one appears defines one—explains why people are moved to pay premium prices for particular brands, why people dress from head to toe in the colors and logos of athletic teams, why people deck out their toddlers in designer outfits. Indeed, without taking this principle into account it is very difficult to explain why so many people living in cities and suburbs are willing to pay fifty thousand dollars for a luxury SUV with all-wheel drive.

The visual rhetoric of Amish tourism uses the Amish to authenticate a vision of an alternative future that resolves important anxieties in middle-American life and may be achieved through the transformation of personal style. To be sure, the Amish understand well the power of style. Their commitment, now more than a century old, to carving out a separate existence by dressing, farming, driving, speaking, and so forth in ways visibly and audibly different from those of the larger culture within which they live serves as irrefutable testimony to their understanding of the power of appearance. They know better than most Americans that it matters how you style your hair, the sort of pants you put on each morning, what vehicle you drive to work. To a great extent, style makes the Amish who they are, insofar as it marks them as other, as a distinctive community living their Christian commitment in a particular way.

As they till their fields or hang their wash out to dry or drive their buggies through town, the Amish not only say much about what they think about technology and its relationship to work, family, and community life. They also raise important questions for the tourist. Even as their presence and ways are used to legitimate the claim of Walnut Creek's visual rhetoric that you can change your life by changing your style, they also wittingly or unwittingly pose a challenge. If their style speaks volumes about their commitments, what does the style of the tourists say about their commitments? What commitments are confessed by the clothes Americans wear, vehicles Americans drive, manner in which Americans speak, and so forth? What does the plethora of flat screen TVs, iPads, and laptops say about work, family, and community? What does one's particular style say, and does it count?

These are powerful questions. Granted, they are probably not the questions heard most loudly amidst the cacophony of signs that make up Walnut Creek's visual rhetoric. Indeed, they may be difficult to hear amidst the promise of plentiful time, gender order, and moral confidence that is Walnut Creek's message to tourists. Still, if Walnut Creek's promises are built upon that basic premise of American consumer culture that a change in style can transform one's life, then perhaps the Amish are speaking more loudly than one might think. Given this premise, how can visitors to Amish Country ignore the questions raised by Amish style? Looking upon them in fascination, as most Americans do, how do observers fail to notice that Amish style speaks to deeply held commitments that are of ultimate consequence to them and that in many ways contest those of US culture? If this Amish witness regarding the importance of style cannot be ignored entirely, then it would seem that tourists to Amish Country are invited to wonder who they are making of themselves, and whether or not it counts.

BERLIN

FARMSTEAD
RESTAURANT

Somerset Rd.

Main St.

Twp Rd 366

AMISH
MENNONITE
HERITAGE
CENTER

62

SOL'S PALACE

BOYD AND
WURTHMANN
RESTAURANT

BERLIN VILLAGE
ANTIQUE MALL

62

Elm St.

Market St.

Twp Rd 358

77

39

N

SCHROCK'S
AMISH
FARM

Tourist sites in the Berlin, Ohio

CHAPTER 4

Technology and Innocence in Berlin

They seem to be getting away from their roots.
—Amish Country tourist as he browsed in a craft mall in Berlin

erlin is the busiest tourist town in Ohio's Amish Country. With
a newly rebuilt grocery / dry goods / hardware store that brings
many Amish to town, and dozens of shops and several restaurants
and inns lining its main street and spilling down side streets that bring
tourists to town, Berlin bustles with commerce, especially between the
months of May and October.[1] So many people visit Berlin during these
months that any attempt to drive through town requires a lot of patience.
In a study conducted in 1998, researchers counted 1,924 cars passing
through the main intersection of the town during business hours.[2] Although this may not sound like a lot of traffic for an urban or even suburban area in the US, for a town with a population of just 685 people,
this is indeed a lot of traffic. Given that the main road through Berlin has
only two lanes and that more than 500 trucks, busses, RVs, tractors, and
Amish buggies also travel the same road, residents and visitors regularly
find themselves sitting in a long line of vehicles waiting to get through
the main intersection in town.[3] This likely comes as a surprise to visitors
anticipating peace and quiet in Amish Country.

Self-identified as the "heart" of Ohio's Amish Country, Berlin is not
only the busiest town in the area. It also claims to be the first in Ohio to
market the Amish to tourists. Since the early 1970s, tourists have been
buying tickets to tour an Amish house and barn at what is now Schrock's
Amish Farm (just one mile east of the center of Berlin on State Route 39).[4]
Berlin's history of tourism cannot explain its popularity as a destination for

Amish Country visitors. To understand why so many tourists are drawn to
Berlin, it is imperative to look at exactly what it offers.

A Virtual Tour of Berlin

For tourists coming from Walnut Creek on State Route 39, it takes only
a few minutes of driving before they see Schrock's Amish Farm on their
right.[5] A few minutes farther down the road and they arrive at the eastern edge of the center of town. From there and for as far as they can see,
Main Street (which overlaps SR 39 as it continues west) is lined with
shops, restaurants, inns, and other tourist businesses. The center of Berlin
(including its Main Street and a few side streets) is home to more than
forty shops, a large grocery store, at least ten inns (including a sixty-nine-
room Comfort Suites and the seventy-eight-room Berlin Grande Hotel),
and four restaurants. Of this plethora of points of interest in Berlin I will
describe just a sampling.

Beginning just east of the intersection of SR 39 and US Route 62,
tourists find on their right (the north side of the street) a cluster of three
barnlike buildings that are home to Berlin Village Gift Barn, which sells
furniture, candles and other interior décor items, and some clothing,[6] and
Country Gatherings, a shop that features reproduction primitive American interior décor and furnishings.[7] Across SR 39, they see Schrock's
Heritage Furniture, which is housed in a false-front building, and Der
Bake Oven (a bakery), in a building that looks a bit like a Swiss chalet. At
the intersection, they find another barnlike structure, painted red, that
is home to the twenty-four-thousand-square-foot Berlin Village Antique
Mall, Cindy's Diner (formerly Route 39 Diner, a 1950s-style restaurant
that serves burgers, hot dogs, and chicken sandwiches as well as roast turkey, beef, and pork dinners), and a candle factory and store. Across SR 39
from this structure they see Sommers General Store, where they can purchase everything from gourmet coffee to John Deere interior décor items
to Amish Country puzzles.

Just one block north on US 62, visitors find the Farmstead Restaurant,
which looks like a giant Amish barn with its white siding and which serves
Amish-style food in a facility with a capacity of three hundred in its main
dining room and banquet facilities. If instead of turning north, tourists
continue down Main Street, they come to another notable restaurant. One

The Berlin Village Antique Mall displays rural associations with its barnlike building

of the oldest in the area, the Boyd and Wurthmann Restaurant has been a favorite among locals (and especially Amish) since 1945.[8] Housed in a flat-front structure, Boyd and Wurthmann serves hearty broasted chicken lunches and many varieties of freshly baked pies; tourists gladly wait in long lines to dine here among the locals.

Continuing down Main Street, tourists pass many shops that are housed in what used to be single-family homes. Many have been significantly altered, renovated, and/or expanded to better accommodate the needs of a shop. A notable example is an early-nineteenth-century house that was so thoroughly renovated in the middle of the twentieth century, in the style of a modern ranch house, as to almost completely obscure the hand-hewn oak beams that hold up its walls.[9] Farther down the block is a feed mill that was completely redone to become the Old Berlin Mill. Now home to three shops, this building retains the relatively simple style of a feed mill. Still farther down Main Street and on the south side of the street, sits Sol's Palace and Sol's Exchange, which together house some four hundred arts and crafts booths in two rectangular structures built to resemble

Sol's Palace, with pseudo—frontier fort walls but a wraparound porch with rocking chairs, houses hundreds of arts and crafts booths

a nineteenth-century frontier fort, with stained wood siding, false fronts, and twin crenelated towers.[10]

A Theme amidst Eclecticism

As this virtual tour suggests, Berlin's architectural environment is not uniform. On the contrary, its built environment includes the all-purpose barn, the American ranch house, the Swiss chalet, and a fake frontier fort. Compared to Walnut Creek's consistent Victorian theme, Berlin's visual cues are eclectic indeed.

That said, certain features dominate Berlin's eclectic style. Flat-front and false-front stores are common. So too are simple two-story, wood-sided buildings without decorative elements like shutters, turned balusters, or large porches. In the past decade or so, barns or newly constructed buildings that resemble barns have been cropping up everywhere. New structures meant to resemble frontier forts and log cabins are also common, with primitive-style features including stained siding and log construction, square porch supports, and stone fireplaces.

Berlin's environment makes repeated references to American frontier architecture. The names of businesses provide additional references to the American frontier. Shop names include language such as "trading company," "exchange," "general store," and "country store," thus calling to mind the trading posts that sold goods to the earliest trappers and settlers and the general stores that replaced them in the nineteenth century. The name of the Farmstead Restaurant suggests the cluster of buildings that included the barn, house, and storage sheds and was the primary site of economic production and home life during the nineteenth century in America. Overnight accommodations in Berlin are often identified as "lodging" rather than "hotel" or "motel" and thereby call to mind a rustic rather than urban or suburban setting.

The merchandise offered in Berlin shops further develops these references. The Catalpa Trading Company, for instance, sells merchandise, including hunting knives and "home remedies," that could have been sold at a frontier trading post. Shops billed as general stores or country stores sell housewares, such as kitchen utensils, pots and pans, and dinnerware; food, including coffee beans, Amish noodles, bottled soda pop, and bulk candy; clothing in the form of Amish Country T-shirts; and miniature "farm implements," like brand-name tractors, hay bailers, and combines. Home décor shops emphasize a primitive style, selling items that look as if they were made by hand and without the benefit of power tools. There are dollhouses constructed of unornamented exterior walls with cutout holes for windows, ragdolls that look as if they were sewn by hand, multicolor braided rugs, and simply decorated hand-painted pottery.

Antiques appear in abundance in Berlin's antique malls, but these are not pricey fine antiques. These are the implements of nineteenth- and twentieth-century farms and country homes. They include old dinnerware, kitchen utensils, furniture, ironing boards, McGuffey Readers, and shop tools. Finally, folk craft items and supplies are the focus of several shops. Throughout the four hundred or so vendor stalls of Sol's Exchange and Sol's Palace, shoppers can find yard ornaments, acrylic paintings of barn scenes, decorated baskets, wood engravings of Bible passages, painted bird feathers, and photographs of local Amish scenes. Some of these items look as though they were made by local craftspeople; many others were clearly mass produced.

By its many references to frontier forts, log cabins, horsemen, hunting

knives, general stores, primitive toys, and the like, Berlin constructs its
dominant visual theme as the American frontier. However, merchandise in
Berlin is presented in a cluttered style, displaying a wide variety of goods
that do not appear to fit the theme. Nearly every available square inch of
space in and around Berlin's shops is filled with all manner of merchandise, much of it unrelated to the frontier. Such proliferation of merchandise that bears no obvious relationship to Berlin's frontier theme seems at
first glance to indicate a marketing approach that simply says put out as
much merchandise as possible wherever possible and never mind about a
theme.

Thus, it was not surprising to hear a shopper (who was standing amidst
displays of miniature porcelain tea cups, plastic key fobs with inspirational
texts on them, and painted bird feathers) say to his companion, "They seem
to be getting away from their roots." Indeed, if "they" are the Amish, then
the shopper has a point. Of course, the Amish do not own these shops,
but this is Amish Country, and the clutter here contrasts sharply with the
plain and simple life of the Amish. This contrast in Berlin echoes the one
in Walnut Creek between the simple lifestyle of the Amish and the ornate
or cluttered style of Amish Country tourism.

The Visual Rhetoric of Tourism in Berlin

Even Walnut Creek's theme is not presented in a seamless way, but Berlin's is set amidst obvious concessions to twenty-first-century life: overnight accommodations include Jacuzzis, a coffee shop advertises free
WiFi, a Burger King at the edge of town offers a drive-thru window, and
so forth. By meeting the expectations and satisfying the preferences of
middle-American tourists, Berlin welcomes tourists as they are. In effect,
these accommodations encourage the tourists to feel comfortable as middle
Americans while they "visit the American frontier."

Notably, Berlin's theme is much more loosely put together than Walnut Creek's. Whereas in Walnut Creek all of the buildings in the town
display some features of Victorian architecture, in Berlin buildings show
a wide variety of architectural styles within and outside of the context
of the frontier theme. Displays in shops also have a more eclectic feel. In
Walnut Creek, the boutique style of displaying merchandise is common;
seemingly unique items are thoughtfully clustered according to themes

like golf, afternoon tea, and the garden. Even where assemblages of items seem cluttered, the displays clearly indicate that great care was given to the selection and positioning of merchandise so as to create a pleasing color palette and well-balanced configuration. By contrast, in Berlin some stalls and shops seem to benefit from thoughtful arrangement of items, but others look haphazardly put together. Multiple copies of the same item may be displayed even when the items are supposed to look handcrafted. The overall look in Berlin resembles a flea market or community garage sale.

This looser approach to store displays in Berlin creates a much less consistent environment than in Walnut Creek. Indeed, in Berlin, one frequently encounters shop themes and merchandise that do not appear to bear any relationship to the American frontier. That said, Berlin's looser approach fits its theme rather well. The architectural diversity and flea market style of displaying merchandise seems appropriate to the context of a theme that evokes ideas of freedom, self-reliance, and individual expression. But, in Berlin there is no attempt to suggest that the tourist is making a return to an earlier time. Instead, loose references to another era invite the tourist, as in Walnut Creek, to enjoy a selective and idealized story of America.

The Frontier Theme

Contemporary language theory talks about floating signifiers—important words or other signifiers that change over time and across space. Race is a good example. A crucial category for organizing society in hierarchical ways, "race" has designated seemingly fixed racial categories evidenced by concrete physical differences. However, as Stuart Hall, renowned sociologist and cultural theorist, has argued, such differences never hold. Whereas it was once thought that skull size or skin color or hair texture could serve as an incontrovertible marker for race, not one of those traits turned out to be a guaranteed indicator of race. Examples could always be found of people who seemed obviously to be members of a certain race yet did not exhibit one of the definitive characteristics of that race. Hall's point is that "race" is not now and never has been a category the boundaries of which can be supported by some nonlinguistic reality. Instead, Hall argues, "race" is a category that humans have invented, the meaning of which changes, or "floats," with time.[11] One reason that the meaning of floating signifiers changes over time is that they are often contested by groups in-terested in challenging the order that such signifiers bring to society.

The term "American frontier" is a floating signifier. Over time it has referred to the Appalachian Mountains, the Great Plains, California, the moon, outer space, and the Internet, as the line marking the progressive transformation of the wild has floated from east to west and beyond. The meaning of "frontier" has been contested as various stories of its signifi-cance have been told or as one or another politician has sought to claim it as a slogan for a presidential campaign. The concept has helped to order American society, not only because it gives meaning to the origins of this nation, but also because it designates cutting edge or outdated, free or cap-tive, open or closed.

To say that Berlin has an American frontier theme is a good start for understanding its visual rhetoric. However, it is impossible to discern the meaning of Berlin's theme until it is known which story of the American frontier is being told there. As it turns out, Berlin clearly favors one story, a story that offers much to the middle-American tourist.

Violent Conquest or Peaceful Settlement?

According to Richard White, an expert on the American West, two sto-ries of the American frontier took hold of the American imagination. One was told by popular showman "Buffalo Bill" Cody and the other by Fred-erick Jackson Turner. Both were told in Chicago in 1893 at the Colum-bian Exposition, both drew heavily upon the conventional wisdom of the day and the popular icons of the American West, and both announced the closure of the American frontier.[12] These two stories continue to serve as the "truth" of the American frontier, both factually and prescriptively. They offer instruction in not only what the frontier was like but also what America is and who Americans should be.[13]

Buffalo Bill told the story of the violent conquest of a land occupied by American Indians. The protagonist in his story was the scout (a white male) who knew "Indian"[14] cultures well and, thus, was able to outsmart his enemy and achieve victory, with the help of his rifle. By contrast, Fred-erick Jackson Turner told the story of the peaceful movement of settlers into a largely unoccupied land. The protagonist in his story was the farmer (also a white male) who, with his axe and plow, created American culture out of untamed nature.[15]

Berlin's frontier theme clearly favors Turner's story over Buffalo Bill's. The focus in Berlin is on the farmstead as the primary site of economic production and a place of domestic tranquility. Architectural references to farming are common in the various barnlike structures and the feed mill. Store themes such as the general store or country store suggest an all-purpose supplier for the needs of farming families. Merchandise that is related to food preparation, home décor, and toys emphasizes domestic activities, while the ubiquitous tractor, whether as a miniature toy, an image within a painting, or the theme of a string of decorative lights, keeps the idea of farming ever before the tourist. Almost as an exclamation point, the Farmstead Restaurant, with both its name and the gigantic proportions of its barnlike structure, underscores that Turner's story is favored here.

The particular manner in which the farmstead appears in Berlin emphasizes peacefulness. Actual barns and barnlike structures in Berlin suggest tranquility because they remind visitors of all of the barns nestled among the hills and valleys of this famously peaceful area. Whether visitors have driven the back roads to experience the quiet or have only read about it, they "know" that barns and farmsteads are peaceful. Moreover, the connection made in Berlin between farming and domestic life (as opposed to connecting it with production and commerce) also suggests tranquility. In Berlin the farmstead is domestic; it is about family. And domestic life in Berlin means creating a home-cooked meal with sturdy utensils, redecorating a room in warm colors and with solid wood furniture, embellishing the exterior of a home with a "Welcome" sign, or rocking to and fro in the shade of a covered porch. In Berlin, the life of the farmstead is creative, welcoming, satisfying, and relaxing.

Other pictorial representations of the frontier also suggest a tranquil setting. One painting, framed reproductions of which are sold in various places in Berlin, is of a man on his horse leading two more horses, each of which carries a pile of sacks. The man and his horses are walking slowly away from a log cabin that sits next to a wooded stream at the foot of a mountain range. Smoke is coming out of the chimney and a warm light can be seen in a window. He is relaxed as he departs, leaving others behind. It is easy to imagine that he is leaving behind his wife and perhaps a young family in order to purchase supplies from a general store some miles off. There is no indication in this image that the frontier is a dangerous or violent place. The viewer experiences no anxiety at the thought that his loved ones will have to manage without him.

Framed copies of this unsigned painting of a peaceful frontier are displayed and sold
throughout Berlin

Sprinkled about Berlin's presentation of the frontier theme are references to a certain Christian discourse that confirms this sense of peace and
tranquility. Throughout Berlin, biblical texts and other common religious
sayings are quoted: on carved wood wall hangings, coffee mugs, refrigera-
tor magnets, key fobs. Often, just a single phrase of the more complete quotation is featured, such as "Give us this day our daily bread," or "This day
the Lord made," or "By His wounds you have been healed." Other times a
whole verse will appear, such as one from Psalm 37: "Take delight in the
Lord, and he will give you the desires of your heart." Still other times a
short series of words is featured, such as "faith, hope, love."[16] Excerpting
text from the Bible is typical of a devotional discourse, popularized by
American Evangelicalism, that emphasizes a simple vertical relationship
between the individual and God as provider, protector, and healer. Re-
contextualized within Berlin's frontier theme, these textual extractions
invite the tourist to see God as the guarantor of personal good fortune for

them as, presumably, was the case on the American frontier. Indeed, like the discourse of manifest destiny, this presentation of biblical and other inspirational texts within an American frontier theme invites the tourist to experience a sense of reassurance that God has good things in store for them as Americans.

In its references to the farmstead, Berlin's preference for the peaceful story of the American frontier seems clear. But what about the fort? Sol's Palace makes obvious references to the frontier fort in its stained siding, square porch supports, and two crenelated towers. Of course, in the nineteenth century, the frontier fort was designed to provide the strongest possible defense against "Indian attacks." The purpose of towers in fort walls was to provide protection and longer sight for scouts watching for an approaching enemy. Inclusion of a building that looks like a fort seems to suggest that Berlin is also telling the violent story of the frontier. Is this so?

Not if the porch on Sol's Palace is taken in account. Running the length of the front of Sol's Palace and continuing down the side that faces Main Street is a deep covered porch. It features long rows of rocking chairs and countless "Welcome" signs. As an architectural feature, a porch serves as a transitional space between inside and outside, provides protection from weather, and facilitates relaxing and socializing. The porch at Sol's Palace provides ample transitional space and protection from the weather and offers a comfortable setting in which to sit down for a rest or, as tourists often do, take a nap. Indeed, the porch at Sol's Palace invites those who are coming in or going out to make that transition between inside and outside in a leisurely manner. Of course, nineteenth-century forts did not include exterior porches or encourage lingering around the periphery. The purpose of a fort was to keep a hostile enemy out. Despite references at Sol's Palace to a frontier fort, this structure seems better designed to serve as a welcome center than a last resort against enemy attack.

As if to underscore the point that this frontier fort has nothing to do with violence, two identical signs for Sol's Palace that are displayed prominently show a pair of smiling Amish men. These cartoon-like characters are holding a sign that reads "Sol's Palace," below which is an image of a farmstead, complete with barn, house, and windmill, nestled among rolling hills. The inclusion of the image of the farmstead links this frontier fort with the peaceful version of the American frontier myth. Even more, the image of two smiling Amish men implies that these nonviolent men approve of Sol's Palace. That being so, how could this frontier fort, even with its towers, possibly be about violence?

Of course, it is not about violence, as one more visual clue and its connection to Turner's story make clear. According to Turner's story of the frontier, white settlers moved into an uninhabited land. With no prior occupants, they were able to transform it into productive agricultural land without violent incident. Given that narrative, it is not surprising that Turner's story includes few references to Indians. Indeed, in order for Turner to tell a story of a peaceful frontier, he is almost obliged to ignore the existence and history of the land's first occupants. In a similar way, Berlin says little about Indians. There is, however, a prominent exception, and he appears within the walls of the fort that is Sol's Palace. He is a life-size figure carved out of wood to look as though he is wearing a headdress and leather outfit. He appears to be smoking a pipe. Although he does carry a hatchet in one hand, the expression on his face indicates that he is much more likely to bury it than wield it. Indeed, so harmless does he appear that the fact that he is standing next to a display of little Amish-attired dolls does not seem incongruous. Hardly an enemy, even the Indian is at peace in Sol's Palace.

The Story Berlin Tells

Through its architecture, merchandise, and images, Berlin reiterates a story of peaceful people who left the Old World or the crowded cities along the Atlantic coast for new opportunities and a better life. This is a story about piling the family, along with a few basic necessities, into a covered wagon and setting out across the Appalachian Mountains. It is a story of leaving behind civilization with all its conveniences, as well as its rigid social structures and limited economic opportunities, for a rugged existence in which a new culture is made by the swing of an axe and the pull of a plow.

According to White, the dynamic that is at the center of this story is a three-step process for recreating civilization. The process begins with regression (the return to a primitive existence), moves through recapitulation (a re-birthing of civilization out of the wild), and ends with regeneration (the renewal of civilization).[17] The problem with civilization, so the story goes, is that it tends over time to become fossilized, so organizational structures (like clan, class, religion, etc.) rigidify social relationships into fixed patterns. Pretty soon, people can no longer move up and down the social hierarchy. The social status into which they are born becomes their destiny. To renew human civilization, organizational structures must be radically transformed. One way to do that is to return to a primitive existence in "the wild." The wild is anything outside of the culture. It is nature, animality, a place where there are no rules. Of course, the frontier is the edge of just this sort of place.

To transform human civilization, says White, human beings must leave all the trappings of civilization behind, including all of its conveniences and comforts as well as its laws and order. They must venture beyond culture (where no soil is yet tilled, no economy guarantees production, no laws curb human behavior, no history shapes the future) so that human civilization may be reborn. Pioneers must go here to regress to a prior form of existence, a more primitive form. Here, too, the pioneers must recapitulate, which is to say, start over. They must return to a moment prior to civilization when everything, including themselves, must be reinvented. Knowledge, assumptions, habits, attitudes, practices—nearly all that made sense and was assumed within culture—are rendered senseless in the wild. They simply do not apply. What makes sense on the frontier is not history, or society, or ethnicity but, instead, the axe and the plow applied to timber and dirt through human sweat and ingenuity. Purged of the trappings of history and culture yet emboldened by freedom, creativity, and work, the pioneers regenerate not only themselves but also human civilization.

White makes a compelling case that this dynamic animates the understanding that Americans have of the western frontier and even their sense of what it means to be an American. It is this three-step process of regeneration through regression and recapitulation that Berlin tells by way of its frontier theme. It does this by exploiting the image of the frontier as a conceptual space and the image of tools, the technology with which the pioneer converted the frontier.

In White's dynamic, the frontier is understood not in the sense of a great expanse of empty space but rather as a delineation that moved in time across the mountains and plains, something that divides civilization from the wild and that juxtaposes the old and the new. On one side of that delineation is civilization as a humanly constructed order that is fossilized into categories, laws, and hierarchies that determine the future. On the other side is the wild, understood as a chaotic space wholly lacking humanly imposed order and in which there are no hierarchies to stifle achievement, no laws to curb freedom, and no categories with which to make sense of the past, present, or future. Everything is possible there; the future is wide open. The frontier functions as a space in between nature and culture. It is a gap between civilization and the wild, society and nature, history and possibility, the old and the new.

As such the frontier is a crucial space, because human beings cannot exist in the wild. Only animals (which is to say, uncultured beings) can live there. Yet human beings need access to the wild. Without the wild, the new, and the unruly, human beings cannot breathe new life into culture, the old, the rigidified. The frontier, then, is that space between nature and culture that provides human beings access to the unruly, the different, the unpredictable, and thereby makes it possible for them to renew civilization.

With the Old World behind them and the wild extending before them, the pioneers shed the burden of history, engaged the wild, and performed the regeneration of human civilization. But the pioneer did not perform this work empty handed. It is the tool in any pioneer's hand that makes him or her into an agent of purpose, ingenuity, and creativity. With the tool, the one standing at the frontier is the pioneer who literally turns dirt into soil, tree into log, nature into culture.[18]

Berlin does not simply tell the story of the peaceful pioneer who settled an unoccupied land, thereby regenerating human civilization. Through its architecture, store themes, and merchandise, it provides a three-dimensional environment in which visitors can experience that story. When middle-American tourists move about Berlin, they are not merely passing through some generic tourism space; they are walking, browsing, and resting amidst a setting of Turner's frontier story and being invited to inhabit that story and become subjects of it.

As I have walked among tourists in Berlin over the last fifteen years, I have noticed that one combination of behavior and speech occurs more than any other. Tourists pick up some tool; it could be anything from a flour sifter to a planer. They hold it in their hands and perhaps attempt to operate it. Then, turning to a companion, they say something like "Oh, look at this. My mother [or father or whoever] used to have one of these." A variation of this behavior is often displayed by younger people who have no memory of the implement in hand. Curious about it, they pick it up, show it to someone else (who is usually older), and ask about it. The response almost invariably is something like, "Oh, my mother [father/ whoever] had one of those. That's a [whatever]."

Tools are important in Berlin. Tractors and related farming equipment in miniature form as well as references to tractor manufacturers are ubiquitous. They appear in craft malls, antique malls, general stores, and toy shops. Full-size kitchen implements—pots and pans, utensils, appliances—appear nearly everywhere as well. Old versions show up in antique malls, reproduction versions appear in general stores, and gourmet versions are featured in specialty kitchen shops. Hand tools, such as pocket knives, socket wrenches, and saws, that are associated with hunting, home repair, and wood working also show up throughout Berlin in both antique and modern versions. They are celebrated in countless references to "handcrafted" items.

Whether an older person picks up a tool, holds it, and remembers someone using it or a younger person asks a question about a tool, tourists throughout Berlin actively engage with the tool—they pick it up, study it, try it out. Central to their experience in Berlin is the tactile, visual, and psychological contact with that important element of Turner's story of the frontier—the hand tool. Thus, tourists in Berlin not only move about an environment that tells that story. They also come to inhabit that story. They take up the very means by which the regeneration of civilization was performed, and they engage with it. By holding hand tools (especially actual nineteenth-century ones), turning them in their hands, and wondering about them or remembering someone else's working hands, tourists are participating in that story. It is as if in taking up those tools they are finding themselves in the position of the pioneers who stood at the edge of history prepared to carve out a new civilization with just that simple tool in their hands.

Middle-American Anxieties about Technology

The relationship Americans have to today's tools, that is, today's technology, is a complicated one. On the one hand, Americans understand tech-

A display of hand tools at one of Berlin's antique malls

nology to augment their power as human beings—to traverse space, increase productivity, access information, send messages, heal bodies, and so
forth. On the other hand, Americans experience technology as stripping
them of power—its speed hurries them, its devices isolate them, its effi-
ciencies downsize them, and its information overwhelms them.

National surveys confirm Americans' collective ambivalence about current technology. In a Gallup poll of 800 Americans conducted in 2004, an
overwhelming majority of participants (98%) said that people need to be
able to use newer forms of technology and have some understanding about
how they work. Yet, the vast majority of respondents (94%) thought that
advanced technology could have both good and bad results. In addition,
although most of the survey participants indicated interest in new tech-

nologies, for example, bioengineering (69%) and robotics (60%), only about half reported that they were actually informed about those technologies (51% and 49% respectively). Most respondents (69%) believed that they as individuals had little or no influence on decisions about the technologies that directly affected them.[19]

This Gallup survey suggests that Americans are ambivalent about technology because they do not think they have much control over it. However, the survey does not reveal much about why Americans feel disempowered by technology. Perhaps a survey is not required to find the answer. Articles on technology in the national press regularly discuss some of the ways in which advanced technology in particular strips Americans of power or makes them feel vulnerable. In these articles, Americans read about how the Internet has changed the labor market so that even in times of low unemployment, wages remain low. They read of managers who are concerned about their liability for employees who might be e-mailing sensitive information and federal judges who are unnerved by the fact that their every keystroke is monitored by government agencies. Their own experience of new technology and work is confirmed by reports that small computers and hand-held communication devices are extending everyone's work day and increasing stress. Their fears are heightened as they hear yet another story about someone whose picture was taken, unbeknownst to them, by way of a cell phone and then was posted on a social networking site for millions of viewers to see. They read that college students are distressed that university administrators are using their residence hall keycards to track where they have been on campus and for how long. They learn that multitasking "rewires" the brain so that people have difficulty focusing on anything. And they discover that even scientists are concerned that all sorts of technology, from computer viruses to clever robots to predator drones, will soon be able to outsmart even the people who created them.[20]

According to Jacques Ellul, author of a seminal book on modern technology, people experience technology as always surpassing their intentions and expectations.[21] They expect it to do one thing but it always ends up doing more. According to Ellul, this is the nature of technology, which is, in its essence, about efficiency. Its single purpose is to produce more results more quickly and with less effort. Because technology is designed and driven by that one goal, he argues, it takes on a life of its own that is relatively autonomous from any other goal or, for that matter, any other encumbrance.[22]

To clarify Ellul's point, consider digital technologies. Digital technologies process information. With time, they have become better at processing more information faster. Their efficiency lies not only in their increasing speed but also in their ever-diminishing size. Over time, they have become able to process more information while taking up less space. The digital camera, for instance, is increasingly able to process more visual information while it has gotten smaller in size. As it has gained efficiency in both of these ways, it has also become easier to integrate into other devices. As digital cameras show up in more and more devices (like cell phones), it grows ever easier to use them on others without their knowledge. People thought that the digital camera was about making it easier for them to take pictures of others. What they have discovered is that, due in part to its increasing efficiency and ever diminishing size, it has become also a tool for others to engage in undetected surveillance of them.[23]

Since technology exceeds intentions and expectations because it is driven by efficiency, if allowed to run its course, technology will keep getting smaller, faster, and more common, according to Ellul. It will show up in more places and often in smaller forms while executing more unanticipated functions. In such a context, Ellul argues, it is not surprising that people do not feel like they are in control of technology.[24] As advanced technology becomes smarter, faster, and more integrated into people's lives in increasingly invisible ways, we will have the strong sense that we are losing control.[25]

Regenerating the Tourist at Berlin's Frontier

The story that Berlin tells is about how those who went before, the pioneers, regained control over their destinies by leaving behind the trappings of culture to regenerate human civilization through hard work with simple tools. It suggests that tourists might regain control of their destinies. Just like the pioneer, they might forge a different relationship to technology. In the context of Berlin's frontier theme, the tourist is offered a few options for doing so. One tourist might refashion her home décor along the lines of a primitive style. Another might take up a hobby that involves nonelectric hand tools. Or they can simply enjoy imagining what it would be like to live as the Amish do. In any case, Berlin provides tourists with the opportunity to envision living as if they, rather than technology, were the agents of their own history.

Inspired to imagine a future in which they control technology and their destiny, tourists become what might be called "pioneer-consumers." As twenty-first century versions of American pioneers, tourists imagine buying simple tools and crafting with their own hands a new living environment, if not a new world. Envisioning such a future, they may begin to feel more self-reliant, more independent, and more free than they did before visiting Berlin and entering its story of regression. As they imagine transforming their lives through simple tools, they may feel as though they better embody "basic American values" like simplicity and self-sacrifice.

As mentioned above, the antiques sold in Berlin are not fine furniture and luxury items. Rather, they are the ordinary artifacts of middle-class daily life. These are the discarded implements of common people. This is important, because it means that what the middle-American tourist is encountering in these antique malls and shops are the kinds of items their parents or grandparents probably used. They are surrounded by the tools of their ancestors. When they pick up an item and wonder what it was used for, they are not considering an item that is altogether strange. More than likely, their parents or grandparents used something just like it. Therefore, their experience of unfamiliarity with the tool is only a matter of the intervention of time.

When visitors to Berlin look at these genuine antique tools and implements, when they take them into their hands to consider their age or use, when they are reminded of someone who used such an item or try to imagine how someone might have used it, they are invited to experience a regression themselves. The frontier theme together with the object they hold in their hand calls to mind another kind of daily life that, comparatively speaking, seems primitive. In this way, they identify, through their contemporary tourist experience and perhaps their own ancestors, with a time in which people made their futures with much simpler tools than the high-tech devices people use today.

Another type of merchandise readily available in Berlin is the simulated antique. Such items are not, strictly speaking, reproductions, because they do not duplicate an item that used to be manufactured, such as a Tiffany lamp or a Depression-glass vase. Instead, simulated antiques are obviously newly made but are designed to call to mind a more primitive living style. Examples are birdhouses, dollhouses, cheese boxes, ceramic pitchers, artificially stained filet crochet doilies, rag dolls, settees, and beds in old-fashioned styles. They are manufactured to *look* as if they were hand painted, glazed, or stitched, and they are often made to look as if they were old. Paint appears to be chipped or worn off, cloth looks as if it is nearly threadbare. These simulated antiques are important for the visual rhetoric of Berlin because they provide an affordable way for the tourist to take the primitive pioneer style home. If a tourist buys, say, a primitive-style birdhouse (which in the context of Berlin's frontier story is a sign of regression), he may then incorporate into his daily life a sign of the promise of regeneration.

A third common type of merchandise in Berlin is folk art or, more often, mass-produced items made to look as though they were folk art. Genuine folk art is also available and may include large bird feathers upon which some creature or scene from the wilderness has been hand painted, photographs by local Amish artists, and acrylic paintings of Amish scenes, such as a Bible meeting, or outdoor scenes. Mass-produced "folk art" includes birdhouses painted with a Harley Davidson theme, pieced quilts manufactured in China, "hand-dipped" candles, and wooden toys. Whether genuine or fake, these folk art items fit well within Berlin's frontier theme because they look like the sort of thing someone made or could make with hand tools. Even more, their appearance implies a process by which someone transforms something (often from nature)—a piece of wood, a feather, dried flowers, an old chair, some leftover fabric—into a work of art.[26]

Browsing among items like these, the tourist is invited to imagine the folk artist at work with his or her tools. The folk artist controls the tools to produce an artifact whose form and appearance is determined by the artist. If the artist has a reasonable degree of skill, he or she has confidence that the item being produced with the tool will be fairly predictable. Indeed, there is little risk that the hammer or the paintbrush or the sewing needle is going to get out of control and produce something surprising. The tourist is encouraged to imagine a circumstance in which the human, rather than the tool, determines the outcome of imagination and will.

If tourists become inspired by displays of "folk art," they need only enter one of the several shops that sell supplies for various arts and crafts projects. Helping Hands, a quilt supply store that also sells ready-made quilts hand stitched by local Amish and Mennonite women, has been in business since 1974 and in 1997 expanded to include a museum for displaying, among other things, Amish and Mennonite quilts.[27] Other arts and craft stores also sell quilt-making supplies, in addition to acrylic paints, yarn, felt, embroidery thread, patterns for counted cross-stitching, knitting, crocheting, and much more. Like Walnut Creek's home décor shops, arts and crafts supply stores in Berlin are largely geared toward women, but several sell farming, woodworking, and repair tools.

Berlin offers its tourists technologies over which they too can experience control.[28] By purchasing and later using a counted cross-stitch kit, a kit for building a birdhouse, or a set of stencils, tourists may achieve a new relationship with technology, one in which they exercise the control and, thereby, are renewed through their own regression to so-called primitive labors.

At first glance, the merchandise for sale in Berlin seems to encourage the tourist to experience a sense of loss. As they stand among the tools of their ancestors, tourists notice how their lives differ from the lives of those who preceded them. If they are anxious about or feel controlled by today's technology, they may focus on how prior generations controlled the tools with which they made their futures. However, when one considers the larger framework within which that merchandise appears—namely, the story of the frontier—it becomes clear that Berlin's story is not about loss but about regeneration through hard work and simplicity, and the tourist is invited to participate in such a regeneration.

The Amish, Technology, and Berlin's Themes

The Frontier Theme

In and around Berlin, the Amish are regularly seen using the sort of technology featured in the story Berlin tells of the American frontier. Although there are exceptions, the technology that the Amish are typically seen using looks primitive to present-day Americans.[29] Their horse and buggy transportation is the most salient example, but there are many others. Among the most visible examples are those used during planting and harvesting seasons, when the Amish are in their fields sowing seeds with horse-drawn plows, loading hay onto a wagon with pitchforks, or harvesting wheat with ground-driven grain binders. Tourists also see Amish playing softball instead of watching television, drying their laundry on a clothesline rather than in a dryer, and lighting their homes with gas rather than electric lamps.[30] As tourists see the Amish using these technologies, especially if they are in or have recently visited Berlin, they may connect the Amish use of simple technology to the story that Berlin's frontier theme tells. In the context of that story of regression and recapitulation, tourists are encouraged to see the Amish as pioneerlike. With their horse-drawn buggies and "primitive" farming implements, the Amish look like living examples of American pioneers.

If they make a link between Berlin's frontier theme and any Amish person who passes by in a horse-drawn buggy, tourists may draw additional conclusions about the Amish, for instance, that the Amish are primitive. Rather than seeing them as a people who engage in complex negotiations with technology, visitors who encounter them in the context of the frontier theme may see the Amish simply as people without advanced technology. As a primitive people who are not dependent on advanced technology, they also signify as hard working, capable, and self-reliant. After all, this is a people (as just about any tourist knows by the conclusion of a visit to Ohio's Amish Country) who, without the benefit of a single power tool, can erect a barn in a day.

Not only do the Amish appear primitive; they appear primitive by choice. Living in a technologically advanced culture, the Amish could at any time plug into the electrical grid and avail themselves of all manner of modern devices. However, most of them do not. In the context of Berlin's frontier theme, then, tourists may imagine that, just like the pioneers, the Amish have chosen to leave behind the newest technology, with all its comforts, conveniences, and unintended effects, so as to regress to an earlier form of human civilization from which they can regenerate American culture.

Of course, tourists may notice that the Amish are not simply primitive but in fact use telephones and ride in cars. Seeing them as contemporary pioneers, tourists may imagine that the Amish are making their way through a recapitulation of human civilization. That is, having fully regressed to a life without any type of advanced technology, they are now slowly moving toward America's technologically advanced society. In this way they may be seen as recapitulating or recreating human civilization afresh following a complete regression. Seen in this way, the Amish seem to be not some bizarre religious sect that rejects the dominant culture but, instead, twenty-first-century pioneers who are in the process of a recapitulation that promises regeneration. From this perspective, the Amish stand in as agents of America's regeneration or, at least, as signs of the promise that such a regeneration is possible.

All this is to say that the Amish are crucial for Berlin's visual rhetoric because it is the Amish who bring to life the story that Berlin tells. When visitors tour Berlin, they move among buildings that remind them of frontier homesteads and forts. They hold tools in their hands that call to mind memories of a grandparent tilling the soil or making apple butter. They purchase implements with which to fashion their own arts and crafts. In all of these ways, they are invited to identify with the American pioneers of more than a century ago. But when they see an Amish man tilling the soil with a horse-drawn plow or Amish woman walking through town in her long dress and bonnet or lighting gas lamps in a small furniture store, they confront the apparent reality that it is possible to live an American pioneer life today. American culture can be thoroughly renewed (the Amish seem to say) right now. The project of regeneration is not locked in the past. It lives and even thrives among the Amish.

Even more, these people who keep that project alive are somewhat like the tourist. They are not complete strangers to middle-American tourists. Although they look and act differently, that is because they have chosen to live the story of the American frontier in the here-and-now. Having chosen to regress, they continue along the trajectory of recapitulation. Walking about in the context of Berlin's story, the Amish signify as pioneers (which is to say, true Americans), and the tourist is encouraged to identify with them. In doing so, tourists may experience vicariously what it is "really" like to pass through that cleansing regression that forges a new relationship to culture and, especially, its controlling technologies.

Berlin's visual rhetoric operates at several levels. First, its architecture, interiors, and merchandise construct a frontier theme that tells a triumphant story about pioneers who renewed human civilization through hard work as they left the conveniences of culture behind to create society anew. Second, within that themed space and amidst the merchandise sold there, tourists are encouraged to imagine themselves as contemporary pioneers who, through their own renewed relationships with technology, might regenerate their culture, or at least their homes. Third, in the context of Berlin's theme and story, tourists are invited to see the Amish not as bizarre relics from another era but as present-day pioneers who prove it is still possible to rebirth human civilization. As primitive versions of the tourist, the Amish signify as a people who have experienced their regression and are on the regenerating path toward a renewed America. Taken together, these three levels of engagement with Berlin's theme and story produce a powerful experience for the tourist. Through Berlin's three-dimensional presentation of its theme, their own tactile engagement with simple tools, and the presence of the pioneer-Amish, tourists are strongly encouraged to envision themselves as no longer mere puppets of technological advances but as the harbingers of a renewed America.

Berlin's 1950s Popular Culture Theme

Earlier it was noted that Berlin's presentation of its frontier theme is not seamless, not as consistent as Walnut Creek's theme. The cracks and gaps in its presentation are helpful because they provide openings through which the tourist can enter the theme as him- or herself, a contemporary middle American. But there is a feature of Berlin's visual rhetoric that constitutes more than a crack or gap: the countless references to American popular culture from the 1950s. So prominent are these references that they constitute a secondary theme to Berlin's dominant frontier theme.

Take, for example, the Catalpa Trading Company's impressive soda fountain. Not a typical soda fountain, this functioning nineteenth-century soda fountain, which was moved from its original location and reassembled complete with marble countertop, occupies a side room that runs the depth of the shop. All around the soda fountain are references to 1950s popular culture, including images of Marilyn Monroe, the Three Stooges, and Lucille Ball. Cindy's Diner makes even stronger connections to 1950s popular culture in America. This diner-style restaurant features metallic-vinyl booth seating, chrome-trimmed tables, and a high-shine black-and-white vinyl floor and offers American comfort food, including cheeseburgers, fries, and milkshakes. The whole restaurant serves as a context for an imaginary return to 1950s America. Beyond these two locations, throughout Berlin there is a great deal of merchandise that contributes to this theme with specific references to brand names, cartoon characters, and Hollywood or other celebrities popular during the 1950s.

The most prominent brand name in Berlin is Coca-Cola. It appears on the sort of items one would expect—such as glass-bottled six packs, vintage pop machines, and tin signs—but also on unexpected items like lamp shades, colanders, and mixing bowls. Other carbonated beverages associated with mid-twentieth-century American life, such as Orange Crush, also appear. Brand names for convenience foods, like Aunt Jemima, Campbell's, and Pillsbury, are seen here as well. They often show up in the form of porcelain reproductions of characters from well-known advertising campaigns of the time.

Oil and gasoline company names and logos connected with the era, such as Sinclair, Gulf, Texaco, and Pennzoil, also appear often in Berlin. These names are frequently seen on metal signs and on tiny metal replicas of mid-century gas pumps (that serve as coin banks). Miniature classic cars are ubiquitous in Berlin. Pictures of models such as Ford Mustang, Chevrolet Chevelle, and Pontiac Firebird appear on signs and lighted wall clocks.

Images of cartoon characters as well as Hollywood, rock 'n' roll, and television stars also can be seen throughout Berlin. Tweety Bird, Mickey Mouse, and Superman appear on reproduction metal lunch boxes and other tins. Mickey Mouse adorns the side of a "retro-style" two-slice toaster. Hollywood and music celebrities from the era, including James Dean, Elvis Presley, and John Wayne, can be seen in forms too numerous to mention. Television shows from the era, like "I Love Lucy," appear on the screens of miniature retro television sets.[31]

Initially, the presence of this 1950s popular culture theme with Berlin's frontier theme is visually jarring. The frontier theme features a primitive style to go along with a story about a regenerative regression that renews human civilization through hard work completed with simple tools; the 1950s popular culture theme emphasizes mass-produced clutter that calls to mind instant gratification through fast cars, convenience foods, and mass-media entertainment. Unlike the frontier theme, the popular culture theme seems to be about easy living. A simple explanation for the inclusion of this secondary theme, which seems to be at odds with the frontier theme, is that Berlin merchants have added to their repertoire of products items that are likely to delight baby boomers, who are probably the largest single age group in their customer population.

While this may be the reason for the 1950s theme, there is a striking commonality between Berlin's frontier theme and its 1950s popular culture theme: technology figures prominently in both. Both themes emphasize technology, whether it is related to farm labor, domestic labor, transportation, advertising, or entertainment. Within the context of the frontier theme, technology transforms nature into culture. As the pioneers stood on the frontier between the wild and human civilization, it was primitive tools that enabled them to transform a society that had become rigid in its rules and fixed in its social hierarchies into one wherein freedom reigned and hardworking individuals determined their own futures. The 1950s popular culture theme represents another frontier, the time before and after the emergence of atomic and digital technologies. As those technologies first appeared, they seemed to hold great promise for solving a great many problems and for giving human beings greater control over their lives and the future.

The 1950s are often remembered as the time before big changes in technology, culture, and politics took hold. American culture likes to romanticize the 1950s as a peaceful era defined by high birth rates, low divorce rates, and a lot of family togetherness, but the 1950s were not altogether quiet and calm. The decade was also a time of change that brought uncertainty and even fear. It was, after all, the time of Senator Joseph McCarthy's televised anti-Communist hearings, the beginnings of the civil rights movement in the Montgomery bus boycott, intense concern about US educational inferiority when the Cold War space race began with the launch of the USSR's Sputnik satellite, and the construction of the national interstate highway system that encouraged a huge population shift from cities to suburbs. The 1950s was also when children crouched under their school desks during atomic bomb drills, and Soviet-backed North Korea invaded South Korea. Technological change played a pivotal role in this decade of change, as the automobile, the television, the jet engine, the transistor, the rocket, the computer, and the hydrogen bomb altered where Americans lived, how they traveled, worked, and played, what they learned in school, and what they feared.

Not surprisingly, Berlin gives no indication that the 1950s was when Americans first realized that they were living in the shadow of a mushroom cloud or in which even the heavens above appeared dominated by the ingenuity and power of the Soviet hammer and sickle. On the contrary, in Berlin the 1950s are constructed as a time when technological progress meant farmers plowing their fields with shiny John Deere tractors, mothers loading up groceries in their new station wagons, and teenagers screaming with delight at Elvis on TV. According to Berlin's secondary theme, technology produced only efficiency, abundance, and pleasure for Americans fortunate enough to be alive at that time.

Berlin tourism purveyors construct a positive relationship between technology and the social, economic, and political life of mid-twentieth-century Americans. This construction employs two rhetorical means. First, the settings of the diner and the soda fountain construct a zeitgeist for the 1950s that is about a moment of innocence, for the individual and for the culture. At the individual level, the 1950s signify as adolescence, or that moment that precedes adulthood and all the responsibilities and awareness that go with it. At the political level, the 1950s represent that time in US history when Americans did not yet fully comprehend the new technologies of war or the effects of televised war and social rebellion. Like two snapshots in a photo album, the diner and the soda fountain invite the tourist to remember an idealized time of innocent goodness without hint of social, economic, or political strife.

Second, within this construction of 1950s America as a place of innocence, technology is constituted as an effect of ingenuity, a force for productivity, and a cause for pleasure. As tourists enjoy lunch at the diner, pick up a miniature classic car, or purchase a Barbie lunch box, they engage technology only as a positive force for increasing efficiency at work, speed on the highway, and pleasure in the living room. In this version of the 1950s, cars signify as the means to go anywhere at anytime in style, tractors translate as the ability to increase productivity on the family farm, and televisions mean wholesome entertainment shared by the whole family. As tourists move about Berlin and interact with the merchandise associated with this theme, they are invited to "remember" an idealized moment when technology was all promise and possibility, not also a cause of environmental degradation, mass destruction, and social control.

Despite the apparent contradiction between the primitive ethos of the frontier primary theme and the media-dominated and industrialized clutter of the 1950s secondary theme, these two themes share a common focus on technology in society. Both themes offer resolutions to middle-American anxieties about their relationship to technology and, specifically, to the manner in which technology seems to control contemporary life. In both cases, these themes provide contexts within which tourists may imagine ways to regain control over technology. The frontier theme offers consumers opportunities to regress to the primitive. The 1950s theme encourages nostalgia for a moment of individual and social innocence.

As visitors experience that nostalgia for innocence, how might the Amish look to them? In the context of Berlin's 1950s popular culture theme, the Amish appear to live as Americans did before the nuclear-digital age and, perhaps even more importantly, to embody the innocence of that moment as well. As a people who depend on the buggy rather than the car, the horse instead of the tractor, the adding machine rather than the computer, the Amish also seem to have figured out how to exercise control over technology. Further, because they are a racially homogeneous people who dress uniformly and modestly, always seem to have numerous small children in tow, and reject divorce, the Amish also appear to be a people who have escaped the profound social, technological, and political upheavals that have occurred since the 1950s. Finally, as a people visibly of the farm, the woodworking shop, and the lumberyard, the Amish seem to have averted entanglements in unseemly worldly concerns like sex scandals, corporate failures, and corrupt politics.

In all of these ways, the Amish appear to visitors as innocent technologically, socially, and politically. They seem to be living proof that it is possible, even in this post–civil rights movement, post–women's movements, post-Vietnam, post-Watergate, post–sexual revolution twenty-first century high-tech culture, to regain innocence in the United States. Understood this way, the Amish are not incongruous with Berlin's 1950s popular culture theme. On the contrary, they appear to embody the possibility of regenerating America once more into that place of freedom in which one may carve out a future of unlimited promise.

But the Amish Are Not Made of Wax

Within the visual rhetoric of the frontier theme and of the 1950s popular culture theme, the Amish signify as earlier versions of today's middle Americans. In the case of the frontier theme, they seem to be twenty-first century pioneers, who, like their eighteenth- and nineteenth-century counterparts, have regressed to a more primitive kind of life dependent on yesterday's technologies. In the case of the 1950s popular culture theme, they seem to represent a cultural memory of an American innocence in

An Amish man and his two sons taking a break from selling hand-woven baskets at
Schrock's Amish Farm

existence prior to the 1960s. Taken together, these themes construct the
Amish as temporally and developmentally prior versions of the middle-
American tourists who are the audience for these constructs. They are
Americans from another era, living amidst technological, political, and social innocence. Represented in this way, the Amish seem to be different
from other Americans only in that they have not progressed as far. Moreover, their difference legitimates tourists' experiences of nostalgia for a future in which Americans regain control over technology, are reborn as a
people, and are once again innocent and good.

This idea that the only real difference between the Amish and the tourists is that contemporary middle Americans are farther along the same historical and cultural path is not new. In a coffee-table style book published
by Doubleday in 1969 that describes (with accompanying photographs)

and comments upon the people and culture of every county and most cities in Ohio, author Dick Perry, who was an award-winning playwright, popular essayist, and novelist, speculates that in the end the Amish will abandon their peculiar ways to become just like the rest of us:

> Will the Amish last? We wish we could say tune in tomorrow, but already the handwriting seems to be on the sides of every hill and valley of the Amish communities . . . some day when we drive along these gravel back roads, power lines will run from every pole into every house. Color television—that awful flattener—will have with laugh-tracks reduced the Amish to the everyday. Horses will no longer snort in barns on ice-cold winter nights. Amish carriages will decorate the lawns of suburban antique stores. And the idea of these Amish and their land will have evolved into a plastic tourist attraction, touted by billboards and brochures. The valley will become a quickie spectacle with a thousand roadside stands. No matter. The history that is against the Amish is against all of us; and so we all live in the wonderland of the supermarket. One day, all too soon, an Amish grandmother and grandfather will wait with sweet patience for fellow Amish to come, sing chants at God, and worship. But they will wait in vain. The others will not arrive. They will be in New Philadelphia, attending the flicks. Sugarcreek—and the outside world—will have won.[32]

Although certain aspects of this prediction ring true, such as the claim that the Amish will be relentlessly marketed to tourists, it is also the case that, forty years after Perry's book was published, the Amish remain unassimilated in many important respects. Although the dominant culture and, in this case, the industry of tourism construct the Amish to appear similar to other Americans in fundamental ways, still the Amish remain strange. Moreover, they are strange in large part because they have insisted on retaining control over their relationship to technology. What is different about their relationship to technology is that, unlike other Americans, they make their decisions about it in community. Rather than assume that the market will decide what technology must be adopted or leave it up to individuals to decide what technology they will allow into their lives, the Amish negotiate the incorporation of technology into daily work and home life as a community of faith that seeks to preserve time for one another, to remain close to the earth, and to enable close personal ties.

They are strange because their unwillingness to go with the flow of the market or the desires of individuals puts them out of step with contemporary life in often bizarre ways: they put their telephones at the end of the drive, run light bulbs on gasoline generators, and set up whole rooms of computers that they will not connect to the Internet. Strange indeed.

However, it is precisely because the Amish are *not* relics from the past but strangers in the present, or, put another way, because they are not made of wax but of flesh, that they encourage tourists' nostalgia for a future in which their ambivalence about technology is resolved. Because the Amish are living examples that human beings can still control technology, they legitimate Berlin's promise that Americans can have a different future. Thus, even as Berlin's visual rhetoric constructs the Amish as primitive versions of middle Americans, the rhetoric also admits that the Amish are significantly different. If the only difference between the Amish and other Americans were that they are not as far along the same historical path as the rest of American society, then they would not hold the promise of a different outcome for that society. If they are truly traveling along the same path that the rest of America has already traversed, then they will end up exactly where the rest of America is. Put simply, if the Amish were not other, then their presence would not help observers imagine a future that is different from the present.

If Berlin's visual rhetoric acknowledges that the Amish are not the same as other Americans and yet it still holds out the promise of a different future for Americans, then a question arises. If the Amish maintain control over technology and, thereby, their world by living in a manner that is very different from the life style of the rest of us, how must we change, individually or collectively, if we are likewise to regain some measure of control over our lives and world? To the extent that any tourist recognizes the strangeness of Amish ways, such a tourist may also wonder whether that cross-stitch kit or primitive-style birdhouse or antique hammer is really going to effect the change that Amish tourism promises. If, in order to maintain control over technology, the Amish must travel at the pace of a horse, light their homes with gas lamps, and keep their tractors stationary in the field or by the barn, then might it take quite a bit more than the purchase of an antique tool or cross-stitch kit or primitive bird house for the tourist to carve out a new relationship to technology in his or her life? As living proof that it is possible to be the agents rather than the objects of technology, the Amish appear to answer with a resounding no. No dinner at the diner, no antique tool, no craft kit is going to transform one's relationship to technology enough to put one back in the driver's seat.

If that is so, are the visitors to Berlin willing to be different enough? Are they willing to resist technology's drive for efficiency and, thereby, be otherwise? Could they unplug this device, turn off that one, limit use of another, resist the temptation to buy the next amazing gadget? If these changes are not possible, what does that say about the degree to which Americans allow themselves to be controlled by high-tech culture? To what extent do Americans choose their own subjection by technology?

These are unsettling questions. They are anything but reassuring. To be sure, they are not the first questions that tourists are encouraged to consider as they move about Berlin. Nevertheless, they may occur to any tourist who can see and take seriously the central proposition of Berlin's powerful visual rhetoric. Berlin's themes of the frontier and 1950s popular culture advance the inspiring proposition that the future could be better than the present, that middle Americans could alter their status of subjugation to technologies, that they could engage their culture as its agents rather than as its objects. But to do so, tourists will have to consider what important and even inconvenient changes they would have to make in their daily lives and the degree to which they are willing to be strangers within their own culture.

SUGARCREEK

93

Cross St.

39

HEINI'S GOURMET
MARKET

Mill St.

Dover Rd.

93

39

Factory St.

Main Street

**HUNTINGTON
BANK**

Broadway St.

**ALPINE HILLS
MUSEUM**

TRAIN DEPOT

N

SWEET BASIL

Ohio Central Railroad

Tourist sites in Sugarcreek, Ohio

CHAPTER 5

Ethnicity and Performance in Sugarcreek

*It's nice to represent my culture and my town. It means more to me since
I'm actually Swiss.*
—Julie Jorg, 2003 Ohio Swiss Festival Queen

Late in 1882, the tracks of the Conotton Valley Railway were laid
in the Sugarcreek Valley. Within a decade, the town of Sugarcreek
emerged and quickly became a center of business and industry.
Over the course of a century, factories that manufactured brooms, wooden
handles, and hand trucks for processing wool and whey appeared in the
town. Retail businesses, such as a large furniture store, fabric stores, a
buggy shop, bookstore, and several car dealerships, flourished during this
time. As roads became more reliable, businesses depended less on the train
for shipping. Yet, even as the train was becoming less important for trans-
porting raw materials and merchandise, it was becoming crucial for Sugarcreek's overall economy.[1] This was because a new and highly successful
industry had come to town in the 1950s: Amish Country tourism.

The Little Switzerland of Ohio

Beginning in 1833, Swiss immigrant cheesemakers arrived in the area
around Sugarcreek.[2] Initially, they produced cheese (the variety that came
to be known as Swiss cheese) for use by their own community. With the
arrival of the railroad and their recognition that local Amish dairy farmers
(who had migrated from southwestern Pennsylvania beginning in 1809),
could provide them a dependable supply of milk, these immigrants got
into the business of manufacturing large quantities of cheese to sell outside

the valley. Sugarcreek's first cheese factory was built in 1885. With the growing popularity of Swiss cheese, other factories followed.

During the 1940s, competition from Wisconsin cheese manufacturers cut demand for Sugarcreek's product.[3] Eager to return to higher profit levels, business leaders in Sugarcreek discussed strategies for increasing demand for their local products without investing a lot of resources in advertising. In 1953, five members of the Ohio Swiss Cheese Association went to Columbus, where they met with officials who were interested in promoting tourism. They made a successful case for the development of what was to become the Ohio Swiss Festival.[4] Held on the fourth Friday and Saturday after Labor Day every year since 1953, the Ohio Swiss Festival features yodelers, Swiss athletic events (like *Steinstossen* or rock throwing and *Schwingfest* or wrestling), polka bands, Swiss foods, and a Swiss cheese contest. Sociologist of the Amish John Hostetler in 1955 described the enthusiastic response to the festival this way: "An estimated 200,000 persons were present to listen to Polka Harmoniers [and] Pop Farver's orchestra, to witness alpenhorn blowing, Swiss flag throwing, and the yodeling Swiss cheese makers . . . The crowd consumed about a ton of hamburger, huge quantities of pies, cakes, soft drinks, and milk products. The Swiss cheese makers sold 13,400 pounds of cheese and a ton of Trail Bologna."[5] With the festival's success at drawing tourists and showcasing Swiss cheese, Sugarcreek became famous as "The Little Switzerland of Ohio."

Seeking to build upon the success of the Ohio Swiss Festival, Ranson Andreas (founder of Andreas Furniture of Sugarcreek, which opened in 1948) dreamed of transforming the whole town of Sugarcreek into a Swiss-like village. As tourism was taking hold in Sugarcreek in the early 1960s, he and artist Tom Miller traveled to Switzerland to study the architecture of Swiss chalets.[6] In 1965 Miller remodeled a downtown building he owned, giving it the first Swiss "face lift" in town, complete with a Swiss chalet–style front featuring his own hand-painted Swiss Alps scene.[7] One by one, other owners of buildings in Sugarcreek followed suit, so that today nearly every building on Main Street (and many on side streets) displays features associated with a Swiss chalet architectural style.[8] As the Swiss look developed, tourism continued to grow in Sugarcreek. In 1971 the Swiss Village Country Store opened as the first business created to target tourists. Others, such as Dutch Valley Restau-

One of the many Tom Miller mural paintings that appear on a variety of buildings
in Sugarcreek, in this case, Huntington Bank

rant (1974), the Dutch Host motel (1974), and Swiss Valley Enterprises
(1975), which offered Amish buggy rides, soon followed.[9]

In the 1990s, however, businesses in Sugarcreek started feeling the effects of competition from nearby tourist towns. In both Berlin and Walnut Creek, entrepreneurs were embarking upon ambitious construction
and renovation projects designed to attract more Amish Country tourists.
Despite increased competition, Sugarcreek was able to sustain high tourist traffic, largely because of its steam engine passenger train. From 1988
to 1998, the Ohio Central Railroad ran the train through Amish Country
between Sugarcreek and Baltic. Tens of thousands of visitors arrived annually to ride this train. Of course, tourists who were drawn by the train
also spent time in the restaurants and shops in the town. Apparently, the
steam engine train stopped running because of unresolved issues regarding parking and public restrooms.[10]

The impact on tourism in Sugarcreek from the loss of the steam train
was quick and devastating. Just a year later, business owners in Sugarcreek
reported that their profits were down 40 percent.[11] But then, the parking

and restroom issues were resolved, and in 2001 the train returned, to the good fortune of business owners and the pleasure of the sixty-five thousand tourists who rode the train annually. In 2004, however, the steam train departed from the depot in Sugarcreek for the last time. The owner of the train attributed the decision to "significant increases in passenger liability insurance premiums combined with insufficient ridership."[12] A dramatic drop in the number of visitors to Sugarcreek followed again, just as it had in 1999.

Like Walnut Creek and Berlin, Sugarcreek offers visitors a themed environment in which to experience Amish Country, but this theme is evidently not as appealing as the other two. Since the steam engine train stopped running, Sugarcreek has failed to attract as many tourists as have the other two towns. Although no scientific study of tourist numbers in Sugarcreek has ever been conducted, informal observations conducted in mid-June and mid-July 2005 indicated that this was the case. Half as many tourists in a two-hour period were counted moving about the whole town of Sugarcreek than were browsing in just one antique mall in a five-minute period in Berlin and than were going in and out of shops in a five-minute interval in Walnut Creek.[13]

The presence of five vacant stores on Sugarcreek's Main Street, all of which once housed businesses with strong connections to tourism, indicated that the comparatively low level of tourist traffic that I observed is not atypical.[14] By comparison, in the more than fifteen years that I have been studying tourism in Ohio's Amish Country, I have not seen a single vacant store (that was not under construction) on the main streets of either Walnut Creek or Berlin. On the contrary, these towns saw such impressive growth in tourist traffic, especially in the last decade of the twentieth century, that extensive renovation, expansion, and construction of tourism businesses was the norm. Significantly, that growth continues into the present.

One obvious explanation of the weakening tourism in Sugarcreek involves the loss of the steam train. The sharp drop in profits among Sugarcreek's tourist businesses following the first and the final terminations of the train strongly indicate that the train was crucial for drawing tourists to Sugarcreek. That said, the fact that neither Berlin nor Walnut Creek has a train yet both continue to thrive as tourist destinations indicates that there must be more to the drop in Sugarcreek's tourist traffic. Keith Rathbun, former president of the Sugarcreek Businessmen's Association and publisher of *The Budget*, a weekly newspaper that serves both the local population and the Amish throughout North America,[15] names two additional factors. The first is that, whereas State Route 39 passes a full mile away from the center of downtown Sugarcreek, it overlaps with Berlin's Main Street, thereby automatically bringing a huge volume of tourists into Berlin. A second factor he identifies is that tourists who have visited Sugarcreek before may pass it by for new experiences in other towns.[16]

Chances are that all of these factors have played a role in Sugarcreek's decline in popularity as a tourist destination. However, given the central role that Sugarcreek's Swiss theme has played in successfully drawing tourists for over a half-century, it makes sense to consider it as a factor as well.[17] Moreover, Sugarcreek's struggle to sustain the interest of visitors may be instructive for understanding Amish Country tourism more generally. Given that the Amish receive as much attention within Sugarcreek's theme as in Walnut Creek's and Berlin's, why is Amish Country tourism working so well in the latter two towns but not in Sugarcreek?

A Virtual Tour of Sugarcreek

First, it is helpful to locate Sugarcreek. The town sits on the western edge of Tuscarawas County, just beyond the border shared with Holmes County to the west. Sugarcreek is only fourteen miles southeast of Berlin and six miles southeast of Walnut Creek. For tourists who drive into Sugarcreek on SR 39 with Berlin and Walnut Creek behind them, the first thing they see is a large wooden sign on the side of the highway which reads "Welcome to Sugarcreek, The Little Switzerland of Ohio." The sign calls to mind a Swiss chalet and features a painted image of a man in Swiss costume tipping his hat in greeting. The dates of the Ohio Swiss Festival are listed prominently at the bottom of the sign.

As travelers pass the welcome sign, they come into a small business district, now part of Sugarcreek but once a separate town known as Shanesville.[18] About a mile northeast of the railroad station and the center of Sugarcreek, this area was never the center of tourism. Nevertheless, it has been home to a variety of businesses in recent years, including a quilt shop, country style home décor shop, tavern, and accounting firm. Over the past decade, retail shops have come and gone. One especially promising ad-

This wooden sign, featuring echoes of a Swiss chalet, welcomes tourists to Sugarcreek

dition was made in 2007. Heini's Gourmet Market opened following a thorough renovation of the interior and exterior of the building. Inside, shoppers can watch the Food Network on a huge flat screen TV as they taste the many samples of Heini's cheese or look over Amish-style noodles and wine made from locally grown grapes.[19]

Most tourists interested in Sugarcreek continue several blocks down Main Street, which splits from SR 39, and arrive in the center of Sugarcreek, where the Ohio Swiss Festival is held each year.[20] If they park their cars here and move through town on foot, they see what they have been encouraged to expect—a town that calls to mind a Swiss village nestled among the foothills of the Alps. Although there are no mountains here, the Swiss-styled buildings tucked into the rolling hills of Tuscarawas County make a strong visual reference to a Swiss village. Indeed, looking down the street, tourists see building after building that features decorative components designed to resemble Swiss chalets—wood siding on front façades, front-gabled roofs, deep overhangs, second-story balconies.[21] Many of these buildings also display boards painted to look like the coats of arms of Switzerland, as well as for the cantons of Berne and Aargau.[22] These buildings house various businesses and tourist attractions, including gift shops, a museum, a chocolate shop, a bookstore, and a tavern.

One of the more elaborately Swiss-styled shops is Alphorn Amish Gifts. Vacant in 2005, it now offers arts and crafts items and some Amish-made furniture. It boasts not only a front gable with wide overhang, a deep balcony under the gable, a similarly deep front porch, and patterned cutout boards under the eaves, but also extensive stick work on exterior walls. One other especially notable building, which sits near the vacant train depot, is home to Huntington Bank. A modern brick structure with large plate glass windows, the bank building nevertheless added over its main entrance a huge gable within which appears a mural of a Swiss Alps scene. Like many other murals and paintings that appear in Sugarcreek, this one was done by local artist Tom Miller. It depicts snow-covered mountains in the background, lush green foothills and a shimmering lake in the middle ground, and a Swiss chalet in the foreground. Notably, the mural also includes a three-dimensional train track upon which moves an actual miniature passenger train, all incorporated into the painting.[23]

Decorative banners hung from light posts read "Welcome," "Sugarcreek," and "Little Switzerland of Ohio." On these banners are simple characterizations of the back end of an Amish buggy, an alphorn, a wheel of Swiss cheese, and Switzerland's coat of arms. Finally, "Swiss" music fills tourists' ears throughout the town by way of an outdoor sound system. With all this, it is easy to imagine that Ranson Andreas, were he alive today, would be pleased to see how thoroughly his dream of recreating a Swiss village in Ohio has been realized.

The Visual Rhetoric of Sugarcreek

While the town is full of references to Switzerland and Swiss culture—buildings that resemble Swiss chalets, Swiss costumes, accordions, alphorns, Swiss cuisine, posters of idyllic Switzerland landscapes—there are also many visible reminders that Sugarcreek is a small town in Ohio. The large signs that appear at the edges of town welcome visitors to "The *Little* Switzerland of *Ohio*" (emphasis added) and to "A Swiss *Village*" (emphasis added) rather than some specific Swiss village. There are not only Swiss but also US and Ohio flags in each of the many red brick flower boxes positioned at regular intervals on the Main Street sidewalks. And a light post in the form of the Statue of Liberty (in miniature, of course) sits just outside a shop. All of these verbal and visual cues alert tourists that they are entering an imaginary Switzerland in the United States, not Switzerland itself or even a recreation of an actual Swiss town.

References to the Amish also appear throughout Sugarcreek. Some notable examples are a large painted plywood silhouette of the back end of an Amish buggy (complete with cutouts of Amish children looking out at observers) that hangs over the entrance to a shop, a display of Amish dolls in a store window, a reconstructed Amish kitchen in the museum, and a mannequin dressed in Amish clothes (who, oddly enough, sat in a shopping cart for many years). These and many more references to the Amish remind visitors that, however well elaborated the Swiss theme, this is Ohio's Amish Country.[24]

Sugarcreek, by exposing tourists to the Swiss and Amish cultures, offers them encounters with ethnic diversity. Engaging with representations of ethnic difference is at the heart of the tourist's experience in Sugarcreek. To understand that experience and its likely impact on the tourist, it is first necessary to consider how middle Americans think and feel about ethnic diversity.

Middle Americans as the Empty Set

White middle Americans[25] know well that their status as a majority population in the United States is changing fast. News reports about the new demographics of the United States are common. In 2007, for instance, the *New York Times* reported on Census Bureau data showing that ethnic minority populations in the United States, which had been on the rise for a long time, had finally crossed the one hundred million mark; one out of every three people in the US is now non-white. Moreover, the article reported, these non-white minority groups are growing a lot faster than white groups.[26]

Not surprisingly, a host of issues and concerns have emerged with these changing demographics. Through countless media reports, white middle Americans have been told that immigration puts an enormous burden on public systems, causes job loss, requires dual-language schools, makes the drug war harder to fight, and enables Islamic terrorism. As media attention intensifies anxiety about immigration, vocal demands increase for

An elaborate Swiss-chalet-style exterior of a banquet hall in Sugarcreek, and one of the many sidewalk flower boxes displaying Swiss, US, and Ohio flags

tightening US borders, building a wall along the entire border between the US and Mexico, establishing English as the national language, limiting the access that US-born children of illegal immigrants have to public services, and criminalizing the failure to carry immigration documents at all times.

Long before white middle Americans realized these demographics were changing, they had already experienced a significant challenge to their status as the normative group in the US. Through the course of the 1960s and 1970s, movements for social change fundamentally challenged the idea that the culture of white middle Americans should set the standard for everyone else. Although initially the civil rights movement took an integrationist approach to challenging racism, later it, along with other social movements of the time, took a strikingly different approach. These social movements argued that the norms of mainstream American culture were neither universal nor good. Instead, they were particular and self-interested. That is, they privileged white people. Rather than seeking integration into white middle-American culture, therefore, these social movements endeavored to celebrate and strengthen their own particular norms, practices, values, and histories. This approach has come to be known as "identity politics," and it posed a powerful challenge to the status of mainstream culture. The white middle American, once presumed to be the normative citizen, or what one scholar has called the iconic subject of US culture, was transformed by the rhetorics of these movements into just one among many types of people who call the United States home.[27]

While white middle Americans are facing this challenge to their iconic status, they are also confronting the reality that their own ethnic particularity has in many cases been obscured. Unlike ethnic and racial groups that are holding on to and reclaiming their ethnic heritage, white middle Americans left theirs behind. In the process of assimilation into America's melting pot, they gave up the language, food, and customs of their immigrant ancestors. This loss was brought into sharp relief when *The Godfather* (1972) appeared on the big screen and *Roots* (1977) commanded attention in living rooms across the country.[28] Of course, both *The Godfather* and *Roots* reiterated the narrative that in the US anyone, no matter their racial or ethnic origins, can achieve the American dream if they work hard and make wise choices. At the same time, however, they also told powerful stories about belonging to a community that was rich in history and tradition and whose members manifested a deep sense of loyalty to one another. With these exceedingly popular stories inviting nostalgia for ethnicity, white middle Americans whose ancestors had immigrated generations earlier and had tried to be more "American" experienced this consequence of assimilation as a loss.[29]

Throughout the latter part of the twentieth century and continuing into the twenty-first, then, white middle Americans have experienced two profound challenges. First, they have been told that they are no longer the norm. Second, they have begun to see that the process by which they and/or their ancestors assimilated into American culture cost them their ethnic heritage. With the first challenge they were demoted from iconic to merely particular; with the second they became bland, dull, common. In a culture that prizes individuality and distinctiveness, white middle Americans signify as the empty set.

The Ohio Swiss Festival: Festival or Spectacle?

Scholars who study festivals point out that festivals include both "event structures" and "social structures."[30] Event structures consist of the sequences of events (such as opening ceremony, rituals, dramatic forms, a feast, dance and music, and a concluding event) that provide structure to a festival. The social structures of festivals emphasize participation. Festival-goers are strongly encouraged to participate in the events of the festival. Participation is central to the purpose of festivals, because festivals are not simply about entertainment. More important than that, they are about inviting community members to work out social tensions and group identity by way of common involvement in celebrations of ethnic heritage, religious devotion, daily labors, and/or valued skills. Community members participate in the event structures—the ceremonies, rituals, dramas, feast, and music/dance—together as a way to bring their social history and contemporary social relations together to shape a common future.

The Ohio Swiss Festival includes the event structures characteristic of a festival. It officially begins with an opening ceremony that takes place at the Sugarcreek American Legion Post and includes a welcome and summary of the program for the festival. It contains two kinds of rituals: coronations and parades. At the conclusion of the first night of the festival, the Grand Champion Cheese Maker and the Ohio Swiss Festival Queen are crowned. On the second day, a parade of antique cars and Swiss-themed floats moves down Main Street. The primary dramatic element at the Ohio Swiss Festival is the Swiss-themed competition. These competitions include the Steintossen (a stone-throwing competition), the Schwingfest (a Swiss-style wrestling competition), yodeling, and cheesemaking. The feast at the festival takes the form of various food booths offering barbequed chicken, bratwurst and sauerkraut sandwiches, apple fritters, and, of course, Swiss cheese. Music is provided throughout the festival at two stages where polka bands and yodelers perform for those who want to dance or listen. Finally, the festival concludes on Saturday night with a three-hour concert.

The Ohio Swiss Festival also reflects the social structures characteristic of festivals insofar as it invites participation on the part of all who attend. However, many of the events are limited to experts (e.g., the yodeling and cheesemaking contests) or to locals (the coronation of the Swiss Festival

Queen). Thus, for many festival events, the vast majority of community members and visitors are spectators rather than full participants.[31]

Since festivals provide an opportunity for a community to work through its tensions, their social structures tend to produce a social meaning that is ultimately about transformation. They do so typically in two ways. First, temporality, or the movement of time, is manipulated by event structures that juxtapose past and present. This can be seen at the Swiss Cheese Festival as Old-World Swiss symbols like Swiss coats of arms, the Berne bear symbol, Swiss costumes, and alphorns appear alongside US and Ohio flags, festivalgoers in contemporary dress, and Christian rap music on stage. Putting signs from the past next to signs of the present invites participants to consider possible tensions between them and projections for the future. One tension that seems apparent at the Swiss Festival is between the musical forms of the past and those of the present. How does Swiss yodeling fit with rap? What does it mean for the future of Swiss culture in Ohio that the descendants of its Swiss immigrants come out in droves to hear the latter but not the former?

Second, festival events and participation encourage social transformation. They do this by performing and celebrating inversions in social order. A festival that takes place within an egalitarian culture (or one that self-identifies as such), for instance, typically includes the coronation of festival royalty. If that festival also takes place in a male-dominated culture, the festival royalty will be a queen rather than a king. The festival in Sugarcreek follows this pattern, as it prominently features the coronation of the Ohio Swiss Festival Queen. Another way that festivals invert egalitarianism is through competitions that establish a clear hierarchy among winners and losers. At the Ohio Swiss Festival, for example, one Grand Champion Cheese Maker is selected from many entrants.

Notably, the Ohio Swiss Festival includes yet another inversion. This one involves showcasing ethnicity in a culture that expects assimilation. By orchestrating an extravagant display of ethnic costumes, food, music, and competition, it overturns the logic of the melting pot, showcasing ethnic particularity to festivalgoers, the vast majority of whom have been thoroughly assimilated into the American mainstream.

Judging from its event structures and social structures, the Ohio Swiss Festival certainly looks like a festival; but those who study festivals would say that, strictly speaking, it is not a real festival. That is because it does not originate from the community. Instead, it belongs to the category of gatherings best understood as "modern constructions, employing festival characteristics but serving the commercial, ideological, or political purposes of self-interested authorities or entrepreneurs."[32] Indeed, the Ohio Swiss Festival belongs firmly in this category, because, as noted above, it was created by business leaders as a cost-effective way to expand Sugarcreek's share in the Swiss cheese market, not as a celebration that arose from a Swiss community residing in the area.

The commercial dimension of the Ohio Swiss Festival is significant for two related reasons. First, it helps explain why participation at the festival is stratified into at least three levels: (1) experts and professionals who participate in competitions, (2) select locals who participate in ceremonies and parades, and (3) locals and tourists who watch and eat. Such stratification of participants makes sense at an event designed as an advertising campaign to increase revenues for area businesses, but it would not at a community festival that provided an opportunity for the people of that community to come together and work out social tensions.

Second, as an advertising event, the Ohio Swiss Festival is structured as a show to be watched by a large audience consisting of community members and tourists. In this way, it is a spectacle, which is to say a "large-scale, extravagant cultural production that is replete with striking visual imagery and dramatic action[,] that is watched by a mass audience,"[33] and that seeks to celebrate (rather than challenge) the "guiding beliefs, values, concerns, and self-understandings" of the community.[34] While there are events (like parades with a queen and competitions with winners and losers) that invert the social order, they occur in the context of a spectacle organized by business leaders and designed to celebrate the social order in its current form. In sum, the Ohio Swiss Festival is a spectacle of a festival that stages social inversions for audiences who, far from being invited to work out social tensions, are expected merely to watch, eat, and applaud.

The Ohio Swiss Festival as Commemorative Event

According to the brochure that promotes it, the Ohio Swiss Festival has always had two aims: to promote the cheese industry and to give tribute to Swiss people. As the brochure puts it: "Conceived with the dual purpose of promoting the Swiss Cheese Industry in Ohio and the Village of Sugarcreek, the festival has been a tribute to the hardworking Swiss people who settled here and established the Swiss Cheese Industry." Its promotion of Swiss cheese is easy to see. Does it also pay tribute to Swiss people? Put another way, is it a commemoration of ethnic origins and ancestry?

According to John Bodnar, a historian who has written extensively on commemorative events and ethnicity, commemorative events are organized by community leaders whose professional and social lives depend on the institutions celebrated by those events. These leaders' purpose in creating such events is "to calm anxiety about change or political events, eliminate citizen indifference toward official concerns, promote exemplary patterns of citizen behavior, and stress citizen duties over rights." Commemorative events achieve this complex purpose by showcasing a particular public memory or story about the past that reassures the community that the status quo is fine, that existing institutions are working on their behalf, and that citizens should continue to act in ways that support the status quo.[35]

Bodnar argues that commemorative events that celebrate ethnicity in the United States changed a great deal over the course of the twentieth century. In the early part of the century, such events focused on the historical individuals who had settled the area, their struggles to thrive in their new context, and the particular social order of their homeland culture. By mid-century that had changed; commemorations of ethnicity started to focus on charming ethnic distinctivenesses that brought financial benefits to the event organizers. As a result, commemorative events came to serve the profit motives of community leaders and to offer little to the ethnic people whose heritage was ostensibly being remembered and celebrated. Another consequence of this change in focus and purpose was a shift in the content of the public memory constructed by the commemoration. Instead of remembering the struggles of their forebears, these profit-driven commemorations constructed ethnicity as merely the food, dance, music, and costume associated with a particular homeland. It is significant that such commemorations of ethnicity posed no challenge to full assimilation into US culture and, indeed, tended simultaneously to embrace American patriotism.[36]

The community leaders and organizations that put together the Ohio Swiss Festival each year (such as the Ohio Swiss Cheese Association, the Sugarcreek Businessmen's Association, and the Village of Sugarcreek) depend upon the ethnic institutions (e.g., cheese manufacturers) that are celebrated in the festival. More to the point, the festival was designed from the start to solve a specific economic problem: the declining market share of Ohio Swiss cheese. Clearly, the festival worked. Smith was able to write in his 1977 history of Sugarcreek, "Upwards of 100,000 people jam their way into Sugarcreek each year to enjoy this two-day fun-fest," and "As much as 30,000 pounds of cheese have been sold at the Festivals and the publicity generated by the event has increased the demand to such an extent that factories have no difficulty in disposing of all the cheese they can make."[37]

Given that profit inspired the Ohio Swiss Festival, it is not surprising that the festival follows the pattern of other ethnic commemorations that were created or re-created after mid-century with similar financial purposes. Indeed, the Ohio Swiss Festival does not tell the story of the many struggles that Swiss pioneers faced as they negotiated differences between the culture of their homeland and that of the United States. Instead, it constructs a public memory of ethnicity that consists of a set of charming distinctivenesses, such as yodeling, stone throwing, and accordion playing. The primary purpose of staging events that showcase these ethnic traditions is to produce pleasure for a paying public. The festival presents an idealized[38] version of Swiss culture in the form of architectural face-lifts, Swiss costumes, and gigantic blocks of Swiss cheese while also celebrating the beauty and ingenuity of the Swiss people in the persons of the Swiss Festival Queen and the Grand Champion Cheese Maker.

The Ohio Swiss Festival conforms to that post-mid-century model of ethnic commemorations in another way—namely, in its embrace of patriotism. It does so by juxtaposing its idealized version of Swiss culture with American patriotic signs and displays. This phenomenon is much in evidence at the opening ceremonies of the festival, when the colors are presented, and in the parade down Main Street, and in the many flower boxes on Main Street that hold US flags. Moreover, anyone visiting the festival who wanders into the Alpine Hills Museum will see an extensive display of images and newspaper clippings from prior Swiss festivals in the same room with many military uniforms that men and women of Swiss origin or ancestry wore as they served the United States in the various wars of the nineteenth and twentieth centuries.

In short, the Ohio Swiss Festival constructs a public memory of how Swiss immigrants and all of their culturally distinctive markers were eas-

ily woven into the fabric of mainstream US culture. The process of inter-
weaving Swiss culture was easy, so the story goes, because in the end the
particular differences that mark Swiss identity do not pose a challenge
to American culture. On the contrary, they function unproblematically as
marketable goods in a consumer economy. Moreover, Swiss distinctivenesses fit seamlessly with US patriotism. As the Alpine Museum amply
shows, whenever a Swiss immigrant to Sugarcreek was called upon to
fight on the side of the United States, their former loyalty to Switzerland
diminished with their newfound allegiance to the United States. In the
context of this public memory of America as melting pot, wherein even
citizens of foreign countries gladly sacrifice their lives for US interests,
the three flags of homeland, nation, and state fly harmoniously in the brick
flower boxes of Sugarcreek.

Tourists' Experiences of the Festival

To attend the Ohio Swiss Festival is to encounter many individuals dressed
in Swiss costume who are yodeling, dancing, playing the alphorn, or just
visiting with family and friends. Many of them are middle-aged and older
adults; some are small children. Visually they are connected by their attire.
They appear to be a multigenerational Swiss community. Those attending
the festival might easily imagine that at least the senior members of this
Swiss community have memories of, say, a grandparent who was the child
of Swiss immigrants in Sugarcreek. Someone like that, a tourist might further imagine, could surely remember family members who spoke Swiss,
made cheese, or played the alphorn. Not only might these older members
of the community have memories of such ethnic particularities, they could
probably also talk to their descendants about the meaning and significance
of these Swiss practices and traditions.

Middle-American tourists who are unsure of their own ethnic roots or
who know of them but cannot name or explain the social customs related
to them may envy these individuals dressed in Swiss costume. If they do,
then they are likely to feel that traditional sort of nostalgia whereby they
long for an idealized version of ethnicity, family, and community. They
want to be like these costumed people who seem to have somehow pre-
served all the beauty and cohesiveness of an ethnic community. While
this kind of nostalgic experience may be pleasurable initially, in the end it

always underscores the tourist's understanding of him- or herself as someone who has no ethnic distinction. Standing amidst people who appear to
be Swiss and to have held on to their heritage, the tourist is likely to feel
unmarked, excessively assimilated, and without history or heritage.

Others may view the performance of ethnicity not as a reminder of
how their people were once also distinctive but, instead, as a display of
the exotic other. If Dean MacCannell, who analyzed tourism in light
of the exotic other, is right, such tourists would experience themselves
as the norm in comparison to which the exotic other signifies as different
or strange. However, white middle Americans who know that they have
been displaced as the normative group by social movements and demographic shifts may long for those bygone days when everyone knew that
the prototypical American was a white person who looked, acted, and believed just like them.

Of course, when MacCannell was researching and writing his seminal book on the tourist (which was first published in 1976), white middle Americans still largely experienced themselves as normative.[39] Thus,
when the tourists he was studying encountered the exotic other, their
position as the iconic citizen of the United States was confirmed. That
felt good. It underscored their normative status and reassured them that
the social order was intact. Today, white middle Americans are no longer
iconic. Thus, when they encounter the exotic other in Sugarcreek, they are
not positioned as the norm. Instead, they are reminded that whereas once
they set the standard, now they are just one cultural group among many
who claim to be Americans. Their experience of the exotic other in Sugarcreek, far from reassuring them that the social order is secure, confirms
their anxiety about having lost that privileged status and highlights the
fact that US culture is in a profound state of flux.

All this to say that tourists are likely to have one of two experiences
at the Ohio Swiss Festival. They may identify with the ethnic subject—
that is, the local in Swiss costume. If they do so, they may recognize that
by contrast they are fully assimilated into US culture and, thus, have lost
track of the ethnic heritage they or their ancestors had. They may experience themselves as without distinction, which is to say, common, unwor-
thy of note, insignificant. The other possibility is that they may see the
local in Swiss costume as an exotic other. Tourists who have this response
may feel nostalgia for that time when people like them were the norm

compared to such exotic others. In this case, they are likely to feel a sense of loss for that iconic status. Putting all this together, it may be said that Sugarcreek tourists face something of an ethnic double whammy. If they identify with the local in Swiss costume, then they experience themselves as having lost their ethnic distinctiveness. If they view the local in Swiss costume as other, then they experience themselves as having lost their once iconic status.

Sugarcreek's Tourism Decline

Understanding the visual rhetoric of Sugarcreek and the Ohio Swiss Festival reveals why Sugarcreek has seen a decline in tourism and why it is less popular than Walnut Creek and Berlin. In 1953, when business leaders in Sugarcreek came up with the idea of hosting a cheese festival and giving the town a Swiss theme, white middle Americans were iconic. When they came to Sugarcreek and encountered locals in Swiss costume engaged in traditional Swiss activities, they were affirmed by the exotic other as the normative subject of US culture. This being so, the fact that they or their ancestors had been assimilated into US culture felt like a good thing. After all, assimilation is what gave them membership in the normative group. However, by the end of the twentieth century, they were no longer iconic. Thus, instead of making white middle Americans feel good about themselves, Sugarcreek's theme and its festival now remind tourists of what they have lost, whether that is their iconic status or their heritage.

Why are Walnut Creek and Berlin having a lot more success in the business of Amish Country tourism? Walnut Creek and Berlin address tourists' anxieties about time, gender, nation, and technology by encouraging visitors to "remember" the past in romanticized ways and then to imagine a better future that is based on that romanticized past. They inspire tourists to experience nostalgia not so much for the past but on behalf of a future that takes its shape from that highly selective and idealized past. Moreover, because that new future has roots in the past (however idealistically rendered) it seems plausible, because it has been done before. The approaches taken by the tourism industry in Walnut Creek and Berlin are both positive and forward-looking, encouraging and reassuring.

Sugarcreek's visual rhetoric also draws upon a romanticized view of the past, but Sugarcreek does not build upon that view toward a future in which anxieties about ethnicity are resolved. While a visitor may experience nostalgia in Sugarcreek, the longing that it inspires is for a past that is forever gone. No strategy for recovering either the iconic status of white middle Americans or their long lost ethnic heritage is offered, no inspiring vision for white middle Americans in a multicultural context is given. Far from resolving tourists' anxieties, Sugarcreek only underscores them. Not surprisingly, tourists prefer Walnut Creek and Berlin, which invite them to imagine alternative futures that resolve their anxieties.

Ethnicity and the Amish

Sugarcreek also features Amish ethnicity.[40] Images calling attention to the Amish presence appear throughout the town. Merchandise representative of or made by the Amish is offered in several stores. And food sold in the town, whether at the Swiss Village Bulk Food store or Beachy's Country Chalet restaurant, includes not only Swiss-style but also Amish-style selections.

Although the Amish are not showcased in any of the official events of the Ohio Swiss Festival, they are, interestingly, referenced in the annual brochure that advertises the festival: "Sugarcreek is located in the rolling hills of western Tuscarawas County . . . It is surrounded by a prosperous farming community, populated largely by the Amish people." Here, the Amish are represented as an ethnic group with strong connections to the culture of farming. More than this, they are constructed in much the same way as the locals who appear in Swiss costume: as a people who have retained the distinctive characteristics and practices of their ancestors. As another ethnic group that has held on to its heritage, the Amish may simply underscore the point that Swiss ethnicity appears to be making in Sugarcreek, namely, that white middle Americans have lost not only their ethnicity but also their normative status.

But is that all there is to say about the Amish in Sugarcreek? Are they just one more patch in the quilt of what has become American multiculturalism? To answer these questions, consider the photograph on the next page, taken at an Ohio Swiss Festival, which shows a portion of the crowd that was lined up on both sides of Main Street to watch a musical group that featured a yodeler. Most of what appears in this photo is just what one would expect: a lot of white middle Americans enjoying a performance of ethnic

A local woman dressed in Swiss costume and an Amish woman with her three small
children watch yodelers perform at the Ohio Swiss Festival

distinctiveness. There is also an older woman dressed in a Swiss costume—
probably a community member—who seems to be having a good time talking with other people in the audience. None of this is surprising. What may
be surprising is the presence of an Amish woman (with what appear to
be her three Amish children) in the audience. Now, one would expect to
see an Amish woman in Sugarcreek. The ubiquitous banners that feature
the silhouette of an Amish buggy, the festival brochure highlighting the
Amish, the Amish food and other merchandise for sale: all of this pre-
pares visitors to see Amish in Sugarcreek. But instead of being the object
of interest, which is clearly how the Amish are positioned by the tourism
industry, this woman and her children are the observers, watching the
spectacle of a different unusual group. They who are typically the show
are here the audience.

As an event that was created by community leaders to promote Swiss cheese and tourism, the Ohio Swiss Festival puts Swiss ethnicity on display for tourists. As a spectacle of ethnicity, audience participation primarily takes the form of watching events in which ethnicity is performed through various Swiss customs and crafts. In this small community, it is to be expected that the performers will be Swiss and look Swiss and the spectators will largely be non-Swiss—and in this case white middle Americans. Given this context, how do the Amish woman and her children, who do not look Swiss, even if their Amish ancestors came from Switzerland, fit in?[41] What makes this Amish woman as a spectator of Swiss ethnicity so strange, and what does this strangeness mean to those who are viewing both the Swiss performers and the Amish woman and her children?

The juxtaposition in the photograph of the Amish woman, in her particular attire, and the woman in Swiss costume points to the issue here. In some sense all people perform their ethnicity or, for those who have long been assimilated into mainstream US culture, their identity. How individuals dress, what sort of vehicle they drive, and how they speak tell others who they are. The Amish, in all sorts of visible ways, tell others who they are and reveal that they are different. More than this, they live and appear as they do whether or not others are watching. If there were no festival, no themed town, no tourists, the Amish woman would still be dressed exactly as she is. Such is not the case for the woman in Swiss costume; she appears as she does because of the festival. Indeed, it is difficult even to imagine that she would dress in that fashion were there no Swiss Festival or similar occasion. She is performing her ethnicity to add authenticity to a staged ethnic commemoration. By contrast, the Amish woman's performance of ethnicity (while undoubtedly a performance) is motivated by faith and community, not the occasion of spectacle.

This photograph underscores the variety among performances of ethnicity and identity. The meaning of the Amish woman's appearance is not the same as that of the woman in Swiss dress, because the former does not signify as one who is purposefully performing her distinctiveness on behalf of a business venture. But the Amish woman's ethnic performance is also different from that of the other locals and the many tourists. Unlike them, she does not signify as a member of mainstream culture; on the contrary, she stands out as one who defies many of the mainstream standards and norms by which most Americans live.

The striking difference between the performance of ethnicity by the Amish woman versus that of the woman in Swiss costume versus the performances of the other locals and the tourists is a powerful reminder that we do have some choice in how we display our identities. While we cannot avoid performing our ethnicities or identities, we do have power to shape the performances of them. For instance, as a "white" person, I may not be able to avoid performing whiteness. Even so, I do have something to do with how I signify as white. It matters whether I perform whiteness with, say, untanned skin, flat-ironed hair, blue contact lenses, and a floral print dress versus bronzed skin, dreadlocks, a flannel shirt, and leggings. Both are performances. Each signifies differently.

Of course, the fact that the Amish have chosen to perform in a fashion that is at odds with social convention inevitably raises questions. Why do they insist on looking so strange? Why not wear a pair of shorts when working out in the yard on a hot summer day? Why not pull on a pair of jeans when heading to work with the construction crew? Why be determined to look so different from everyone else? What is the point? Why make these choices?

The answers to these questions are to be found in the motivation for the performance, its purpose. For the Amish, the purpose is the whole point of the performance. A woman wears her cape dress and white prayer covering and a man wears his broadfall pants and solid color shirt to make visible their convictions regarding simplicity, community, and humility. They wear plain clothes, drive buggies, speak Pennsylvania Dutch, and so forth because they believe that making their commitments visible serves as a witness to the reality of the Kingdom of God in the world. Unlike most Americans, theirs is a performance born out of religious faith rather than, say, the intent to impress or, in the case of the Ohio Swiss Festival, the desire to sell more cheese.

For the Amish, the performance of identity is about making visible the fact that the ways of the world—including individualism, pride, and competition—are not the only option. Of course, some of their performances in Sugarcreek and elsewhere in Amish Country could easily raise questions for the tourists. Why do they perform their identities in the ways that they do? What purposes lead them to perform their identities in this way? At the end of the day, do these purposes have meaning?

By raising questions like these, the Amish invite tourists to consider whether they might want to shape their own performance to new purposes that are distinctive and that hold real meaning. The presence of the Amish woman at the festival raises yet another question, one about spectatorship. That is the question I explore in the final chapter.

Nostalgia for sale at Sommers' General Store in Berlin

CHAPTER 6

Nostalgia and the Power of
Amish Witness

The good news about this recession is that the Amish are becoming more Amish.
With less cash in their pockets, their gardens are getting big again.
—New Order Amish man

Amish Country tourism attracts more than 19 million people every year and generates over $2 billion of economic benefit to the areas surrounding the three largest Amish settlements in the world, those in Pennsylvania, Indiana, and Ohio. The question this book has probed is why. Why do so many middle Americans spend a fair amount of time and a lot of money in Amish Country? Why is Amish Country tourism so appealing?

The Appeal of Amish Tourism

This examination of the visual rhetorical features of three prominent tourist towns in Ohio's Amish Country has revealed that each town's rhetorical elements are based on a theme and tell a story or retell a popular myth that the tourist is invited to experience. Perhaps the single most important characteristic of Amish Country tourism that has become apparent is that it is designed in strategic ways for a particular audience. Throughout these three towns, tourists are welcomed as they are, which is to say, as middle Americans who, among other things, enjoy certain modern conveniences, require ample parking, and like to shop and eat. Even more importantly, tourists of Amish Country are approached as people with specific con-

cerns regarding middle-American life. Amish Country tourism addresses
these concerns through complex and compelling visual rhetorics that offer
symbolic resolutions to middle-American anxieties.

In particular, Amish Country tourism offers these resolutions by constructing themed environments that tell stories. In all three towns the
stories take the form of idealized versions of a presumably shared past, a
past that is imagined as holding the answer to troubles in the present. Put
simply, nostalgia is crucial in the appeal of Amish Country tourism. The
comparison of two highly successful towns along side another whose tourism industry is struggling reveals a fundamental difference in the nature
of the forms of nostalgia employed. Walnut Creek and Berlin tell stories
about the past that encourage tourists to imagine how they might change
their lives and, thereby, alter their future. This nostalgia for the future is
a nostalgia of hope. By contrast, the nostalgia of Sugarcreek is only about
the past. According to the story told in Sugarcreek, the answers to contemporary concerns are found in bygone days, but no means are offered
for recovering them in the present. With the answers locked in the past,
Sugarcreek's nostalgia is about loss. Not surprisingly, a tourism theme that
idealizes the past on behalf of a better future is much more appealing to
middle-American tourists than one that says that their better days are behind them.

One of the most striking aspects of Amish Country tourism is the contrast between the elaborately, sometimes ornately, themed environments
created for the tourists and the plain and simple life of the Amish. But a
close reading of the three towns reveals that, while the aesthetic in each
town contrasts sharply with Amish simplicity, the stories and solutions
offered by them draw upon aspects of Amish life. Indeed, the Amish are
essential, especially in Walnut Creek and Berlin, for legitimating the symbolic resolutions made available by these two towns. The Amish demon-
strate that it is possible to slow down your life, to regain clarity about gender differences, and to reassert control over technology. Thus, they make
the answers provided by Amish Country tourism in Walnut Creek and
Berlin seem plausible.

The Amish are used by these environments as living proof that the solutions offered will work, but they would not serve as successful examples
if they were not pursuing their distinctive ways for other reasons. First,
in order for the Amish to legitimate an alternative future, they must be

other. If they were essentially the same as the middle-American tourists who come to Amish Country then they could not signify something different; yet, as people who are truly different, there really is no knowing what they might mean or say to the visitors. Second, the Amish have their own visual rhetoric, or what they call their witness. That witness is born out of a set of faith commitments that are different from the worldview of most middle Americans. Although their witness may not be as loud as the stories told by Amish Country tourism, it just may be that they can be heard.

The Unrepresented Reality in Amish Country Tourism

While much of what has been gleaned from this rhetorical analysis is particular to Amish Country tourism, three implications emerge for understanding tourism more generally.

The first is that all forms of tourism are not the same. That is to say, while all tourist destinations are mediations of reality, not all mediate to the same degree or in the same ways. Some mediations still promise access to the strange other; some mediations traffic in the pleasure of the obviously fake. Amish Country is the former sort, purporting to give access to the world of the Amish; Disney World is the latter, promising a mediation that is even better than the real, what theorists have called the "hyper-real."[1] In Amish Country, the tourist gets a curious mix of imperfectly themed environment and actual Amish people. In Disney World the tourist is presented with a small town or an animal kingdom or an American frontier that is so perfect as to be a place, to quote the Disney World website, "where fairytale dreams come true." Two mediations of reality, but in the one there is some hint of the real and in the other there is a very polished fake.

The second implication of this analysis closely relates to the first. While, as Dean MacCannell argued, tourism cannot fully deliver on its promise of authenticity, this does not mean that nothing important happens at a tourist destination. While MacCannell would agree on this point—what made his book seminal was that he took tourism seriously so as to theorize its dynamics and functions—he did not consider the possibility that although the tourist does not have an authentic experience of the other, they might have a significant encounter that (perhaps greatly) exceeds the boundaries of tourism's mediation. This possibility is much greater with the sort of tourism that takes place "on location" than with the sort that offers the hyperreal. Although Amish Country tourists may not gain access to who the Amish "really are," they may still encounter the otherness of the Amish in a manner that matters.

Finally, tourism involves a double dynamic in its processes of signification. On the one hand, tourism represents the strange other in ways designed to please the tourist. On the other hand, because the subject being observed can never be fully represented by any signifying system, something about that other is always left out—a remainder. What Amish Country tourism cannot fully take into account are the ways in which the visible witness of the Amish challenge the very stories told by Amish Country tourism. To understand any particular instance of tourism it is necessary to be on the lookout for that remainder, because whatever tourism cannot account for is likely to be precisely the otherness of the other that says something important, perhaps even something unsettling.

The Amish and the Tourist's Camera

This final example from Amish Country applies to all three towns that have been considered in this book, and beyond them to all Amish tourist locations. Indeed, it can serve as a metonym for what has been said above about tourist destinations, tourists, and the other.

If a tourist entering Ohio's Amish Country does not know upon arrival, they will surely learn fast that the Amish do not want to have their picture taken. In tourist magazines, newspapers, and brochures as well as the many signs that appear at area shops, visitors are repeatedly instructed not to photograph the Amish. For instance, at the livestock auction in Mount Hope, a sign hangs above the main auction area saying that no photographs or video may be taken. Sometimes the notification is accompanied by an explanation as to why the Amish avoid the camera. When photographs of the Amish appear in tourist publications they typically carry a disclaimer stating that the photographer who took the pictures has a longstanding relationship with the people and had permission from the Amish to photograph them.

Tourist materials that explain the Amish prohibition against photography frequently say that the Amish avoid the camera for religious reasons. Donald Kraybill puts it this way: "The well-known Amish taboo against personal photographs is legitimated by a biblical command: 'You shall not make for yourself a graven image or a likeness of anything' (Ex. 20:4). In the latter part of the nineteenth century, as photography was becoming popular, the Amish applied the biblical injunction against 'likenesses' to photographs. Their aversion to photographs of individuals was a way of suppressing pride. If people pose for a photograph, they want to exalt themselves and are taking themselves too seriously."[2] The Amish avoid having their picture taken by tourists not merely because they find it bothersome (though they undoubtedly feel that too) but because having one's picture taken is seen as putting oneself forward, as if one were better than others. In a community that depends upon conformity, humility, and yieldedness, an expression of pride in any form has no place.

For anyone who has visited Amish Country or learned about the Amish, looking upon the photograph above of the Amish woman at the Ohio Swiss Festival (or perhaps any of the other photographs in this book that include Amish persons) may raise questions. Given the Amish prohibition against photography, was I wrong to take this picture? Did I violate this woman's religious convictions and communal commitments? If so, what does it mean for anyone to look at it? By looking at this photograph of her, do viewers participate in making her seem prideful?

As to whether this photograph put the Amish woman in violation of her community's prohibition, the answer is no. I took this photograph in a particular manner so as to ensure that she could not be said to have broken the rule. Because she is not facing the camera, and therefore has no awareness that she is being photographed, and because she appears in a large crowd as just one person among many, she would not be seen by her community as putting herself forward in any way.[3] However, looking at this photograph may make one feel uneasy, and for good reason. While most people probably do not know the specifics of this Amish prohibition, chances are that many are aware that one should not take photographs of Amish people.

The fact that tourists know they should not photograph the Amish is important because taking pictures is crucial for tourists. It is not an accident that the prototypical image of a tourist is of someone with a camera hanging from his or her neck. To understand why this is so and, more importantly, to appreciate its significance for Amish Country tourism requires a brief consideration of some theory concerning tourists and their cameras.

In his book *The Tourist Gaze*, John Urry argues that photography is "emblematic of the tourist." The whole project "of being seen and recorded and seeing others and recording them" is at the center of the tourist experience. Photography provides the opportunity for the tourist to become the subject of knowledge and memory, insofar as the tourist objectifies whoever or whatever is being photographed by constructing the subject within the frame of the photographic image.[4] Urry puts it this way: "To photograph is in some way to appropriate the object being photographed. It is a power/knowledge relationship . . . Photography tames the object of the gaze, the most striking examples being of exotic cultures."[5]

As MacCannell explains, tourism is about encountering difference. Tourists want to experience a mode of living that is unlike their own. Sometimes they go to places like tropical islands where they can expect to see "exotic" people who dress, eat, speak, and dance differently than they do. Sometimes they visit tourist attractions, like wax museums, in which they are promised access to historical figures who lived in another time. The point is that tourists do not tour that which they already know. They seek out the different, the strange, the other. In doing so they open themselves to encountering something unsettling.

Take, for example, middle-American tourists visiting a tropical island. While there, they may observe the people of that island living at a slower pace and on considerably less income than they do. The islanders may nevertheless appear to be quite content. Seeing this different way of living may raise questions about the tourists' own lives. They may wonder whether working long hours, being stressed out by mortgage payments, having too little time to spend with loved ones, and so forth is a good way to live. Asking questions like these may unsettle what was once their taken-for-granted mode of being in the world. Tourists of such a location may start to think that they have it all wrong.

Here is where the camera becomes important. The camera gives people the power to capture, and thus control, the meaning of the other, whose different way of being in the world raises questions about how one lives one's own life. In taking a person's picture, the photographer stops the other's movement, makes the other a static object of the photographer's gaze, and fixes the other as a point of interest. More than this, the photog-

rapher—zooming in, zooming out, and thus framing the other in a particular way—exercises a great deal of control as to how the other appears in
the photograph. Further, as a tourist takes a picture, he or she can imagine
some future evening when family or friends are being shown photographs
from the trip. The tourist photographer can anticipate telling them all
about these "exotic" people, in the process serving as possessor of knowledge about this extraordinary other. In sum, the camera is crucial to tourists because it allows them to encounter the potentially unsettling other
while simultaneously feeling, as the image of the other is captured, as if
they are in control.

The designers of Disney World know how important the camera is
for tourists. That is why visitors to the Magic Kingdom encounter signs
throughout the park that inform them that a certain location is a perfect
"picture spot." As tourists arrive on Main Street USA, with its bustling
shops and daily parade (which may raise unsettling questions about the
vitality of exurban living), they are directed to the perfect location from
which to objectify the scene. Likewise, Disney characters (who roam the
park with their oversized heads and shoes, as well as permanent smiles
that might terrify as much as delight) are well trained to strike just the
right pose for the tourist's camera.[6] Thus, in case any of Disney World's
elaborately designed experiences of the extraordinary happen to produce
unsettled feelings in visitors, the park gives tourists ample opportunity
to reestablish control, and thus order, with the camera. Actually, it may
very well be this play between encountering the strange or unsettling and
shooting it (with just a camera, of course) that brings so much pleasure to
tourists.

But this is not the case for the tourist in Amish Country. Amish Country tourism does construct the Amish as living proof that the stories told
within these tourist towns are plausible, and the themed environments of
Ohio's Amish Country do an effective job of suggesting that eating that
Amish-style dinner or buying that coverlet or taking home that 1950s-
style toaster will change the tourist's life. However, those visual rhetorics are not completely successful, because even amidst these elaborately
themed environments, the Amish remain strange. Indeed, they must remain somewhat strange. If they are not out of the ordinary in their slower
life, clear gender categories, and control of technology—if they are not visibly strange with their horses and buggies, plain clothes, and gas lamps—

then they cannot legitimate the vision of an alternative future that brings hope to the tourist.

Given that the Amish remain strange to tourists and, thereby, have the power to contest the order and meaning of the tourists' lives, it is not surprising to discover that tourists want desperately to take photographs of them. As we have seen, they will even go so far as to run down the middle of a main street just to get a picture of the back end of an Amish buggy. Like the visitor to Disney World, tourists of Amish Country want to take control of the very strange Amish.

But they cannot. They can take pictures of an Amish buggy, barn, or bailer, but they cannot take a picture of the face of the other, who, through their strange ways, have the power to unsettle the status quo. And, in fact, the tourists do refrain from photographing Amish persons.[7] Tourists are often seen photographing a horse and buggy parked at a hitching post or an Amish person farming in the distance, but in the fifteen years I have been studying tourism in Ohio's Amish Country, I have never, for instance, seen a tourist attempt to take a picture of the Amish man who gives buggy rides in Walnut Creek. This restraint is remarkable, given that the buggy driver is an easy target, since he spends most of his day sitting in a chair along the main street in town.

It makes a great deal of sense that the Amish prohibition against being photographed would frustrate the tourist. Tourists encounter the strangeness of the Amish, a strangeness that has the power to challenge the tourists' understanding of the world, yet they are denied the promise that they might be able to domesticate it. Armed with cameras, they could render the Amish quaint or beautiful or childlike or something else of the tourists' imagining. Without cameras, they are much more likely to truly notice the strangeness of the Amish. And if that happens, then the questions that the Amish pose through their very visible witness will remain alive for those who are observing them.

With Eyes to See

To be sure, Amish Country tourism does not give the tourist the Amish as such. Instead, it offers representations of the Amish that largely serve the interests of Amish Country tourism. But that is not all. It also affords tourists the opportunity to witness the visibly strange ways of the Amish, and those ways contest the stories told and the resolutions offered by Amish Country tourism. Thus, although the Amish may not speak out to challenge the way they are represented by Amish Country tourism, that does not mean that they are not "speaking." While the Amish may not be prone to verbal commentary on tourism or on "the English," their visible manner of being in the world raises fascinating, and disturbing, questions about the character and meaning of current American life styles.

With this final example of the otherness of the Amish, I am reminded of the conversation I recounted in the preface that I and my companions had with a group of New Order Amish men. In that conversation, I asked the men what they thought of Amish Country tourism, and I was surprised by their answer. I had read in Amish publications of Amish frustration with the silly questions tourists often ask, such as whether the Amish are a cult, whether they worship Satan, or whether their men have multiple wives. So, I expected them to talk about how silly and annoying tourists are. Instead, they spoke with compassion and empathy about how hard it must be to live in the world, with all of its pressures and stress. They talked about their perception that life in the world, as opposed to Amish life, was rushed all of the time. They talked about feeling bad that tourists do not have time for their families, do not generally enjoy their work, and often feel lost. They then went on to describe their own lives and how fortunate they are to live according to the Amish way. They finished by saying that rather than being bothered by tourists, they see tourism as an opportunity to offer a witness of the Kingdom of God to people who may be looking for answers to fundamental questions about their lives. They said that, although they do not want to put on a show for tourists, they do see everyday activities that bring them into contact with tourists as important opportunities to make visible another way of being in the world, a way that is peaceful and fulfilling.

When one passes through Amish Country and sees fiberglass Amish horses inside hotel water parks and silhouettes of Amish buggies on everything from signs in the parking lots of outlet malls to shot glasses to potato chip bags, it is tempting to conclude that Amish Country tourism is just another example of one group of people (tourism entrepreneurs) lightening the wallets of another group of people (tourists) by taking advantage of still another group (the Amish). But if one takes seriously the fact that millions of tourists travel to Amish Country every year and apparently like what they encounter there, and if one listens carefully to Amish who see themselves speaking through their daily lives in important ways to people in search of answers, then it is obvious that Amish Country tourism can be more than it first seems.

Put another way, there is a sense in which the Amish are succeeding in the witness that those New Order men described. The Amish are demonstrating that it is possible to live in ways that transgress the expectations of consumer culture even amidst its seemingly overwhelming influence. In the context of Amish Country tourism, this witness is transformed into legitimation of the stories that that tourism tells and of the appeals it makes for tourists to buy more stuff. Still, this witness nevertheless makes its voice heard because of the truly strange beliefs and curious practices of the Amish. Indeed, the otherness of the Amish strongly suggests that bringing forth that slower, more peaceful, more humane future might take more than laying down some cash for an antique plane or lace tablecloth or peanut butter pie. It seems to me that, for as long as we have eyes to see the Amish as strange, they will ask us whether we have the courage or the creativity or the vision or the faith to embrace a future that we have not yet seen and in which we become, in the context of this all-consuming culture, truly strange ourselves.

Notes

Introduction

1. Although not precise, the term "Amish Country" is meaningful. Used heavily by the tourism industry, it designates areas where relatively large numbers of Amish live and where tourist attractions have emerged to take advantage of the presence of the Amish population. I use the term here in much the same manner that the tourism industry does. By "Amish Country" I do not mean *any* area where Amish live but rather those areas where Amish live and where tourism with them as the focus has taken hold.

2. For those unfamiliar with the varieties of Amish, the New Order Amish are more change minded than Old Order Amish groups. Unlike the "Old Oder," for instance, the New Order have pocket doors rather than roll-down curtains and rubber wheels rather than steel wheels on their buggies.

3. This brief description of signs and sign systems is based in the work of Ferdinand de Saussure, the French linguist who pioneered structuralism as a theory for understanding language, literature, and culture. See Saussure, *Course in General Linguistics*. For an accessible introduction to Saussure's work as it relates to the study of culture, see Fiske, *Introduction to Communication Studies*.

4. Because I am interested in how the Amish are represented to visitors, my approach is similar to that of the scholars who contributed to Diane Zimmerman Umble and David Weaver-Zercher's collection on the Amish and the media. In that volume, some of the contributors (myself included—published under the name Susan Biesecker) reflect on how the Amish have been represented in Hollywood films, other documentaries, television reality shows, Amish Country tourism, and so forth. Other scholars in that volume talk about how the Amish represent themselves in the media. See Umble and Weaver-Zercher, *The Amish and the Media*.

5. By "myth" is meant a story that a culture tells to make sense of itself and the world in a particular, and usually reassuring, way. Often myth is understood as a story that is false. That is not the focus of the meaning here. Myths may be true or false. What is important about myths is not so much their truth or falsehood but how they structure the way people understand their world and their place in it. For a fuller explanation of myth and its relationship to culture and meaning, see Barthes, *Mythologies*.

6. In their recent book, *An Amish Paradox*, Charles Hurst and David McConnell do much to fill this gap in Amish studies. Their sociological-anthropological study of the many varieties of Amish in the counties of Holmes and Wayne in eastern Ohio reports on extensive interviews and observational research. Their research makes a valuable contribution to current understanding of the effects that, especially, economic changes are having on Amish life and culture.

7. Data supporting the impressive growth that Amish Country tourism was bringing to the Amish settlement in Ohio were presented in a special twenty-eight-page supplement of the local newspaper (*The Bargain Hunter*) called "Progressing in New Directions in 1996," which documented expansions of businesses that specifically served tourists, including Amish-style restaurants, a bakery, a flea market, a furniture store, and an antique mall. The publication cited additional signs of growth, including a new bank, a Burger King restaurant, a McDonald's restaurant, a hospital, and a construction company. *Progressing in New Directions in 1996*, Graphic Publications, February 27 to March 4, 1996.

8. Initially, the study of visual rhetoric focused on two-dimensional images. See, for instance, Hariman and Lucaites, "Performing Civic Identity" and "Public Identity and Collective Memory in U.S. Iconic Photography." While such research continues, other rhetorical scholars have expanded the purview of visual rhetoric to include environments, such as museums and memorials. See, for instance, Barbara Biesecker, "Remembering World War II"; Blair and Michel, "The AIDS Memorial Quilt and the Contemporary Culture of Public Commemoration" and "Reproducing Civil Rights Tactics" Dickinson, Ott, and Aoki, "Memory and Myth at the Buffalo Bill Museum" and "Spaces of Remembering and Forgetting." For an introduction to the communication subfield of visual rhetoric, see Olson, Finnegan, and Hope, *Visual Rhetoric*.

9. Scholars, commentators, and practitioners have been writing about rhetoric for thousands of years, so there are many resources available on the subject. For single-authored general introductions to rhetorical theory, see Hauser, *Introduction to Rhetorical Theory*, and Campbell, *The Rhetorical Act*. To read what a variety of scholars in the field have had to say about rhetorical theory, see Lucaites, Condit, and Caudhill, *Contemporary Rhetorical Theory*. See also Rosteck, *At the Intersection*, for a collection of essays that emphasizes the relationship between rhetorical studies and cultural

studies. The field of rhetoric supports several journals that publish scholarly articles on the subject. Just three of the more prominent periodicals are *Quarterly Journal of Speech*, *Communication and Critical/Cultural Studies*, and *Rhetoric Society Quarterly*.

10. I borrow the concept of symbolic resolution from Jameson, *The Political Unconscious*.

11. I develop the argument that the visual rhetoric of Amish Country tourism offers visitors an experience of a nostalgic longing for a future in which these anxieties and issues are resolved. I borrow the concept of "nostalgia for a future" from Barbara Biesecker, who theorizes about the relationships among memory, identity, politics, and visual rhetoric. In her essay "Remembering World War II," Biesecker reads the recent visual rhetorics of World War II (as seen in film, memorials, and a commemorative book) as technologies of "transmogrification" that transform an event into an experience of a constructed past as an idealized future. When experiencing the operations of these visual rhetorics, she argues, Americans do not remember the war but, instead, take up a mode of being in a present that anticipates a future idealized by a particular and constructed memory of the past. In my readings of the visual rhetorics of Amish Country tourism, I attend to the ways these rhetorics invite the tourist to adopt a mode of being (or a certain nostalgia for a particular idealized future) in which the symbolic resolutions offered by Amish Country tourism appear to bring peace, satisfaction, and moral assurance to middle-Americans. See Biesecker, "Remembering World War II," esp. pp. 398–406.

Chapter 1. Who Are the Amish?

1. It should be noted that the Reformers sought initially to reform the Catholic Church (thus, the name Reformation) rather than to create an alternative to it.

2. For an insightful account of the relationship between Protestantism and pluralism, see William Trollinger, "Evangelicalism and Religious Pluralism."

3. Although there were no "states" in the sixteenth century, I use the term for convenience to designate a civic authority that governs a particular region.

4. For an in-depth rhetorical analysis of the debates among Radical Reformers concerning taking up the sword and separation of church and state, see Gerald Biesecker-Mast, *Separation and the Sword*.

5. I use the term "nonviolence" here rather than "pacifism" or "nonresistance" because it highlights the contrast between the Kingdom of God, which is characterized by peace and reconciliation, and the world, which is characterized by human justice and violence. For an Anabaptist theology that centers the atonement in Jesus' nonviolent salvific action, see Weaver, *The Nonviolent Atonement*. For an Anabaptist theology written on behalf of a Spirit-driven, nonviolent church based in defenseless Christianity, see Mast and Weaver, *Defenseless Christianity*.

6. The last recorded execution of an Anabaptist, that of Hans Landis, occurred in 1614. However, Anabaptists were persecuted throughout the seventeenth century in Switzerland (where the Anabaptists who later became Amish came from); they were forced into galley slavery, imprisoned, and/or exiled. A record of the stories of thousands of these persons can be found in van Braght, *Martyrs Mirror*. Although the authorities sought to decrease the influence and popularity of Anabaptists by staging huge public spectacles of torture and execution, the displays often had just the opposite effect. For an analysis of the visual rhetoric of martyrdom among Anabaptists, see my essay, Susan Biesecker-Mast, "Visible Church."

7. Simons's writings are collected in Simons, *Complete Writings*. For a general introduction to the history of Mennonites, see Dyck, *Introduction to Mennonite History*; Smith, *Smith's Story of the Mennonites*; and Loewen and Nolt, *Through Fire and Water*. For a history of the Mennonites in Europe, see Lapp and Snyder, *Testing Faith and Tradition*. For a contemporary history of US Mennonites and their relationship to the state, see Bush, *Two Kingdoms, Two Loyalties*. For a searchable encyclopedia with information on Anabaptist groups including Amish and Mennonites, and Menno Simons in particular, visit the *Global Anabaptist Mennonite Encyclopedia Online* at www.gameo.org.

8. Van Braght, *Martyrs Mirror*, 6–15.

9. It is significant that Amman was not arguing on behalf of a new practice but, rather, was advocating that the Swiss Anabaptists enforce a longstanding practice. Indeed, one of the seven articles of faith included in the first confession of faith adopted by the sixteenth-century Anabaptists (in 1527) articulated the importance of shunning (the ban) for keeping their Christian community pure. The subsequent revision of that confession, known as the Dortrecht confession (written in 1632), stressed even more than did the first confession the importance of the ban. The Dortrecht confession remains the confession of faith of the Amish today. Both confessions can be found in their entirety at "Encyclopedia Index" at www.gameo .org.

10. For a scholarly account of Amman's critique of the Swiss Anabaptists and the schism that followed, as well as primary sources related to it, see Roth, *Letters of the Amish Division*. For a fuller account of the origins of the Amish, see Kraybill, *Riddle of Amish Culture*, 24–26.

11. Nolt and Meyers, *Plain Diversity*, 24.

12. For a clear explanation of the connections among Amish practices and Amish faith, see Kraybill, *Riddle of Amish Culture*.

13. To borrow a phrase from John Howard Yoder, what Jesus' victory over death on the cross showed was that the peace and reconciliation of God ran with the very "grain of the universe." See Yoder, "Armaments and Eschatology," 58. Stanley Hauerwas, whose work depends heavily on Yoder, borrows Yoder's phrase in his book,

With the Grain. For an extended discussion of Anabaptist theology made relevant for twentieth-century Christians, see Yoder, *Politics of Jesus*.

14. For the definitive scholarly statement on the Schleitheim Brotherly Union, see Gerald Biesecker-Mast, *Separation and the Sword*, 97–132.

15. The term now favored for this extension of nonviolence is "defenselessness." See Mast and Weaver, *Defenseless Christianity*.

16. For extended discussions of these Amish commitments, see Kraybill, *Riddle of Amish Culture*; Kraybill, Nolt, and Weaver-Zercher, *Amish Grace*; and Nolt and Meyers, *Plain Diversity*.

17. I describe Old Order Amish life in what might be called its traditional form—that is, in the agrarian form that it took during much of the last century or so and that continues for many Amish today. I focus on this traditional form because that is the mode of Amish life that is featured in Amish Country tourism. My description depends relies heavily upon Kraybill's scholarship, especially in *Riddle of Amish Culture*. It also makes use of my observations of Old Order Amish in Ohio. For in-depth descriptions of the diversity of Amish life and the complex interaction of the Amish with modern culture, see Kraybill, *Riddle of Amish Culture*; Kraybill and Olshan, *The Amish Struggle with Modernity*; Nolt and Meyers, *Plain Diversity*; Hurst and McConnell, *Amish Paradox*; Hostetler, *Amish Society*; and Nolt, "Who Are the Real Amish?"

18. For a description and explanation of the process by which the Amish make decisions about whether to incorporate or reject a technology, see Kraybill, "War against Progress."

19. Kraybill, *Riddle of Amish Culture*, 13.

20. Ibid., 10–17.

21. Ibid., 88.

22. Ibid., 162–177. For a lengthier treatment of this controversy, see Meyers, "Education and Schooling," 87–106. For additional scholarly essays on a range of issues over which the Amish and the state negotiated, see Kraybill, *Amish and the State*.

23. For a scholarly treatment of Old Order Amish education in the contemporary context, see Johnson-Weiner, *Train Up a Child*.

24. Female Amish youth do not purchase cars, and they tend to continue wearing Amish clothes through Rumspringa. A powerful documentary film about Rumspringa, titled *Devil's Playground*, is available on DVD. For scholarly commentary on that film, see Eitzen, "Reel Amish." For a book-length, scholarly study of Amish youth, see Stevick, *Growing Up Amish*.

25. For more on Amish courting and marriage practices, see Stevick, *Growing Up Amish*.

26. "The Twelve Largest Amish Settlements (2009)."

27. For a more detailed discussion of excommunication and shunning as currently practiced among the Amish in the Holmes-Wayne settlement, see Hurst and McConnell, *Amish Paradox*.

28. Nolt and Meyers, in *Plain Diversity* (56–58), refer to these visible distinctions as "symbolic separators."

29. Although there is much uniformity in Amish dress, it does vary among Amish groups. For more on the relative uniformity and the subtle differences in Amish dress, see Scott, *Why Do They Dress That Way?* and Kraybill, *Riddle of Amish Culture*, 60–70.

30. The exact look and shape of the prayer covering varies slightly from one settlement to another. In the Lancaster settlement, the covering is stiff but sheer and puffy. It has a heart-like shape when viewed from the back. In the Holmes-Wayne settlement, by contrast, the covering is made of a much thicker and stiffer material and has a round shape when seen from the back.

31. For more on the messages of Amish dress, see Kraybill, *Riddle of Amish Culture*, 57–60.

32. For a scholarly history and analysis of how the Amish negotiated their relationship with the telephone, see Umble, *Holding the Line*.

33. The Amish do ride in automobiles and when going longer distances often hire taxis that serve the Amish. They also ride in buses and trains. They do not fly in airplanes.

34. Kraybill, *Riddle of Amish Culture*, 227–231.

35. Ibid., 70–72.

36. By Dutch they mean *Deitsch*, German, not Dutch as in from Holland. Some Old Order Amish in Indiana speak a Swiss-German dialect.

37. A Pennsylvania German translation of the New Testament (Hershberger and Hershberger, *Es Nei Teshtament*) was published in 1993, and then revised in 2002 with the addition of the Psalms and Proverbs, by a publisher near the Holmes-Wayne settlement. Thus, the dialect now also serves as a language of the Bible.

38. Kraybill, *Riddle of Amish Culture*, 225–228.

39. Nolt and Meyers, *Plain Diversity*, 3; Kraybill, *Riddle of Amish Culture*, 240–241. See Kraybill and Nolt, *Amish Enterprise*, for a full discussion of how the Amish have responded to the move away from farming and the effects it has had on Amish life.

40. Kraybill, *Riddle of Amish Culture*, 243–244.

41. Ibid., 242.

42. In *Riddle of Amish Culture*, Kraybill describes the strategies developed to deal with non-farming work and the Amish reasoning behind them, 244–248.

43. Amish informant at Keim Lumber, April 7, 2010.

44. For the impact of factory work on the Indiana Amish in particular, see Nolt and Meyers, *Plain Diversity*, 87–90.

45. Kraybill, *Riddle of Amish Culture*, 267.

Chapter 2. Tourism in Amish Country

1. Paul Boyer, in "Understanding the Amish," argues that, over the years, the way non-Amish Americans have viewed the Amish has involved both idealization and vilification and has depended on what non-Amish Americans needed at any given moment, be that a romantic fantasy of life back on the farm or a scapegoat for hard times on the farm.

2. For a discussion of smaller Amish tourism locations, see Luthy, "Origin and Growth of Amish Tourism."

3. For these and other statistics concerning the size and growth of the Amish population in the United States, see "Twelve Largest Amish Settlements (2010)." Measured in terms of population rather than numbers of districts, Lancaster County is the largest (29,535) and the Holmes-Wayne settlement is a very close second (29,510).

4. Kraybill, *Riddle of Amish Culture*, 10.

5. The quoted volume of tourists represents significant growth in Amish Country tourism over time, from about 1.5 million in 1963 (Kraybill, *Riddle of Amish Culture*, 240). According to the Pennsylvania Dutch Convention and Visitors Bureau, Amish tourism (in 2007) generated not only $818 million in direct economic impact but nearly $460 million in indirect economic impact. By direct impact is meant "value added (sum of wages, taxes, profit and capital depreciation) of those sectors that interact directly with the visitor." By indirect economic impact is meant "the benefit to suppliers to those direct sectors (e.g., food suppliers to a restaurant)." In addition, travel and tourism generates about $460 million in tax revenues. Pennsylvania Dutch Convention and Visitors Bureau, "Tourism Fact Sheet."

It should be noted that accurate comparison of tourism's economic impact in the three locales is difficult, given that in each instance the numbers are generated by different entities: for Lancaster County, the Pennsylvania Dutch Convention and Visitors Bureau; for Holmes County, the Holmes County Chamber of Commerce; and, for Elkhart County, Certec Inc. See notes 6 and 7.

6. These figures (which are for all tourism, but tourism in Holmes County is largely Amish Country tourism) were obtained from Shasta Mast, executive director of the Holmes County Chamber of Commerce and Visitors Bureau, in telephone conversations with the author, June 10 and August 12, 2009, quoting from *The Economic Impact Report for Travel and Tourism in Holmes County* (2004). The quoted volume of tourism represents significant growth in Amish Country tourism since the

mid-1990s, when about 1 million tourists visited annually (Kreps et al., "Impact of Tourism," 360). In this case, direct economic impact refers to the total travel expenditures of tourists to Holmes County Amish areas annually. The annual economic impact of this tourism on Holmes County includes direct impacts on employment (3,000 jobs) and wages ($46 million) as well as indirect impacts on employment (1,400 jobs) and wages ($32.4 million). The annual direct impact on state taxes is $6.5 million and on local taxes is $3.6 million. The annual indirect impact on state taxes is $5.5 million and on local taxes is $4.1 million.

7. According to a 2007 study of the economic impact of all tourism in Elkhart County, of the 4.2 million annual visitors to the county, 2.6 million were "destination" visitors and 1.6 million were "pass-through" travelers. Of the $358.6 million generated by tourism, $243.9 million were direct expenditures. Tourism generated 5,239 jobs through direct and indirect expenditures. Finally, tourism produced more than $85.7 million in tax revenues, with $31 million going to the state, $16.7 million to local government, and $37.9 million to the federal government. These statistics were given to me by Mike Huber, destination and development manager of the Elkhart Convention and Visitors Bureau, as reported in an unpublished report, *Economic Impact of Elkhart County's Tourism and Travel Industry, 2005 and 2007*, produced by Certec Inc., a consulting firm.

8. Weaver-Zercher, *Amish in American Imagination*, chapter 2.

9. Weaver-Zercher, *Amish in American Imagination*, 67. David Walbert confirms the importance of the school dispute for the development of Amish Country tourism (*Garden Spot*, chapter 2).

10. One novel that appeared was *Rosanna of the Amish*, by Joseph W. Yoder. First published in 1940, the book remains in print today. According to David Luthy, 360,000 copies of the book had been printed by 1994 ("Origin and Growth of Amish Tourism," 116–117).

11. According to Weaver-Zercher, early tourism in Lancaster County had three forms: the guided tour, the self-guided tour, and staged attractions (*Amish in American Imagination*, 93–95).

12. See chapter 3 in Weaver-Zercher, *Amish in American Imagination* for a description of the musical *Plain and Fancy* and a discussion of the ways in which it both provided a positive representation of the Amish to a culture already interested in them and also reassured Americans of their own moral superiority.

13. Luthy, "Origin and Growth of Amish Tourism," 114.

14. *Witness*, released by Paramount, grossed more than $100 million. As David Luthy puts it, "The tremendous impact of this movie on tourism in Lancaster County is difficult to fully measure" ("Origin and Growth of Amish Tourism," 114). For an account of the representation of the Amish in the film, of the controversy surrounding it, and of the role that Mennonite interpreters played in that controversy, see Weaver-Zercher, *Amish in American Imagination*, chapter 5.

15. Luthy, "Origin and Growth of Amish Tourism," 125.

16. Ibid., 127.

17. Because of Lancaster County's proximity to larger metropolitan areas, the visitors to the Lancaster settlement are somewhat more diverse in terms of race and class than those to the midwestern settlements.

18. By "white" I mean non-Hispanic white. Hispanic-American tourists are even more rare, at least in Ohio's Amish Country, than are Asian-American and African-American tourists. In his 2000 survey of 734 subjects, Thomas Meyers found that only 3 percent of tourists to Indiana's Amish Country were non-white (Meyers, "Amish Tourism," 111).

19. In his 2000 survey Thomas Meyers also found that 62 percent of the tourists in Indiana's Amish Country were over the age of fifty ("Amish Tourism," 111).

20. In the Lancaster area, unlike both the Elkhart-LaGrange and Holmes-Wayne settlements, it is more common to see luxury sedans and vehicles made by foreign car makers. This difference likely reflects the national difference in car ownership on the coasts versus within the Midwest. Frank Langfitt argues that "there are two U.S. auto markets. One is Middle America, places like the Great Lakes and the Plains states, where people prefer trucks and SUVs, where GM excels—and where more than half the vehicles on the road come from Detroit. Then there are the coasts. Here, foreign brands like Honda and Toyota can account for up to 70 percent of sales" (Frank Langfitt, "GM Seeks to Overcome Perceptions on the Coasts," NPR: All Things Considered, June 11, 2009, www.npr.org/templates/story/story.php?storyid=105263320.

21. Kreps and Lunsford, "1998 Holmes County."

22. According to Thomas Meyers's study of Amish Country tourism in Indiana, "the majority of the respondents [tourists interviewed] were from the Midwest with 31 percent from Michigan, 30 percent from Indiana and 10 percent from Ohio" ("Amish Tourism," 111).

23. In its first issue of 1970, Time Magazine declared "middle Americans" to be the man/woman of the year for 1969. In the cover story that accompanied the declaration, "middle Americans" were described in detail in all their economic, educational, and attitudinal characteristics. The description remains remarkably accurate today. "Middle Americans," Time Magazine, January 5, 1970, www.time.com/.

24. The first Amish-style restaurant to serve tourists in the Lancaster area was Miller's Dutch Restaurant, which opened in 1931. The first such restaurant to open in the Holmes-Wayne settlement was Der Dutchman of Walnut Creek in 1970. Das Dutchman Essenhaus was the first of this type to open in the Elkhart-LaGrange settlement, in 1971. Luthy, "Origin and Growth of Amish Tourism," 120, 127. A commemorative cookbook with accompanying history of the restaurant, Der Dutchman's Amish Kitchen, is available at all Der Dutchman restaurants.

25. Kraybill, *The Riddle of Amish Culture*, 290–291.

26. Weaver-Zercher, *Amish in American Imagination*, 93–94; Luthy, "Origin and Growth of Amish Tourism," 119.

27. For a history and interpretation of "the first freestanding, paid-admission Amish tourist attraction," the Amish Farm and House in Lancaster County, see Walbert, *Garden Spot*, 84–86.

28. One of the common myths retold in the Lancaster area is that Amish fathers paint their fence gates blue to indicate that they have a daughter available for marriage. This is not so, but the propagation of this myth was likely assisted by the publication of a booklet that featured on its cover an Amish man standing in front of a blue gate. Luthy, "Origin and Growth," 115.

29. For a history and interpretation of how so much misinformation about the Amish has been generated and spread, see Weaver-Zercher, *Amish in American Imagination*, chapter 4.

30. For a history of the fascinating dispute among Holmes County business owners, Mennonite Church leaders, and the cyclorama's artist over the painting that became so contentious as to cause the canvas itself to end up in jail not once but twice, see my essay, Susan Biesecker-Mast, "Behalt."

31. The Beachy Amish are a more change-minded group who, unlike the Old Order and New Order Amish, drive automobiles, though only plain ones. For more information on the variety of Amish groups, see Kraybill, "Plotting Social Change."

32. Scholars of the Amish have noted that "Amish" has become a brand in the United States. See, for instance, Nolt and Meyers, *Plain Diversity*, 1.

33. At the Blue Gate restaurant and its associated stores, tourists may purchase such things as kitchen cabinets, interior décor items, locally made furniture, and inspirational wall hangings. On the second floor of the Blue Gate restaurant, visitors may purchase tickets to attend a show in an auditorium that seats 550 when configured one way and more than a thousand in a different configuration. Performances include gospel music as well as musicals and plays with Christian themes.

34. Photographs displayed prominently in the open staircase within the mall show Amish men at work building the structure. The manner in which their work is framed and photographed in this series of photos suggests an Amish barn raising. For a description and discussion of Amish barn raisings, see Kraybill, *Riddle of Amish Culture*, 142–143, 154–155.

35. Festivals have been a prominent feature of Amish Country tourism for decades. For a history of the early festivals and a discussion of their function, see Weaver-Zercher, *Amish in American Imagination*, chapter 2, and Walbert, *Garden Spot*, chapter 3.

36. Meyers first makes this argument in a 2003 essay, "Amish Tourism." He and Steven Nolt reiterate it in their 2007 book, *Plain Diversity*. In the essay, Meyers

reports that a small portion of his subjects expressed a desire to encounter a more peaceful, tranquil, and therefore—they felt—more deeply American kind of life by visiting Amish Country. By contrast, 85 percent of the tourists interviewed for his study said that their first reason for traveling to Amish Country was to shop ("Amish Tourism," 116). Meyers's argument resonates with the theory of the "post-tourist" developed separately by Jonathan Culler and John Urry. They argue that contemporary tourists no longer seek authenticity but the perfection of the fake, as in Disney World's Main Street or Safari. See Culler, "Semiotics of Tourism," and Urry, *Tourist Gaze*.

37. Meyers, "Amish Tourism," quote on p. 126. Nolt and Meyers, in *Plain Diversity* (94–95) point out that this kind of tourism does serve a purpose for the Amish, which other scholars have also noted, in that it maintains the boundaries between Amish culture and its mainstream counterpart. Thus, it strengthens the sense among the Amish that they are different from the world. It also encourages the Amish to value their more traditional ways even as they face the pressures of an always changing and modernizing world.

38. The gross domestic product in the United States in 2006 was $13.247 trillion and personal consumption expenditures were $9.269 trillion. Using these figures as a guide, personal consumption makes up approximately 70 percent of GDP. *Statistical Abstract of the United States: 2008*, 127th edition, table 645.

39. For a scholarly consideration of shopping as an activity through which human beings nurture relationships and construct identities, see, Miller, *Theory of Shopping*.

40. For MacCannell "modern life" is characteristic of human beings who understand that all is not what it seems. Moderns know that theirs is a mediated world in which reality is represented to them and in which they cannot assume that what they see or what they are told is true. Similarly, moderns know that their true self is not readily accessible to them. This awareness of the opaqueness of culture and the self is important for tourism. According to MacCannell, modern tourists desire access to people who are premodern and, thereby, have a simple, unmediated experience of themselves and the rest of reality. For MacCannell's argument about the importance of studying tourism, see *The Tourist*, 1–16.

41. For more on MacCannell's approach to studying tourism, see my essay, Susan Biesecker, "Heritage versus History," 113–115.

42. Buck, "Boundary Maintenance Revisited," 232.

43. Ibid., 233.

44. Hostetler, *Amish Society*, 317, 321.

45. On more than one occasion Hostetler spoke for the Amish and, more specifically, wrote as if their opinions matched his. For an account of the way in which Hostetler spoke for the Amish in the controversy over the filming of *Witness*, see Weaver-Zercher, *Amish in American Imagination*, chapter 5.

46. Kraybill, *Riddle of Amish Culture*, 289. MacCannell, in *The Tourist*, was the first to theorize the role of front stage and back stage performances.

47. For this and other ways in which tourism strengthens Amish community, see Kraybill, *Riddle of Amish Culture*, 289–293.

48. For Weaver-Zercher's history of the representation of the Amish, see chapters 1 to 3 of *Amish in American Imagination*. For Walbert's history, which is very similar to Weaver-Zercher's, see *Garden Spot*, chapter 2. For Walbert's point on the relationship between popular representations and tourist curiosity, see *Garden Spot*, 84. For Weaver-Zercher's argument on this point, see *Amish in American Imagination*, 67.

49. Although Weaver-Zercher and Walbert do not take as dark a view of the Amish Country tourist as Hostetler does, they do point out certain ironies that most visitors apparently fail to notice. Walbert, for instance, observes that, although tourists make the trip to Lancaster County to encounter the simplicity of rural life, they insist on staying in well-appointed hotels and inns (*Garden Spot*, 92). Similarly, Weaver-Zercher comments that, whereas visitors to Amish Country are drawn there because they want to experience something of the simple life, these same visitors also want to engage in "accumulation, excess, and display" and that the tension between these conflicting desires results, ironically, in the conspicuous consumption of "the simple life" (*Amish in American Imagination*, 84–85). A poignant and humorous look at some of the ironies of Amish Country tourism is presented in the 1987 documentary film *The Amish and Us*, which critiques the Amish Country tourism industry and how it is endangering the rural life of the Amish in Lancaster County.

50. Walbert, *Garden Spot*, Epilogue.

51. Ibid., 68, 100.

52. Weaver-Zercher argues, for instance, that Americans enjoyed the musical *Plain and Fancy* in large measure because it depicted a peaceful alternative to their fearful experience of the Cold War (*Amish in American Imagination*, 109).

53. Weaver-Zercher, *Amish in American Imagination*, 93.

54. For an analysis of the news, publication, and entertainment media that takes into account both the advantages that large media outlets have in shaping the way that Americans understand their world and the often underappreciated ways in which marginal voices contest those media constructions, see Fiske, *Media Matters*.

55. In Umble and Weaver-Zercher's edited volume, *The Amish and the Media*, scholars attend to the ways the Amish have endeavored through print publications to shape how others understand them.

56. This theoretical point, that no system of signification can ever fully fix the meaning of a signifier, is now widely accepted by theorists and critics who work in literature, rhetoric and composition, communication, social history, social theory,

and other fields. Arguably the two most important theorists of this view are Jacques Derrida and Michel Foucault. See, for instance, Derrida, *Of Grammatology* and Foucault, *Archaeology of Knowledge*. For an accessible introduction to Derrida's theory, see Caputo, *Deconstruction in a Nutshell*.

57. For an analysis of tourism in Mount Hope that compares it to more popular tourist destinations, see my essay, Susan Biesecker, "Heritage versus History."

Chapter 3. Time and Gender in Walnut Creek

Epigraph. Lehman's Hardware, which has its main store in Kidron, Ohio, and a smaller store in Mt. Hope, sells nonelectric appliances, like refrigerators, stoves, and washing machines, as well as housewares, hardware, and gas lamps, especially to the Amish. In 1999, Lehman's Hardware gained national media attention as people around the world stocked up on generators and other nonelectrical supplies from Lehman's in case public power supplies were affected by electronic problems at the turn of the century.

1. A restaurant has been in operation at Der Dutchman's location since 1960. In 1969 Emanuel Mullet, Robert Miller, and Dan Lehman purchased Dutchman's Restaurant. Later, they transferred ownership to the Dutch Corporation, which over time came to own numerous restaurants, gift shops, and inns not only in Holmes County but also in Bellefontaine, Ohio; Plain City, Ohio; and Sarasota, Florida. Der Dutchman was expanded or remodeled numerous times between 1972 and 1998. These changes included expansions of the kitchen, dining, and banquet areas as well as additions of a bakery and gift shop. For a brief history of Der Dutchman restaurant, see Der Dutchman, *Der Dutchman's Cooking*, v–viii. See also, Dutchman Hospitality, "About the Company," at www.dhgroup.com.

2. Originally, Carlisle Gifts was named Carlisle House Gifts and Carlisle Inn was named Carlisle Village Inn.

3. During the peak of the season, the restaurant serves from thirty-five hundred to four thousand customers on a Saturday (office manager of Der Dutchman phone interview by author, January 18, 2005).

4. Dutchman Hospitality, "About the Company," www.dhgroup.com.

5. Additional restaurants and inns also serve visitors in Walnut Creek. Rebecca's Bistro features light meals and gourmet coffee, and The Inn at Walnut Creek has twenty-one rooms. The Inn at Walnut Creek is full throughout the week during the month of October and every weekend from Memorial Day to the end of October (front desk employee at the inn, phone interview by author, June 24, 2008).

6. Installation of a traffic light at the intersection of Routes 39 and 515 in the spring of 2003 testifies to the growth in traffic into and out of Walnut Creek.

7. The cemetery was initially set aside as the final resting place for Jonas Stutz-

man, the first white settler to the area, who happened to be Amish. A portion of this cemetery was razed in 1964 to accommodate the construction of the SR 39 by-pass around Walnut Creek. From an infrastructural perspective, that change made it possible for Walnut Creek to be developed into a quaint town. Unfortunately, in the course of construction, Stutzman's remains were scattered. Now a headstone in a nearby cemetery marks an empty grave as his. Stahura, *Holmes County, Ohio,* 19.

8. There are other Amish Country tourist businesses on the outskirts of Walnut Creek, such as Walnut Creek Cheese (a large complex on SR 39 just east of Walnut Creek in which kitchen ware, cookbooks, bulk foods, preserves, meat, cheese, etc. are sold and in which some of these food items are made), Hillcrest Orchard (an Amish-owned apple orchard located about a mile north of Walnut Creek on TR 444), Walnut Creek Furniture (a large store on SR 39 just west of Walnut Creek which sells Amish-made solid-wood furniture along with upholstered furniture from national manufacturers), and Schrock's of Walnut Creek (also located on SR 39 just west of Walnut Creek, where custom cabinets, grandfather clocks, and Mission-style furniture are made by the Amish and sold). Although these businesses are major tourist attractions worthy of study, I have focused this study on the centers of each of three main Amish tourist towns.

9. For many years, the Farmer's Wife was located in the house that the gallery now inhabits. Owned by what was then the Dutch Corporation, the Farmer's Wife was a small gift shop that sold lace tablecloths, garden decorations, and other decorating items that varied by season.

10. McAlester and McAlester, *Field Guide,* 263–268.

11. Of course, the Dutch Corporation, which then owned several key enterprises, exercised a great deal of influence over the Victorian look of the town, as it built, renovated, and expanded its properties.

12. As Stephen Scott points out, many Amish houses are actually characterized by an asymmetry that results from multiple additions having been made over time with seemingly little concern for exterior appearance. This ad hoc asymmetry is different from the planned asymmetry of the themed buildings of Walnut Creek. The asymmetry of Walnut Creek shops and inns is designed to echo the asymmetry that was an element of the ornate style of the Victorian era. For a more detailed discussion of the architecture of Amish houses in Pennsylvania, Ohio, and Indiana, see Scott, *Amish Houses and Barns.*

13. Some Amish (especially those working in the construction of non-Amish houses) have started to adopt the building styles of their neighbors. Scott, *Amish Houses and Barns,* 8–9.

14. Interior décor and exterior details of Amish houses are often regulated by the Ordnung, the set of standards used in a given Amish church district; styles thus vary to some extent. For more on variations in the Ordnung, see Nolt and Meyers, *Plain Diversity,* 38–53.

15. Walnut Creek is not Disney World. Disney World is famous for creating illusions that are designed to resist as much as possible the intrusion of the real world. A revealing discussion of the lengths to which the Disney Corporation goes to protect these illusions can be found in Kuenz, "Working at the Rat."

16. A few especially notable histories of America in the late nineteenth and early twentieth centuries that discuss the cultural transformations of the time are Dawley, *Struggles for Justice*; Lears, *Rebirth of a Nation*; Painter, *Standing at Armageddon*; Schlereth, *Victorian America*; Trachtenberg, *Incorporation of America*; and Wiebe, *Search for Order*.

17. Regarding the dramatic changes in farming, Schlereth argues that between 1870 and 1920 "mechanization, 'cash-crop' farming, and stock trading in commodities entangled independent, local farmers in an international network of storing, shipping, and selling" (*Victorian America*, 45). Importantly, as Lears contends, all this change had profound effects on Americans as they sought new meaning in a rapidly transforming world: "As daily life became more subject to the systematic demands of the modern corporation, the quest for revitalization became a search for release from the predictable rhythms of the everyday" (*Rebirth of a Nation*, 1). Indeed, as Wiebe convincingly argues, these changes transformed not only economic and political systems but also the most basic organization of life: "America during the nineteenth century was a society of island communities . . . Already by the 1870s the autonomy of the community was badly eroded . . . the outlines of an alternative system rather quickly took shape early in the twentieth century. By contrast to the personal, informal ways of the community, the new scheme was derived from the regulative, hierarchical needs of urban-industrial life. Through rules with impersonal sanctions, it sought continuity and predictability in a world of endless change. It assigned far greater power to government . . . and it encouraged the centralization of authority" (*Search for Order*, xiii–xiv). For more on these profound economic changes, see Lears, *Rebirth of a Nation*, chapter 4, and Trachtenberg, *Incorporation of America*, 38–69.

18. For more on the women's movements at this time, see Dawley, *Struggles for Justice*, 77–85, and Painter, *Standing at Armageddon*, 36–52. For a history of the broader changes women experienced during this time, see Dawley, 85–97. For histories of the United States' shift to an imperial power, see Lears, *Rebirth of a Nation*, chapter 7, and Painter, *Standing at Armageddon*, 141–169.

19. One prominent voice in this debate arguing that Americans are working more is Juliet Schorr (*Overspent American*). An argument that Americans actually had more free time in the 1990s than in the 1960s is found in Robinson and Godbey, *Time for Life*.

20. Robinson and Godbey, *Time for Life*, 34.

21. Ibid., 38–39.

22. David Walbert presents an alternative reading of the meaning of food in

Amish Country tourism, emphasizing its connection to rural life (*Garden Spot*, chapter 4).

23. For an introduction to at least one prominent part of the slow food movement (which is dedicated to biodiversity, taste education, and slowing down the pace of life) and a description of its mission and its realization in a gastronomic university, grassroots organizational structure, and many conferences and festivals, visit the home page of Slow Food USA at www.slowfoodusa.org.

24. Vicki VanNatta, marketing manager for Dutch Hospitality Group (corporate owner of Der Dutchman of Walnut Creek), interview with author, June 22, 2011. The description that follows is based on that interview.

25. Der Dutchman is not a participant in the slow food movement. However, the moniker "slow food" seems appropriate here, since the story of food being told by Der Dutchman is about experiencing a slower pace in the manner of food preparation and consumption. Many smaller eating establishments do meet the criteria of the movement. For instance, at Mrs. Yoder's Kitchen in Mt. Hope, much of the food is purchased from a produce auction that sells food grown locally on Amish farms. Gloria Yoder, owner of Mrs. Yoder's Kitchen, interview with author, January 3, 2005.

26. There is some indication that the management of Carlisle Gifts is moving away from tea sets as a retail emphasis. Overall, however, the sorts of merchandise on sale at Carlisle Gifts have remained fairly constant.

27. I am using the common term "buggy" although, as Kraybill points out, the vehicle I am referring to is more precisely and accurately referred to as a carriage. Kraybill, *Riddle of Amish Culture*, 74–76.

28. Kraybill, *Riddle of Amish Culture*, 72.

29. Non-Amish Americans' equation of slowness of life with simplicity is inaccurate. Amish life in contemporary America is quite complex.

30. According to US Department of Labor statistics, women "held the majority of nonfarm payroll jobs in January [2010]. They also did so in February, March, November and December of last year [2009]." Catherine Rampell, "Women Now a Majority in American Workplace," *New York Times*, February 5, 2010 (www.nytimes.com). For a discussion of the significance and implications of this historic change, see Hannah Rosin, "End of Men" *Atlantic Monthly*, July–August 2010.

31. According to the US Department of Labor, 63 percent of married-couple families in 1995 and again in 2001 included two employed parents (US Department of Labor: Bureau of Labor Statistics, "Employment Characteristics of Families: 1996," and "Employment Characteristics of Families in 2002"). Although the titles of these two reports refer to 1996 and 2002, respectively, they each include all of the employment data from the previous year (1995 and 2001).

32. Washington Post, Kaiser Foundation, and Harvard University, "Gender

Poll," *Washington Post*, March 26, 1998, www.washingtonpost.com/. This survey was based on random telephone interviews with 1,202 US adults.

33. Judith Warner (journalist, former columnist for the *New York Times*, and author of numerous articles and books on women's issues and American culture) reports that men who are married to women who have turned to full-time homemaking and childrearing feel good about the fact that their children are receiving the focused care of their mothers but regret the loss of income. Judith Warner, "Guess Who's Left Holding the Briefcase? (It's Not Mom.)," *New York Times*, June 20, 2004, www.nytimes.com/.

34. Space and gender have been intertwined for over three centuries in such a way as to provide what Barbara Biesecker has called a "grid of intelligibility" for understanding gender roles. For Biesecker, a grid of intelligibility is a relatively organized weave of conceptual lines that make sense of the world by associating certain terms and disassociating others. Resistance occurs when that weave or that grid is disrupted such that old lines of making sense tangle and potentially new lines emerge. See Barbara Biesecker, "Michel Foucault."

35. Satterthwaite, *Going Shopping*, 134.

36. Of course, department stores are not revolutionary spaces in which woman and man regularly undergo radical transformation. However, as spaces in which the distinction between private and public are blurred, there is possibility now and again for disruptions to conventional understandings.

37. The small front dining room was the only dining area in the original restaurant. Vicki VanNatta, marketing manager for Dutch Hospitality Group (corporate owner of Der Dutchman of Walnut Creek), interview with author, June 22, 2011.

38. As a *New York Times* article reported, given the kind of physical labor that both men and women among the Amish do, they do not have to worry about obesity despite their high-fat, high-calorie diet. Eric Nagourney, "Among Amish, Work Is Workout," *New York Times*, January 13, 2004, sec. 1.

39. Vicki VanNatta, marketing manager for Dutch Hospitality Group (corporate owner of Der Dutchman of Walnut Creek), interview with author, June 22, 2011. According to Ms. VanNatta, the one man who currently works in the kitchen, and has done so for over a decade, is the only one who has ever worked there.

40. Gender as referred to here is a social category, not a biological one, since a female may exhibit one or more masculine traits, just as a male may exhibit one or more feminine characteristics.

41. Daniel Miller argues that in general women shop on behalf of others first and only after having done so do they indulge in purchasing a "treat" for themselves. Read this way, the section in Carlisle Gifts that is dedicated to scented creams, soaps, and lotions may be seen as women's invitation to indulgence amidst a

broader shopping experience undertaken on behalf of the family. See Miller, *Theory of Shopping*, 40–49.

42. Kraybill, *Riddle of Amish Culture*, 272–276.

43. Ibid., 272–280.

44. Susan Page, "Bush's Disapproval Rating Worst of Any President in 70 Years," *USA Today*, April 22, 2008, www.usatoday.com. According to this article, Bush's approval rating had not reached 50 percent since May 2005 and never made it above 40 percent after September 2006.

45. Floyd Norris, "Off the Charts: A Rare Case of Confident Consumers Disapproving of a President," *New York Times*, June 9, 2007, www.nytimes.com.

46. "Poll Finds New US Pessimism about Iraq War," *Toronto Star*, December 10, 2006, www.thestar.com/.

47. Susan Page, "Opposition to Iraq War is divided after 5 years," *USA Today*, March 13, 2008, www.usatoday.com/.

48. Susan Page, "Many in Global Poll See Pollution as Biggest Threat," *USA Today*, June 28, 2007, www.usatoday.com/. The original report of the survey can be found at "Global Unease with Major World Powers and Leaders," *Pew Global Attitudes Project*, June 27, 2007, http://pewresearch.org.

49. Thomas Kinkade, *Thomas Kinkade: Painter of Light*, Limited Edition Comprehensive Catalog (Morgan Hill, CA: Media Arts Group, 2003), 39.

50. This rhetoric is consistent with that of Amish and Mennonites in earlier periods of patriotism and war. During World War II, for instance, Amish and Mennonites conveyed their appreciation for the nation through alternative public service even as they refused military service. Their message was that although they could not fight or serve in a military capacity for the war, they were loyal to their country. For a history of Mennonites' relationship to conscription especially during World War II, see Bush, *Two Kingdoms, Two Loyalties*. See also Hershberger, *Mennonite Church*.

51. In the summer of 1999, for instance, the global economy seemed to benefit the US worker, insofar as the jobless rate remained below 5 percent for two years. As one *Washington Times* editorial put it, the continuing increase in jobs "confirms that the rising tide continues to lift more and more boats." "Rational Exuberance," editorial, *Washington Times*, July 6, 1999, www.washingtontimes.com/.

52. An April 2005 *New York Times* editorial, for instance, lamented the fact that job creation had been slowing for the previous six months and wages had been stagnant or falling for a year. Reports such as these appeared to confirm the theory that a global economy is bad for US workers. "Ungainful Employment," editorial, *New York Times*, April 4, 2005, www.nytimes.com/. Interestingly, back in 1999 when the economy appeared to be booming in all sectors within the context of the global economy, the US unemployment rate was low at just 4.1 percent. Unfortunately

for middle Americans, however, the demand for US workers did not translate into higher wages. Even as the jobless rate in the US was at a thirty-year low, wages for workers below the rank of supervisor increased only one cent per hour during the previous month. Louis Uchitelle, "Jobless Rate Drops to 4.1% as Wages Rise by 1 Cent an Hour," *New York Times*, November 6, 1999, www.nytimes.com/.

53. By 2006, middle-American ambivalence was showing up in newspaper reports. In April of that year, one *New York Times* article reported apparent contradictions both in the economy and in the experiences of American consumers. The automobile industry was in trouble, gas prices were on the rise as were mortgage rates, the housing market was starting to slip, and workers' wages were not keeping up with inflation. Still, the US economy continued to grow at a robust 5 percent, and the number of jobs was increasing fast, even in construction, despite rising interest rates. As to the role of the global economy in all this, the wisdom at that time was that although the US economy had some serious problems, the global economy and its demand for US exports were keeping the US economy strong. Interestingly, in that same article it was reported that, according to a CBS poll, while 55 percent of Americans rated the economy as good, 66 percent said the country was on the wrong track. David Leonhardt and Vikas Bajaj, "U.S. Economy Is Still Growing at Rapid Pace," *New York Times*, April 28, 2006, www.nytimes.com/.

54. As the first decade of the twenty-first century came to a close, the US economy experienced the deepest economic downturn since the Great Depression. That downturn was strongly related to the global economy. Thus, the ambivalence and even anxiety of middle Americans about the global economy and its relationship to the US economy during the 1990s and early years of the current century, despite reassuring popular commentary, were reasonable.

55. About a quarter of a mile down State Route 39, east toward Sugarcreek, the tourist will come upon Walnut Creek Cheese's new home. This miniature "village" (as it is called in their promotional materials) includes similar visual access to laboring Amish women. Through an opening over which hangs a sign that reads "Walnut Creek Kitchen Viewing Gallery," tourists may watch Amish women making food products to be sold in the store.

56. This view of Amish men making solid wood cabinets and grandfather clocks is available from the showroom of Schrock's of Walnut Creek, a custom cabinetmaking business.

57. Continuing weakness in the US economy may challenge the plausibility of Walnut Creek's visual rhetoric. Business owners report that tourist traffic decreased in the latter years of the first decade of the twenty-first century but then improved. Time will tell if an economic upturn will return Amish tourism to its previous levels or if the visual rhetoric of tourism will need to change in response to larger economic trends.

58. By narratives I mean the stories or myths that Walnut Creek's visual rhetoric tells about time, gender, and nation that may be true or false but that seem to promise a better future for middle Americans.

59. Kinkade, *Thomas Kinkade: Painter of Light*, 38–39.

Chapter 4. Technology and Innocence in Berlin

1. German Village, a twenty-nine-thousand-square-foot grocery, dry goods, and hardware store that opened in 1973 and had served a large Amish clientele, burned to the ground in 2003. Within a year, it was rebuilt in that same location.

2. According to the study, Berlin had the heaviest traffic of all the tourist towns in Holmes County. Kreps and Lunsford, "1998 Holmes County Traffic Count." The results of this survey were made available to me by the Holmes County Chamber of Commerce, located in Millersburg. The survey has not been repeated, but similar traffic densities continue to be seen in Berlin on the weekends during summer and autumn.

3. The data on the number of vehicles other than cars comes from Kreps and Lunsford, "1998 Holmes Country Traffic Count." The population for Berlin comes from "Berlin, Ohio Census Data and Community Profile," www.americantowns.com/oh/berlin-information#data.

4. The farm has been under Schrock's management since 1988. Joanne Hershberger, interview with author, June 30, 2008.

5. Schrock's Amish Farm offers tours of two Amish houses (a main house, where a mother and father and children would live, and a daudy house, which would be occupied by the grandmother and grandfather who had lived in the main house), buggy rides, and farm animals available for petting. More a village than a farm, it also includes a quilt shop, woodcrafts shop, pottery shop, a large Christmas shop, an antique mall, a craft mall, and a diner. Across a large parking lot from all of these attractions stands a false-front building that is home to even more shops.

6. Originally, the building housing the Village Gift Barn was a dairy barn owned by Eli Yoder, an Amish farmer. In 1988 it was transformed into a shop by John Yoder, Eli's son, and Steve Schlabach (husband of its current owner) and named Berlin Country Market. The building was again renovated and in June of 2000 opened as Berlin Village Gift Barn. It was significantly expanded and the exterior was updated in 2006. The establishment is now owned by Ruth Schlabach. Information from Ruth Schlabach, e-mail communication with author, July 8, 2008.

7. Country Gatherings moved into its current location from the lower level of Berlin Village Gift Barn in 2004. The building in which it is currently located was built to house a farmers' market before it was remodeled to be a shop. It was again remodeled in 2007. Ruth Schlabach, e-mail communication with author, July 8, 2008.

8. Berlin Sesquicentennial Historical Committee, *Sesquicentennial History*, 93.

9. So thorough was this renovation that it was not until Raymond Hagood, the owner of the shop currently housed in the building, pointed out a hand-hewn oak load-bearing beam inside the store that I recognized the true age of the structure. Raymond Hagood, interview with author, August 21, 2004.

10. A crenelated tower imitates the look of a castle tower and is not characteristic of frontier forts in the American West.

11. Stuart Hall offers an especially accessible and clear explanation of the notion of race as a floating signifier in a lecture that was video recorded by Sut Jhally. See, Hall, *Race*. In this lecture, Hall identifies those discourses of truth (or those understood by a culture to have the status of truth) which support ideas that a single physical difference can distinguish an entire race. The discourses of truth that he talks about are philosophy, theology, and science. For a sustained, theoretical discussion of the production and workings of such discourses of truth, see Foucault, *Archaeology of Knowledge*. For a reading of a discourse of truth about sexuality, see Foucault, *History of Sexuality*. Elsewhere, Hall talks about race as a signifer that changes over time, for instance, in Stuart Hall, "Old and New Identities, Old and New Ethnicities."

12. White, "Frederick Jackson Turner," 9.

13. For an example of a contemporary reiteration of Turner's story, see "Frontier Life in U.S. History," *Encylopedia Americana*, 2003.

14. I put the word "Indian" in quotation marks here because I am summarizing White's argument, and that is the term he uses.

15. White, "Frederick Jackson Turner," 9. For a history of the uses of these two stories about the frontier in the political rhetorics of Franklin Delano Roosevelt, John F. Kennedy, Ronald Reagan, and Michael Dukakis, as well as in popular discourses about technology, see Limerick, "Adventures of the Frontier." These two dominant stories of the frontier have, of course, been contested, as scholars and others have attempted to rewrite the story of the frontier from the perspective of Indians. Not surprisingly, given the place the frontier has in American identity, that effort to rewrite the story has been strongly resisted.

16. Much of the merchandise described here is manufactured by P. Graham Dunn. This merchandise also appears in the P. Graham Dunn gallery in Walnut Creek.

17. White excellently describes this story and its animating dynamic of regression and regeneration. White, "Frederick Jackson Turner," 15.

18. I am extending White's argument here, but in ways I think he would find in keeping with his argument.

19. Lowell C. Rose et al., "A Report of the Second Survey Conducted by the Gallup Organization for the International Technology Education Association," In-

ternational Technology Education Association, www.iteaconnect.org/. An identical survey had been conducted in 2001 with similar results. In another national poll, one conducted by Virginia Commonwealth University in 2003, which was a repeat of a study conducted in 2001 and 2002, Americans overwhelmingly opposed certain technologies, for instance, human cloning (even if they were well informed about it), and were not convinced that scientists knew enough to make such technologies safe. The survey results indicate that 84 percent of Americans opposed human cloning and 77 percent of Americans said that scientists did not know enough about it to make it safe even in the treatment of disease. Cary Funk, "VCU Life Sciences Survey," www.vcu.edu/.

20. For sample articles on each of these topics (all published in the *New York Times* and posted on www.nytimes.com), see "Technology Is Heightening Job Worries, Greenspan Says," July 12, 2000; Marci Alboher Nusbaum, "Executive Life: New Kind of Snooping Arrives at the Office," July 13, 2003; Neil A. Lewis, "Rebels in Black Robes Recoil at Surveillance of Computers," August 8, 2001; John Schwartz, "Always at Work and Anxious: Employees' Health Suffering," September 5, 2004; Matt Richtell, "Hooked on Gadgets and Paying a Mental Price," June 7, 2010; Avi Salzman, "On Campus, a Security Card and More," October 5, 2003; Amy Harmon, "Privacy on Hold: Smile, You're on Candid Cellphone Camera," October 12, 2003; John Markoff and Ken Conley, "*Ay Robot*: Scientists Worry That Machines May Outsmart Man," July 26, 2009.

21. Although Jacques Ellul's book, *The Technological Society*, was first published in 1964, his insights into the character of the relationship between human beings and technology remain relevant today and continue to be widely referenced in scholarly work.

22. Ellul calls this feature of technology "automatism." Ellul, *Technological Society*, 133.

23. Edward Tenner details some of the unintended effects of technology in his many articles and several books on the subject. See especially Tenner, *Why Things Bite Back*. While Tenner recognizes the power of technology to shape human life, as Ellul does, he also wants to take into account the improvisational character of people's relationship to technology by which people adapt to technology and also change it. See Tenner, *Our Own Devices*.

24. Ellul is not a technological determinist. Things could be otherwise, he says, but to make them so would require a radical transformation in the nature of technology, altering today's technologies' goal to forever increase their own efficiency. For a collection of essays designed to empower individuals to disrupt the controlling character of technology, see Katz, Light, and Thompson, *Controlling Technology*.

25. Philosopher of society and culture, Albert Borgmann, makes a similar argument specifically about people's relationship to information technology when he

writes: "Yet with all these gains [from information technology] we sometimes feel like the sorcerer's apprentice, unable to contain the powers we have summoned and afraid of drowning in the flood we have loosed. And much like the apprentice we are unable to find the words that would restore calm and order, misspeaking ourselves when we try to get control of our situation." Borgmann, *Holding on to Reality*, 4. In his best-selling book, *The Shallows: What the Internet Is Doing to Our Brains*, Nicholas Carr argues even more strongly than Borgmann not just that we may be losing control over technology but that technology (and especially the Internet) is significantly altering our brain physiology and function, so that we are having increasing difficulty reading deeply. As our brains adjust to the demands of the Internet's constant interruptions, they are less able to pay attention to any one thing for very long.

26. Many of these items are actually hand made, but not in the manner potential purchasers may be imagining. The quilts from China, for instance, are often hand stitched, but the fact that they are hand stitched in China conveys a message of underpaid factory labor rather than craftsmanship. Notably, these quilts from China are priced much lower than the Amish hand-stitched quilts that are also sold in Berlin.

27. The Helping Hands Quilt Shop was started by Alma Mullet when she decided to move her quilting supplies to a building on Berlin's Main Street that her husband, Emanuel Mullet (mentioned in chapter 3 as one of the original owners of Der Dutchman restaurant), no longer needed. Almost immediately thereafter, many Amish and Mennonite women joined her. Within months she was selling quilts made by herself and her friends for one hundred dollars each. The shop used 10 percent of each sale to help someone in need. Since that modest beginning, Helping Hands has purchased an x-ray machine for a mission hospital in India, built a local counseling facility, and served as a longtime supporter of Mennonite Central Committee, a relief organization supported by various Mennonite denominations. More information on Alma Mullet's life and her quilt shop is recorded in "The Rich Tapestry of Alma Mullet's Life," *Ohio Amish Country Guide* New Philadelphia, OH: Kirkpatrick Advertising, 2008), 28–29.

28. Any arts and crafts supplies store sells technology over which the consumer can imagine having control. The point here is that in the context of Berlin's frontier theme, this relationship with technology means something more, as it connects with a story (made plausible by the Amish in the area) about how human society is regenerated through engagement with the elements of a primitive life.

29. It is important to remember that Amish can be seen using modern technology like forklifts (at a lumberyard), computers (in a publishing house), and precision power tools (in cabinet-making shops). For recent scholarship on the use of technology by the Amish in the Holmes-Wayne settlement, see Hurst and McConnell, *Amish Paradox*.

30. For more on Amish use of nonelectric technology, see Scott and Pellman, *Living without Electricity*.

31. The 1950s popular culture theme is no more seamless than the Western frontier theme. Alongside references to Marilyn Monroe, James Dean, and Lucille Ball there are also references to *The Wizard of Oz* (which was released in 1939) and Barney Fife, a character in the Andy Griffith Show (which first aired in 1960).

32. Perry, *Ohio*, 147–149.

Chapter 5. Ethnicity and Performance in Sugarcreek

1. The Belden Brick Company is one materials producer that continues to function in Sugarcreek. It uses the Ohio Central Railroad, which still runs through the town, for shipping some of its bricks. Leslie A. Kaser, curator and director of the Alpine Hills Museum in Sugarcreek, interview with author, June 20, 2005.

2. This brief account of the emergence and development of tourism in Sugarcreek depends on George R. Smith's history of Sugarcreek and my interview with Leslie Kaser (see n. 1). Smith, *History of Sugarcreek*, 91.

3. Smith, *History of Sugarcreek*, 102. The competition from Wisconsin cheesemakers was made known to me by Leslie Kaser (see n. 1).

4. Smith, *History of Sugarcreek*, 103.

5. Hostetler, "Why Is Everybody Interested?" 190–191. According to George Smith, "upwards of 100,000 people jam their way into Sugarcreek each year to enjoy this two-day fun fest." Smith, *History of Sugarcreek*, 104. Smith's counts are not dated in his text but, given that his history was published in 1977, likely refer to festivals held in the 1960s and/or 1970s.

6. Leslie A. Kaser, interview with author, June 9, 2005.

7. Smith, *History of Sugarcreek*, 84.

8. Other businesses that were remodeled in this way include the Swiss Hat Restaurant (1971), Goshen Dairy store (1972), Edelwiess Inn (1974), Sunoco station (1974), Shell service station (mid-1970s), and Village Tire and Service (some time between 1973 and 1975). Smith, *History of Sugarcreek*, 72–94.

9. Ibid.

10. Ann Swinderman, "Ohio Central Departure to Impact Area Economy," *The Budget*, May 28, 2003.

11. Ibid.

12. Bill Strawn, press release, 2004. This announcement remained posted on the train depot in Sugarcreek for several years after the train's final departure from Sugarcreek.

13. These observations were made on Monday, June 13, 2005. I visited all three towns that day. All observations were made during business hours (in the morn-

ing and afternoon). I counted people out of doors who were moving into and out of shops, browsing merchandise, and carrying shopping bags. People in plain dress (Amish or conservative Mennonite) were not counted, as I assumed they were not tourists. I repeated my observations on June 13, 2008, and found the same differences in the numbers of people moving about these three towns.

14. The five vacant businesses on Main Street in Sugarcreek were the Goshen Dairy (which sold ice cream cones to tourists), the Edelweiss Inn (a restaurant and tavern that featured imported beer), Changing Seasons (a gift shop that specialized in electronic pictures), a building at the corner of Broadway and Main that once housed a gas and service station, and Stardust Café (a restaurant built just a year or so earlier in a folk Victorian style). All of the buildings that were vacant in 2005 were not so in 2008. However, most of the businesses that have opened in Sugarcreek since 2005 do not target tourists. They are the administrative offices for the Ohio Central Railroad (which is located in the building that used to be home to Goshen Dairy), two discount stores (in stores that were once gift shops), a catering service, and a Christian educational and training organization for business leaders (the last two in the building that housed the Stardust Café). Only two buildings in Sugarcreek that were vacant in 2005 have since been reoccupied by businesses aimed at tourists: Edelweiss Inn and the Alphorn.

15. *The Budget* has served Sugarcreek, as well as Amish and Mennonite communities throughout the United States and beyond, since 1890. For a history of *The Budget*, see Smith, *History of Sugarcreek*. Smith was publisher of *The Budget* for many years.

16. According to Rathbun's assessment in 2005, the whole area of Holmes, Wayne, and Tuscarawas counties, including Berlin, Walnut Creek, and Sugarcreek, had seen a slight slowdown in tourism during the previous few years. Keith Rathbun, interview with author, June 13, 2005.

17. Rathbun described a project to revitalize Sugarcreek that was in the works and that involved hiring a consulting firm to design plans for the revitalization. Keith Rathbun, personal interview, June 13, 2005. The effort was also reported in *The Budget*. See, Ann Swinderman, "Cars, Music and Good Times," *The Budget*, June 8, 2005. This effort did not involve altering the Swiss theme of Sugarcreek's Main Street. The project's aim, to improve the appearance of Sugarcreek, suggests that leaders in the community recognized that the presentation of the Swiss theme (the town's visual rhetoric) was important for tourism.

18. The town of Shanesville merged with Sugarcreek in 1968. Smith, *History of Sugarcreek*, 8.

19. Heini's Gourmet Market is owned by Bunker Hill Cheese Company, which also owns Heini's Cheese Chalet, where cheese has been made and sold since 1935. For more information on Heini's Cheese Chalet and the new store in Sugarcreek,

see "Artisan Cheese Produced in Ohio's Amish Country since 1935!" Bunker Hill Cheese Co. Inc., www.heinis.com/.

20. Travelers who, instead of taking Main Street, continue on SR 39 (Dover Road), pass Belden Brick, a long-time manufacturing interest in Sugarcreek. Beyond that they see a McDonalds that has taken on Sugarcreek's Swiss theme, sporting bright yellow decorative cutout boards under the eaves and large exterior murals depicting scenes of Swiss mountains and valleys. As recently as the mid-1990s, employees wore Swiss-styled uniforms and served a "Swiss burger" topped with Swiss cheese.

21. The Swiss chalet style was popularized by landscape architect and horticulturalist A. J. Downing in his book of country house designs, which was first published in 1850. For descriptions of the Swiss chalet style, especially as it has been adapted to US settings, see McAlester, *Field Guide*, 231–233. For Downing's description, see Downing, *Architecture of Country Houses*.

22. The decorative coats of arms are actually symbols reflecting the flags for each area and rendered in the shape of coats of arms, not the localities' actual heraldic shields. The reason for putting them in that shape is unclear. Berne was the origin of several families that immigrated to the Sugar Creek Valley. Aargau apparently was not. At one time, a series of such signs was hung across the false balcony of one of the buildings. It may be that along the way someone picked the symbol of Aargau for other than historical reasons. Patricia Kaser, Information Coordinator for the Alpine Hills Museum, phone interview with author, June 23, 2005.

23. Tom Miller's murals are well known throughout Ohio's Amish Country. A self-taught artist, he painted many murals of Swiss scenes on exterior and interior walls of restaurants, cheese houses, grocery stores, banks, and the like. Many appear in Sugarcreek but they also can be found in Walnut Creek, Bunker Hill, and elsewhere. For more on Miller's work and life, see Bill Mayr, "Mural Majority: Tom Miller Made His Name Creating Scenes in Ohio's Amish Country," *Columbus Dispatch*, July 9, 2006, www.dispatch.com/.

24. The Amish mannequin in the shopping cart always seemed to me an interestingly ironic statement about the relationship between consumer culture and the Amish in Amish Country. In the summer of 2008, the Amish mannequin was seen sitting in a plastic outdoor chair, next to a statue of a howling wolf. Why he was taken out of the shopping cart and put next to a howling wolf remains a puzzle.

25. Again my definition of "white" here does not include Hispanics.

26. One among countless newspaper articles devoted to this demographic shift, its causes, and potential social effects, is Sam Roberts, "New Demographic Racial Gap Emerges," *New York Times*, May 17, 2007, www.nytimes.com. In that article, Roberts reported that in the year between July 1, 2005, and July 1, 2006, the number of Hispanics grew by 3.4 percent. The growth among Asians followed closely

at 3.2 percent. By contrast, the white population increased by only .3 percent. As has also been well documented and reported, this change is due both to higher birth rates among non-white people, especially among Hispanic Americans, and to immigration across the United States' southern border.

27. In this exposition I depend on the work of Lauren Berlant and, in particular, on her argument that white US citizens are in crisis, largely because they have been removed from the position of the iconic citizen (*Queen of America*, 1–24). Another excellent source that provides historical perspective on what "white" has meant over time in the United States and elsewhere is Painter, *History of White People*.

28. According to a January 18, 2002, Associated Press article, *Roots* was seen by as many as 130 million people. Lynn Elber, "Roots Changed the Face of TV: Anniversary Special Looks at Legacy of Seminal Miniseries 25 Years Later," *The (Montreal) Gazette*, January 18, 2002, www.montrealgazette.com.

29. The popularity of such stories continued, for instance, in HBO's hit series, *The Sopranos*. For analyses of *The Sopranos* and its continuity and discontinuity with American ideology, see Simon, *Tony Soprano's America*. See also Lavery, *Reading the Sopranos*.

30. The characterization of festivals that follows depends on Beverly J. Stoeltje's summary of the scholarship on festivals. See Stoelje, "Festival," 161–166.

31. Although community members and visitors primarily participate through watching, most do join in the feast and some participate in the stone-throwing contest and/or dance to the polka music.

32. Stoeltje, "Festival," 161.

33. Manning, "Spectacle," 137.

34. Ibid.

35. Bodnar, *Remaking America*, 15. Bodnar's book contains a complete discussion of this view of commemorative events and their relationship to public.

36. Ibid., 55, 77.

37. Smith, *History of Sugarcreek*, 104.

38. This use of the term "idealized," common in the field of rhetoric, is meant to convey that the version of Swiss culture seen at the festival is an ideal (rather than real) form. It was created in the 1950s in response to a particular set of exigencies at that time and in Sugarcreek. In this sense, though idealized, it is historical, for it was created at a particular moment in time.

39. The history of middle Americans' growing awareness of their loss of normative status is, of course, complex. It is part historical, part sociological, part psychological. For an especially insightful analysis of this shift, see Lauren Berlant, *Queen of America*, Introduction. There she argues that it was with the rise of the Reagan Right that middle Americans began to become convinced of this change in their status.

40. Throughout this section, I make a distinction between Swiss ethnicity and Amish ethnicity. Although many Amish trace their ancestry to Switzerland, their ethnicity is not Swiss in the sense celebrated in Sugarcreek. Thus, even though both groups trace their origins to Switzerland, they do not have the same ethnic roots and, therefore, are not the of same ethnicity.

41. Amish ethnicity goes beyond place or culture of origin to a history, recounted in chapter 1, of persecution as a religious group. So, even if the woman in this picture happened to descend from people who once lived in Switzerland, she would not likely think of herself as Swiss but as a descendant of the Anabaptists who were persecuted for their beliefs in the sixteenth and seventeenth centuries.

Chapter 6. Nostalgia and the Power of Amish Witness

Epigraph. New Order Amish guide, interview with author, April 18, 2009.

1. For a discussion of the hyperreal in tourism, see Urry, *Tourist Gaze*.

2. Kraybill, *Riddle of Amish Culture*, 41.

3. The other photographs included in this book were also taken in such a way (from behind, at a distance, or as the Amish person was looking away) so as not to involve the active participation or awareness of the people being photographed. That said, I confess that as I took these photographs I felt some unease about whether I might be taking advantage of my awareness of the particulars of the rule to get an image that ought not be captured. For a filmmaker's take on the challenges of photographing the Amish, see Eitzen, "Reel Amish."

4. See Urry, *Tourist Gaze*, chapter 7. For classic theorizations of the camera and its power to objectify the subject in its frame, see Barthes, *Camera Lucida*, and Sontag, *On Photography*.

5. To see these quotations in context as well as more on Urry's point about power and photography, see *Tourist Gaze*, 11, 138, and chapter 7.

6. In an essay about Disney World, tourists, and the camera, Karen Klugman, who is a photographer, writes: "With amazing speed and efficiency, Mickey and Minnie processed the passersby. They would size up their subjects, quickly locate the recording device, and strike up a pose." Klugman, "Reality Revisited," 44.

7. In his film *The Amish and Us*, Dirk Eitzen documents that Lancaster County tourists do take pictures of the Amish and sometimes are even intrusive about it. I have not seen such behavior in Ohio, Indiana, or Pennsylvania.

Bibliography

Bibliographical information for sources that do not appear in this list (interviews, newspaper articles, and encyclopedia entries, for example) is provided in the notes.

Barthes, Roland. *Camera Lucida: Reflections on Photography.* Translated by Richard Howard. New York: Hill and Wang, 1981.

———. *Mythologies.* Translated by Annette Lavers. New York: Hill and Wang, 1972.

Berlant, Lauren. *The Queen of America Goes to Washington City: Essays on Sex and Citizenship.* Durham, NC: Duke University Press, 1997.

Berlin Sesquicentennial Historical Committee. *Sesquicentennial History of the Berlin Community: 1816–1966, Berlin, Ohio.* Sugarcreek, OH: Middaugh Printers, 1966.

Biesecker, Barbara. "Michel Foucault and the Question of Rhetoric." *Philosophy and Rhetoric* 25, no. 4 (1992): 351–364.

———. "Remembering World War II: The Rhetoric and Politics of National Commemoration at the Turn of the 21st Century." *Quarterly Journal of Speech* 88, no. 4 (2002): 393–409.

Biesecker, Susan. "Heritage Versus History: Amish Tourism in Two Ohio Towns." In Umble and Weaver-Zercher, *The Amish and the Media,* 111–130.

Biesecker-Mast, Gerald. *Separation and the Sword in Anabaptist Persuasion: Radical Confessional Rhetoric from Schleitheim to Dordrecht.* Telford, PA: Cascadia Publishing, 2006.

Biesecker-Mast, Susan. "Behalt: A Rhetoric of Remembrance and Transformation." *Mennonite Quarterly Review* 73, no. 3 (1999): 601–614.

———. "The Visible Church in a Visual Culture." *Brethren in Christ, History, and Life* 27, no. 3 (2004): 217–253.

Blair, Carole, and Neil Michel. "The AIDS Memorial Quilt and the Contemporary Culture of Public Commemoration." *Rhetoric and Public Affairs* 10, no. 4 (2007): 595–626.

———. "Reproducing Civil Rights Tactics: The Rhetorical Performances of the Civil Rights Memorial." *Rhetoric Society Quarterly* 30, no. 2 (2000): 30–55.

Bodnar, John. *Remaking America: Public Memory, Commemoration, and Patriotism in the Twentieth Century.* Princeton, NJ: Princeton University Press, 1992.

Borgmann, Albert. *Holding on to Reality: The Nature of Information at the Turn of the Millennium.* Chicago, IL: University of Chicago Press, 1999.

Boyer, Paul S. "Understanding the Amish in Twenty-First-Century America." *Mennonite Quarterly Review* 82, no. 3 (2008): 359–376.

Buck, Roy C. "Boundary Maintenance Revisited: Tourist Experience in an Old Order Amish Community." *Rural Sociology* 43, no. 2 (1978): 221–234.

Bush, Perry. *Two Kingdoms, Two Loyalties: Mennonite Pacifism in Modern America.* Baltimore, MD: Johns Hopkins University Press, 1998.

Campbell, Karlyn Kohrs. *The Rhetorical Act.* Belmont, CA: Wadsworth, 1996.

Caputo, John D., ed. *Deconstruction in a Nutshell: A Conversation with Jacques Derrida.* New York: Fordham University Press, 1997.

Carr, Nicholas. *The Shallows: What the Internet Is Doing to Our Brains.* New York: W. W. Norton, 2010.

Ching, Francis D. K. *A Visual Dictionary of Architecture.* New York: Van Nostrand Reinhold, 1995.

Culler, Jonathan. "The Semiotics of Tourism." *American Journal of Semiotics* 1, no. 1–2 (1981): 26–140.

Dawley, Alan. *Struggles for Justice: Social Responsibility and the Liberal State.* Cambridge, MA: Belknap Press of Harvard University Press, 1991.

Der Dutchman. *Der Dutchman's Amish Kitchen Cooking: A Collection of Recipes from Der Dutchman Restaurant, Friends, and Employees.* 30th anniversary ed. Sugarcreek, OH: Carlisle Printing, 2000.

Derrida, Jacques. *Of Grammatology.* Translated by Gayatri Chakravorty Spivak. Baltimore, MD: Johns Hopkins University Press, 1998.

Devil's Playground. Film. Directed by Lucy Walker. Stick Figure Productions, 2001.

Dickinson, Greg, Brian L. Ott, and Eric Aoki. "Memory and Myth at the Buffalo Bill Museum." *Western Journal of Communication* 69, no. 2 (2005): 85–108.

———. "Spaces of Remembering and Forgetting: The Reverent Eye/I at the Plains Indian Museum." *Communication and Critical/Cultural Studies* 3, no. 1 (2006): 27–47.

Downing, A. J. *The Architecture of Country Houses.* New York: Da Capo Press, 1968.

Dyck, Cornelius J. *An Introduction to Mennonite History: A Popular History of the Anabaptists and Mennonites.* Scottdale, PA: Herald Press, 1993.

Eitzen, Dirk. *The Amish and Us.* Film. Directed by Dirk Etizen. Santa Monica, CA: Direct Cinema Limited, 1987.

———. "Reel Amish: The Amish in Documentaries." In Umble and Weaver-Zercher, *The Amish and the Media,* 43–64.

Ellul, Jacques. *The Technological Society.* Translated by John Wilkinson. New York: Vintage Books, 1964.

Fiske, John. *Introduction to Communication Studies.* 2nd ed. New York: Routledge, 1990.

———. *Media Matters: Everyday Culture and Political Change.* Minneapolis: University of Minnesota Press, 1994.

Foucault, Michel. *The Archaeology of Knowledge and the Discourse on Language.* Translated by A. M. Sheridan Smith. New York: Pantheon Books, 1972.

———. *The History of Sexuality: Volume I: An Introduction.* Translated by Robert Hurley. New York: Vintage Books, 1980.

Global Anabaptist Mennonite Encyclopedia Online. www.gameo.org.

Grossman, James R., ed. *The Frontier in American Culture: An Exhibition at the Newberry Library, August 26, 1994–January 7, 1995.* Berkeley: University of California Press, 1994.

Hall, Stuart. "Old and New Identities, Old and New Ethnicities." In *Theories of Race and Racism: A Reader,* edited by Les Black and John Solomos, 144–153. New York: Routledge, 2000.

———. *Race: The Floating Signifier.* Film. Directed by Sut Jhally. North Hampton, MA: Media Education Foundation, 1996.

Hariman, Robert, and John Louis Lucaites. "Performing Civic Identity: The Iconic Photograph of the Flag Raising on Iwo Jima." *Quarterly Journal of Speech* 88, no. 4 (2002): 363–392.

———. "Public Identity and Collective Memory in U.S. Iconic Photography: The Image of 'Accidental Napalm.'" *Critical Studies in Media Communication* 20, no. 1 (2003): 35–66.

Hauerwas, Stanley. *With the Grain of the Universe: The Church's Witness and Natural Theology.* Grand Rapids, MI: Brazos Press, 2001.

Hauser, Gerard A. *Introduction to Rhetorical Theory.* Philadelphia, PA: Harper and Row, 1986.

Hershberger, Guy F. *The Mennonite Church in the Second World War.* Scottdale, PA: Mennonite Publishing House, 1951.

Hershberger, Henry D., and Ruth Hershberger, trans. *Es Nei Teshtament: Mitt di Psaltah un Shpricha.* Rev. ed. South Holland, IL: Bible League, 2002.

Hostetler, John A. *Amish Society.* 4th ed. Baltimore, MD: Johns Hopkins University Press, 1993.

————. "Why Is Everybody Interested in the Pennsylvania Dutch?" (1955). In Weaver-Zercher, *Writing the Amish*, 188–196.

Hurst, Charles E., and David L. McConnell. *An Amish Paradox: Diversity and Change in the World's Largest Amish Community.* Baltimore, MD: Johns Hopkins University Press, 2010.

Jameson, Fredric. *The Political Unconscious: Narrative as Socially Symbolic Act.* Ithaca, NY: Cornell University Press, 1982.

Johnson-Weiner, Karen M. *Train Up a Child: Old Order Amish and Mennonite Schools.* Baltimore, MD: Johns Hopkins University Press, 2007.

Katz, Eric, Andrew Light, and William Thompson, eds. *Controlling Technology: Contemporary Issues.* Amherst, NY: Prometheus Books, 2003.

Klugman, Karen. "Reality Revisited." In Project on Disney, *Inside the Mouse*, 12–33.

Kraybill, Donald B., ed. *The Amish and the State.* 2nd ed. Baltimore, MD: Johns Hopkins University Press, 2003.

————. "Plotting Social Change Across Four Affiliations." In Kraybill and Olshan, *The Amish Struggle with Modernity*, 53–74.

————. *The Riddle of Amish Culture.* Rev. ed. Baltimore, MD: Johns Hopkins University Press, 2001.

————. "War against Progress: Coping with Social Change." In Kraybill and Olshan, *The Amish Struggle with Modernity*, 35–50.

Kraybill, Donald B., and Steven M. Nolt. *Amish Enterprise: From Plows to Profits.* 2nd ed. Baltimore, MD: Johns Hopkins University Press, 2004.

Kraybill, Donald B., Steven M. Nolt, and David L. Weaver-Zercher. *Amish Grace: How Forgiveness Transcended Tragedy.* San Francisco, CA: John Wiley and Sons, 2007.

Kraybill, Donald B., and Marc A. Olshan, eds. *The Amish Struggle with Modernity.* Hanover, NH: New England University Press, 1994.

Kreps, George, and Shirley Lunsford. "1998 Holmes County Traffic Count Survey." 1998.

Kreps, George M., Joseph F. Donnermeyer, Charles Hurst, Robert Blair, and Marty Kreps. "The Impact of Tourism on the Amish Subculture: A Case Study." *Community Development Journal* 32, no. 4 (1997): 354–367.

Kuenz, Jane. "Working at the Rat." In Project on Disney, *Inside the Mouse*, 110–162.

Lapp, John A., and C. Arnold Snyder, eds. *Testing Faith and Tradition: Europe.* Global Mennonite History Series. Intercourse, PA: Good Books, 2006.

Lavery, David, ed. *Reading the Sopranos: Hit TV from HBO.* New York: Palgrave Macmillan, 2006.

Lears, Jackson. *Rebirth of a Nation: The Making of Modern America, 1877–1920.* New York: HarperCollins, 2009.

Limerick, Patricia Nelson. "The Adventures of the Frontier in the Twentieth Century." In Grossman, *The Frontier in American Culture*, 67–95.

Loewen, Harry, and Steven M. Nolt, with Carol Duerksen and Elwood Yoder. *Through Fire and Water: An Overview of Mennonite History*. Scottdale, PA: Herald Press, 1996.

Lucaites, John Louis, Celeste Condit, and Sally Caudhill, eds. *Contemporary Rhetorical Theory: A Reader*. New York: Guilford Press, 1999.

Luthy, David. "The Origin and Growth of Amish Tourism." In Kraybill and Olshan, *The Amish Struggle with Modernity*, 113–129.

MacCannell, Dean. *The Tourist: A New Theory of the Leisure Class*. New York: Schocken Books, 1989.

Manning, Frank E. "Spectacle." In *International Encyclopedia of Communications*, edited by Erik Barnouw et al. New York: Oxford University Press, 1989.

Mast, Gerald J., and J. Denny Weaver. *Defenseless Christianity: Anabaptism for a Nonviolent Church*. Telford, PA: Cascadia Press, 2009.

McAlester, Virgina, and Lee McAlester. *A Field Guide to American Houses*. New York: Alfred A. Knopf, 2002.

Meyers, Thomas J. "Amish Tourism: 'Visiting Shipshewana Is Better than Going to the Mall.'" *Mennonite Quarterly Review* 77, no. 1 (2003): 109–126.

———. "Education and Schooling." In Kraybill, *The Amish and the State*, 87–106.

Miller, Daniel. *A Theory of Shopping*. Ithaca, NY: Cornell University Press, 1998.

Nolt, Steven M. "Who Are the Real Amish?: Rethinking Diversity and Identity among a Separate People." *Mennonite Quarterly Review* 82, no. 3 (2008): 377–394.

Nolt, Steven M., and Thomas J. Meyers. *Plain Diversity: Amish Cultures and Identities*. Baltimore, MD: Johns Hopkins University Press, 2007.

Olson, Lester C., Cara Finnegan, and Diane S. Hope, eds. *Visual Rhetoric: A Reader in Communication and American Culture*. Thousand Oaks, CA: Sage Publications, 2008.

Painter, Nell Irvin. *The History of White People*. New York: W. W. Norton, 2010.

———. *Standing at Armageddon: The United States, 1877–1919*. New York: W. W. Norton, 1987.

Pennsylvania Dutch Convention and Visitors Bureau. "Tourism Fact Sheet," Lancaster County, PA. www.padutchcountry.com/.

Perry, Dick. *Ohio: A Personal Portrait of the 17th State*. Garden City, NY: Doubleday, 1969.

Project on Disney, *Inside the Mouse: Work and Play at Disney World*. Durham, NC: Duke University Press, 1995.

Robinson, John P., and Geoffrey Godbey. *Time for Life: The Surprising Ways Ameri-*

cans Use Their Time. University Park: Pennsylvania State University Press, 1997.

Rosteck, Thomas, ed. *At the Intersection: Cultural Studies and Rhetorical Studies.* New York: Guilford Press, 1999.

Roth, John, ed. and trans. *Letters of the Amish Division: A Sourcebook.* Goshen, IN: Mennonite Historical Society, 1993.

Satterthwaite, Ann. *Going Shopping: Consumer Choices and Community Consequences.* New Haven, CT: Yale University Press, 2001.

Saussure, Ferdinand de. *Course in General Linguistics.* Edited by Charles Bally and Albert Sechehaye in collaboration with Albert Reidlinger. Translated by Wade Baskin. New York: Philosophical Library, 1959.

Schlereth, Thomas. *Victorian America: Transformations in Everyday Life, 1876–1915.* New York: HarperCollins, 1991.

Schorr, Juliet B. *The Overspent American: Upscaling, Downshifting, and the New Consumer.* New York: Basic Books, 1998.

Scott, Stephen. *Amish Houses and Barns.* Intercourse, PA: Good Books, 2001.

———. *Why Do They Dress That Way?* Intercourse, PA: Good Books, 1986.

Scott, Stephen, and Kenneth Pellman. *Living without Electricity.* Intercourse, PA: Good Books, 1990.

Simon, David. *Tony Soprano's America: The Criminal Side of the American Dream.* Boulder, CO: Westview Press, 2002.

Simons, Menno. *The Complete Writings of Menno Simons: Circa 1496–1561.* Edited by J. C. Wenger. Translated by Leonard Verduin. Scottdale, PA: Herald Press, 1984.

Smith, C. Henry. *Smith's Story of the Mennonites.* Newton, KS: Faith and Life Press, 1981.

Smith, George R. *A History in Word and Picture of the Village of Sugarcreek and the Parent Village of Shanesville.* Sugarcreek, OH: Alpine Hills Historical Museum, 1977.

Sontag, Susan. *On Photography.* New York: Farrar, Straus and Giroux, 1977.

Stahura, Barbara. *Holmes County, Ohio: Celebrating 175 Years.* Paducah, KY: Turner Publishing, 1999.

Stevick, Richard A. *Growing Up Amish: The Teenage Years.* Baltimore, MD: Johns Hopkins University Press, 2007.

Stoelje, Beverly J., "Festival." In *International Encyclopedia of Communications,* edited by Erik Barnouw et al. New York: Oxford University Press, 1989.

Tenner, Edward. *Our Own Devices: The Past and Future of Body Technologies.* New York: Alfred A. Knopf, 2003.

———. *Why Things Bite Back: Technology and the Revenge of Unintended Consequences.* New York: Vintage Books, 1996.

Trachtenberg, Alan. *The Incorporation of America: Culture and Society in the Gilded Age.* New York: Hill and Wang, 1982.

Trollinger, William Vance, Jr. "Evangelicalism and Religious Pluralism in Contemporary America: Diversity Without, Diversity Within, and Maintaining the Borders." In *Religious Pluralism in the United States, 1945–Present,* edited by Charles Cohen and Ronald Numbers. New York: Oxford University Press, forthcoming.

"The Twelve Largest Amish Settlements" (2010). Young Center for Anabaptist and Pietist Studies, Elizabethtown College. www2.etown.edu/amishstudies/Largest_Settlements_2010.asp.

Umble, Diane Zimmerman. *Holding the Line: The Telephone in Old Order Mennonite and Amish Life.* Baltimore, MD: Johns Hopkins University Press, 1996.

Umble, Diane Zimmerman, and David L. Weaver-Zercher, eds. *The Amish and the Media.* Baltimore, MD: Johns Hopkins University Press, 2008.

Urry, John. *The Tourist Gaze: Leisure and Travel in Contemporary Societies.* London: Sage Publications, 1990.

US Department of Labor: Bureau of Labor Statistics. "Employment Characteristics of Families: 1996." www.bls.gov/news/release/history/famee_061697.txt.

———. "Employment Characteristics of Families in 2002." www.bls.gov/news.release/history/famee_07092003.txt.

van Braght, Thieleman J. *The Bloody Theater or Martyrs Mirror of the Defenseless Christians.* Scottdale, PA: Herald Press, 1997.

Walbert, David. *Garden Spot: Lancaster County, the Old Order Amish, and the Selling of Rural America.* New York: Oxford University Press, 2002.

Weaver, J. Denny. *The Nonviolent Atonement.* Grand Rapids, MI: William B. Eerdmans Publishing Company, 2001.

Weaver-Zercher, David. *The Amish in the American Imagination.* Baltimore, MD: Johns Hopkins University Press, 2001.

———, ed. *Writing the Amish: The Worlds of John A. Hostetler.* University Park: Pennsylvania State University Press, 2005.

White, Richard. "Frederick Jackson Turner and Buffalo Bill," In Grossman, *The Frontier in American Culture,* 7–55.

Wiebe, Robert. *The Search for Order: 1877–1920.* New York: Hill and Wang, 1967.

Yoder, John Howard. "Armaments and Eschatology." *Studies in Christian Ethics* 1, no. 1 (1988), 43–61.

———. *The Politics of Jesus.* 2nd ed. Grand Rapids, MI: William B. Eerdmans Publishing Company, 1994.

Index

Page numbers in *italics* indicate a photograph or map.

Werner O. Packull, *Hutterite Beginnings: Communitarian Experiments during the Reformation*

Benjamin W. Redekop and Calvin W. Redekop, eds., *Power, Authority, and the Anabaptist Tradition*

Calvin Redekop, Stephen C. Ainlay, and Robert Siemens, *Mennonite Entrepreneurs*

Calvin Redekop, ed., *Creation and the Environment: An Anabaptist Perspective on a Sustainable World*

Steven D. Reschly, *The Amish on the Iowa Prairie, 1840 to 1910*

Kimberly D. Schmidt, Diane Zimmerman Umble, and Steven D. Reschly, *Strangers at Home: Amish and Mennonite Women in History*

Diane Zimmerman Umble, *Holding the Line: The Telephone in Old Order Mennonite and Amish Life*

David Weaver-Zercher, *The Amish in the American Imagination*